The African American
SONNET

The African American SONNET

A LITERARY HISTORY

TIMO MÜLLER

UNIVERSITY PRESS OF MISSISSIPPI / JACKSON

Margaret Walker Alexander Series in African American Studies

www.upress.state.ms.us

The University Press of Mississippi is a member of
the Association of American University Presses.

First printing 2018

∞

Library of Congress Cataloging-in-Publication Data

Names: Müller, Timo, author.
Title: The African American sonnet: a literary history / Timo Müller.
Description: Jackson: University Press of Mississippi, [2018] | Series:
Margaret Walker Alexander Series in African American Studies | Includes
bibliographical references and index. |
Identifiers: LCCN 2018009306 (print) | LCCN 2018009999 (ebook) | ISBN
9781496817846 (epub single) | ISBN 9781496817853 (epub institutional) |
ISBN 9781496817860 (pdf single) | ISBN 9781496817877 (pdf institutional)
| ISBN 9781496817839 (cloth: alk. paper)
Subjects: LCSH: American poetry—African American authors—History and
criticism. | African Americans—Intellectual life. | LCGFT: Literary
criticism.
Classification: LCC PS153.N5 (ebook) | LCC PS153.N5 M85 2018 (print) | DDC
811.009/896073—dc23
LC record available at https://lccn.loc.gov/2018009306

British Library Cataloging-in-Publication Data available

Contents

Acknowledgments

Tracing the development of a venerable poetic form through more than two centuries of African American poetry has been an adventurous, rewarding process. This book began as a research project under the guidance of Hubert Zapf, whose generous support and intellectual scope have laid the foundations for my academic work. Martin Middeke and Oliver Scheiding provided helpful comments on the initial version of my manuscript and valuable advice in many situations. At the University of Augsburg I benefitted from stimulating discussions with Christoph Henke, David Kerler, Michael Sauter, and the participants of the literary studies research colloquia. A substantial portion of the book was written during a one-year visiting fellowship at Harvard University, which was made possible by the generous interest of Henry Louis Gates, Eliza New, and Stephen Whitfield. During this period I greatly benefited from the thoughtful responses and inspiring ideas of Homi Bhabha, Stephen Burt, and Helen Vendler. For their support during the revision and publication process I am grateful to Udo Hebel and my colleagues at the University of Regensburg.

The book is based on the first systematic corpus of African American sonnets, which I compiled by going through thousands of books, journals, and manuscripts. For their assistance in procuring these sources I am obliged to the staff of Beinecke Library (Yale), the British Library (London), John Hay Library (Brown), the Library of Congress (Washington, DC), the Manuscript, Archive, and Rare Book Library (Emory), the Robert W. Woodruff Library (Atlanta University Center), the Schomburg Center for Research in Black Culture (New York), and Widener Library (Harvard). For financial support along the way I thank the Fritz Thyssen Foundation, Beinecke Library, and the British Association of American Studies. I am grateful to Vijay Shah, my editor at the University Press of Mississippi, for believing in my work and guiding me through the vagaries of a transatlantic publication process. I would also like to thank the two anonymous readers for the press who provided valuable feedback on the manuscript. My research assistants Verena Baier, Nadine

Ellinger, Luis Groitl, Allison Haskins, and Nicole Mittelstädt helped prepare the manuscript for publication.

Academic work tends to make demands on personal life, and I am grateful to those who have borne with me over the years. My parents have supported me and my work without hesitation. My friends at home and abroad shared the good times and helped me through the bad. Above all I want to thank my partner Julia, who has taught me things I never knew and helped me in ways I could never have imagined.

The African American
SONNET

Introduction

TROUBLING SPACES

When Albery Allson Whitman, a minister and former slave, published his first collection of poetry in 1877, he inaugurated an unlikely genre: the African American sonnet.[1] This was an altogether remarkable event. An ethnic group that had largely been excluded from intellectual life was beginning to appropriate one of the most venerable traditions in Western literature. A group whose capabilities had widely been disparaged was demonstrating its mastery of one of the most complex poetic forms in the language. A group whose cultural heritage had mainly relied on oral transmission was turning to one of the most durable genres in written literature. It was a development few were prepared to acknowledge or accept—as June Jordan, herself a writer of sonnets, would put it many years later, it was "not natural" (*On Call* 87–98). The African American sonnet was ignored, even denounced, by white and black scholars alike. But it persisted, and developed into a continuous, productive tradition. Drawing on more than a thousand sonnets by hundreds of poets, this study traces the African American sonnet tradition from its nineteenth-century beginnings to the present. It aims to demonstrate that closer attention to this tradition modifies our understanding of key developments in African American literary history.

Somewhat surprisingly, the first sonnet to which an African American signed his name seems entirely unconcerned with the culture, tradition, or current situation of African Americans. Whitman's "Sonnet: The Montenegrin" (227–28) pays tribute to the Montenegrin struggle for independence from the Ottoman Empire, which was reaching its decisive stage in the Montenegrin-Ottoman war of 1876–1878.

> Undaunted watcher of the mountain track,
> Tho' surging cohorts like a sea below,
> Against thy cliff-walled homes their thunders throw;

Proud, whilst thy rock fastness answers back
The fierce, long menace of the Turk's attack,
Thy eagle ken above the tumult flies,
The hostile plain spurns, and its prowess black,
And lights on strongholds terraced in the skies;
There thou wilt quicker than the roe-buck bound,
If bolder dangers mount to force thy pass;
But not till thou a signal brave hast wound,
That hears responses from each peak around,
And calls thy comrade clans-in-arms, to mass
In high defence, when battle stern begins—
Then who can conquer the Montenegrins?

At a second glance the poem establishes an implicit but compelling analogy between the oppressed yet "undaunted" Montenegrins in the Ottoman Empire and the black minority in the United States. The analogy acquires additional force through Whitman's appropriation of the sonnet. Generally associated with the white European tradition, the sonnet here becomes a space that the black poet, like the Montenegrins, occupies in "defence" against the oppressor. Whitman's poem lays claim to the sonnet form in its title and opens with a conventional Petrarchan quatrain. It begins to reshape the form in the second quatrain, which shifts to cross rhyme in order to accommodate the spatial/racial rhyme "attack/black." A more radical revision occurs at the end of the poem, where Whitman oversteps the conventional boundaries of the sonnet by adding a fifteenth line and turns that line into a suggestive assertion of the oppressed minority's powers of resistance.

The sonnet has not always been defined by structural criteria, but in the English tradition it had stable boundaries from the beginning. Its fourteen lines were divided into an octave and a sestet or three quatrains and a couplet by the rhyme scheme, often reinforced by syntax and layout. In the twentieth century poets began to dismantle these criteria but continued to allude to the sonnet tradition. They retained the fourteen lines, reproduced classic structural units, or marked their texts as sonnets in the title or through inclusion in a sonnet sequence.[2] "Sonnet: The Montenegrin" follows most of the traditional rules, but the fifteenth line transcends and redefines the conventional boundaries of the sonnet. The territorial conflict the poem recounts is redoubled as Whitman asserts his control over the sonnet form and turns the white European tradition it represents into an occupied space. Moreover, both the topic of his poem and its genre history evoke forces that transcend national boundaries, which reinforces Whitman's critique of racial oppression in the United States.

From Whitman onward, the following chapters suggest, many African American sonnets can be described as troubling spaces in American literary history. Their authors conceived the sonnet as a space that can be occupied, reshaped, and expanded. They created sonnets that trouble the boundaries of the form itself but also the boundaries erected by the conventions, traditions, and histories the form evokes. As June Jordan notes, the sonnet was one of the spaces blacks were supposed to stay out of but ventured into anyway. And many who ventured in, most famously perhaps Countee Cullen in "Yet Do I Marvel" (1925), did so on the assumption that their mere presence would question the ideology of racial difference on which American culture was founded. The history of the African American sonnet is thus also a series of challenges to boundaries of language, perception, and convention.

The African American Sonnet: A Literary History deliberately works with these spatial metaphors because they evoke a long, influential tradition of conceiving the sonnet in spatial terms—a tradition that African American poets have engaged and revised. The most influential manifestation of this spatial conception in anglophone literature is the prefatory sonnet to William Wordsworth's *Poems, in Two Volumes* (1807, 661–63):

Nuns fret not at their Convent's narrow room;
And Hermits are contented with their Cells;
And Students with their pensive Citadels:
Maids at the Wheel, the Weaver at his Loom,
Sit blithe and happy; Bees that soar for bloom,
High as the highest Peak of Furness Fells,
Will murmur by the hour in Foxglove bells:
In truth, the prison, unto which we doom
Ourselves, no prison is: and hence for me,
In sundry moods, 'twas pastime to be bound
Within the Sonnet's scanty plot of ground:
Pleas'd if some Souls (for such there needs must be)
Who have felt the weight of too much liberty,
Should find short solace there, as I have found.

The spatial image of the "narrow room" goes through a series of variations in the opening lines of the sonnet, reaching its most clearly negative variant—the sonnet as a prison—at the end of the octave. Instead of observing the conventional boundary between octave and sestet, however, the poem breaks this "prison" with the enjambment of "doom / Ourselves" in lines 8 and 9—a revisionary practice Albery Allson Whitman would adopt for the African

American sonnet. The sestet then develops a more positive variant of the narrow room, the "scanty plot of ground." Wordsworth draws on a substantial prior tradition of spatial figurations of the sonnet, from Shakespeare's sonnet-tombs and monuments to Donne's "well-wrought urn" and the tectonic conception of the form in early German Romanticism.[3] He adds to this tradition by making the spatial understanding explicit and by specifying it in two important ways.

On the one hand, Wordsworth foregrounds the tension between freedom and restriction engendered by the stable boundaries of the form. Its bounded space becomes a social parable in that it models the balance of individual and collective concerns—of liberty and restraint—that Wordsworth found lacking in the England of his time. Most African American poets were familiar with Wordsworth's poetry given his stature since the early nineteenth century, but they were rarely acquainted with the problem of "too much liberty." As a consequence they tended to appropriate the transgressive rather than the confining impulse Wordsworth ascribes to the sonnet. Less obviously but no less momentously, they engaged with the other influential aspect of Wordsworth's spatial conception: the analogy between the sonnet and the nation. The reference to the Furness Fells situates Wordsworth's prefatory sonnet in rural England. Like many of the 1807 *Poems,* the prefatory sonnet depicts the bounded liberty of the sonnet as characteristic of England and opposed to both the excessive liberty of the French Revolution and the threat created by that excess: Napoleonic dictatorship. Wordsworth's analogy between the boundaries of the sonnet and the boundaries of the English nation blends the aesthetic with the political to valorize unity and caution against the threats of excess within and aggression from the outside.[4]

This linkage of rural and national imagery came to pervade the vocabulary of sonnet criticism in the nineteenth century. Literary histories from the period describe the sonnet as a flower "transplanted" from Italy into an English "soil" and "clime" (Wagner, *A Moment's Monument* 121). The nationalist dimension of such metaphors is most openly acknowledged in the *Lectures on the British Poets* (1859) by Henry Reed, a literary scholar and Wordsworth's American editor. Starting from his impression that the sonnet continues to create "an *un-English* feeling" among readers, Reed seeks to prove the thoroughly national character of the English sonnet. "Our literary territory," he asserts, "is held absolutely, or it had better be relinquished entirely" (357–59). The Wordsworthian vocabulary of soil and belonging appears in African American sonnets such as Herbert Clark Johnson's *Poems from Flat Creek* (1943) and James A. Emanuel's "For a Farmer" (1964). It exerts a palpable influence on the work of Claude McKay, who shaped and popularized the African American sonnet to a degree comparable to Wordsworth in the English sonnet. McKay echoes his precursor in the opening lines of his sonnet "Labor's Day" (1919): "Once poets in their safe and calm retreat / Essayed the singing of the fertile soil" (*Complete Poems* 137, lines 1–2). Moreover, as Sonya Posmentier has pointed out, cultivation is a nodal concept in McKay's aesthetic, where it brings together concerns related to agriculture, personality formation, and the maintenance of traditional customs in a new country. The example of McKay shows, however, that African American poets evoked the boundedness of the sonnet not so much to assert national or cultural belonging, as to trouble the limitations such concepts imply.

African American literary critics drew on the spatial conception of the sonnet as well, and with a similarly transgressive impulse. In the Black Arts period, the concept of the sonnet as a prison was cited as evidence of the stultifying effect of Western forms on the black artist. In *Blackness and the Adventure of Western Culture* (1972), George Kent demanded the revalorization of African American traditions on the grounds that they were "a resource—not a prison" (10–11). Later critics tended to emphasize the productive aspects of the sonnet space. With its "strict conventions of representation," Marcellus Blount argues in a seminal 1990 article, the sonnet "provides an ideal forum for affirmation and contestation, as poets define themselves within and against the terms of what Wordsworth called the sonnet's 'scanty plot of ground.' As contested ground, these sonnets enact . . . struggles for identity in Afro-American art" (227). Both of these assessments share a spatial conception of the sonnet. Kent emphasizes the limitations the form imposes on African American self-expression, while Blount stresses the discursive negotiations that unfold in this "contested ground."

The notion that literary forms can be occupied and reshaped is not limited to discussions of the sonnet. It is deeply embedded in African American literary criticism from the twentieth and twenty-first centuries. A classic manifestation is Henry Louis Gates's *The Signifying Monkey* (1988), which argues that the black literary tradition has been shaped by the playful revision of precursor texts.[5] Gates argues that when used deliberately, signifying

> functions to redress an imbalance of power, to clear a space, rhetorically. To achieve occupancy in this desired space, the [Signifying] Monkey rewrites the received order by exploiting the Lion's hubris and his inability to read the figurative other than as the literal. Writers Signify upon each other's texts by rewriting the received textual tradition. . . . This sort of Signifyin(g) revision serves, if successful, to create a space for the revising text. (124)

In Gates's account both the textual tradition as a whole and individual texts are understood in spatial terms, and revising a form amounts to transforming this spatial configuration. The dynamics Gates describes unfold with particular force in the sonnet—because of the spatial boundaries of the form but also because, as the scholar Daniel Robinson puts it, a sonnet "is always an allusion to every other poem of its kind ever written" (71). In choosing a form conventionally associated with the European heritage and white cultural privilege, black writers engage a number of American traditions—literature, poetry, high culture—that had not only excluded them but sometimes defined themselves in opposition to them. An exceptionally durable manifestation of these traditions, the sonnet becomes a synecdoche whose appropriation can be understood as transgressing and reshaping the boundaries of that tradition.

The most prominent discussion of the sonnet in an African American context, Rita Dove's foreword to her collection *Mother Love* (1995) illustrates how poets working with the form engage these dynamics. Titled "An Intact World," the foreword begins:

> "Sonnet" literally means "little song." The sonnet is a *heile Welt*, an intact world where everything is in sync, from the stars down to the tiniest mite on a blade of grass. And if the "true" sonnet reflects the music of the spheres, it then follows that any variation from the strictly Petrarchan or Shakespearean forms represents a world gone awry.
>
> Or does it? Can't form also be a talisman against disintegration? The sonnet defends itself against the vicissitudes of fortune by its charmed structure, its beautiful bubble. All the while, though, chaos is lurking outside the gate. (xiii)

Dove follows Wordsworth in conceiving the sonnet as a site of freedom and imprisonment at the same time. Whereas Wordsworth seeks to resolve these contradictory ideas in a problematic notion of voluntary confinement and folkloristic belonging, Dove foregrounds the disruptive effect of a poet's transgressions on the ontological implications of bounded form. The enjambment Wordsworth employs to refute the notion that boundaries equal imprisonment can be seen as one instance of this effect, which Dove regards as more destabilizing than Wordsworth suggests. If the formal framework is as strict as that of the sonnet, she argues, "any variation" of the traditional rules breaks apart the construct of the intact world and evokes "a world gone awry." This approach effectively combines the ideas of the sonnet as a space and of formal revision as an act of occupying and reshaping that space.

A more decisive modification of the spatial conception is put forward in Fred Moten's *In the Break: The Aesthetics of the Black Radical Tradition* (2003), which examines the politics of the form against the background of the radical aesthetics of jazz and black nationalism in the 1950s and 1960s. According to Moten, innovative African American cultural production at this time takes shape "in the break" between containment and excess: between the limitations enforced against African Americans and their taking freedom with these limitations. Moten takes the concept of the break from syncopation and improvisation in jazz music but stresses its spatial connotations when applied to literary forms. Observing that Amiri Baraka, soon to become the figurehead of black cultural nationalism, called Billie Holiday "the Dark Lady of the Sonnets," Moten suggests that a bounded form like the sonnet exemplifies the creative potential of restriction and transgression: "Something held within these forms also exceeds them" (120). While Dove retains the Wordsworthian notion of the sonnet space as refuge and regards the disruption of its boundaries as dangerous and liberating at the same time, Moten welcomes disruption as the very source of political and aesthetic innovation.

Few other theorists of African American literature have even mentioned the sonnet, let alone discussed it in any detail. The history of the African American sonnet tradition has met with similarly scant attention. A few individual sonnets such as McKay's "If We Must Die" have been thoroughly examined, and well-known poets who wrote sonnets—Paul Laurence Dunbar, McKay, Cullen, Langston Hughes, Gwendolyn Brooks, Robert Hayden, and Rita Dove—have been the subject of individual studies. Only a handful of essays and book chapters have approached the African American sonnet as a distinct phenomenon. Following Blount's abovementioned "Caged Birds: Race and Gender in the Sonnet" (1990), two essays, Antonella Francini's "Sonnet vs. Sonnet: The Fourteen Lines in African American Poetry" (2003) and Jeff Westover's "African American Sonnets: Voicing Justice and Personal Dignity" (2012), attempted surveys of the tradition. Jon Woodson's *Anthems, Sonnets, and Chants: Recovering the African American Poetry of the 1930s* (2011) includes a chapter on self-fashioning in the 1930s sonnet, and Edward Brunner's essay "Inventing an Ancestor: The Scholar-Poet and the Sonnet" (2013) traces the negotiation of African American history in contemporary sonnet sequences.

While these scholars have done important work in raising awareness of the very existence of an African American sonnet tradition, their efforts necessarily remain limited in scope and method. Even the surveys by Francini and Westover cover only a fraction of the available material, and Woodson's small selection of sonnets from the 1930s is hardly representative even of that decade. The present study, by contrast, relies on a corpus of over a thousand sonnets compiled in extensive archival research. Instead of focusing on a few canonic poets, it bases its claims on a survey of all sonnets published in volumes by

African American poets listed in the Library of Congress catalog. Given the sheer breadth of the material under consideration—at the time of this writing close to four hundred African American poets have published sonnets—the study cannot reference all sonnets from this corpus. It significantly extends our understanding of the African American sonnet tradition, however, by positioning outstanding achievements like "If We Must Die" against similar efforts of forgotten contemporaries and by revalorizing the contribution of little-known poets like Cordelia Ray, Leslie Pinckney Hill, and Joe H. Mitchell.

In elucidating this material, *The African American Sonnet: A Literary History* employs what Anthony Reed calls a "situated formalism" (8). It examines the formal strategies poets developed to engage the cultural and historical circumstances they negotiate in their texts. Reed positions this approach against the tendency to locate texts "within a preemptive black tradition or black social location" and arrive at one-sided readings as a result (7). This tendency is particularly risky when studying a culturally hybrid form like the African American sonnet, which has often been at odds with preemptive notions of black art and identity. A situated formalism can best capture the variety of perspectives the sonnet has offered on the themes, forms, and politics of African American poetry since the late nineteenth century. In tracing how these perspectives shaped and were shaped by the sonnet, *The African American Sonnet: A Literary History* charts a historical poetics of the African American sonnet tradition. It shares the interest of scholars such as Simon Jarvis, Yopie Prins, and Ivy G. Wilson in the cultural functions of poetic forms and genres, including the conviction that these functions are specific to historical periods. While scholars of historical poetics have produced an impressive body of work on nineteenth-century poetry in particular, the sonnet has not yet been examined from that angle, even though its durability and recognizability affords a unique lens onto the changing roles of a particular genre.[6]

The six chapters of this study examine the historically specific ways in which African American poets have troubled the space of the sonnet, and conversely, in which the sonnet has troubled received notions of African American writing. Chapter 1 traces the emergence of the sonnet in African American literature to the pervasive influence of genteel conventions, which have widely been regarded as conservative or even stultifying but which provided black poets with opportunities for self-assertion in the public sphere. The sonnet was a favorite genre among the genteel establishment and the chapter shows how poets pushed the boundaries of black expression by appropriating the form to subvert racial stereotypes, develop a black poetic subjectivity, and participate in the debate over the memory of the Civil War.

The sonnet moved to the center of African American literature in the Harlem Renaissance. Chapter 2 argues that this development was one of continuity rather than rupture with genteel conventions. Drawing on previously neglected material, the chapter situates McKay's epochal sonnet "If We Must Die" (1919) in the gradual transformation of the protest sonnet over the decade. In a second step, it draws attention to the important role of genteel conventions in shaping the subversive variety of protest that younger poets such as Cullen, Sterling Brown, and Helene Johnson explored in the mid-twenties. The ambivalent position of the sonnet in between gentility and protest, the chapter argues, is behind the difficulties that scholars like Houston A. Baker have faced in assessing the interplay of formal mastery and deformative self-assertion in the Harlem Renaissance sonnet.

In the late nineteenth and early twentieth centuries the transnational history and genteel credentials of the sonnet provided African American poets with a perspective beyond the racist boundaries they were facing in the United States. McKay, Cullen, and other leading figures of the Harlem Renaissance explored the liberatory potential of transnationality in their lives and works. A closer look at their less-known sonnets, some of which remained unpublished until the early twenty-first century, reveals that these explorations did not end with the onset of the Great Depression, as many histories of the Harlem Renaissance suggest. Chapter 3 demonstrates that African American poetry of the 1930s, which scholars have discussed primarily in national and leftist frameworks, sustained a range of transnational conversations that were incited by poets' travels and also by the Pan-Africanist sentiments that emerged around the Italo-Ethiopian War of 1935–36.

The political affiliations of most African American poets at that time seem to have discouraged the continuing exploration of the modernist experimental techniques that Jean Toomer and Langston Hughes had pioneered in the twenties. When Hughes returned to modernist experimentation and combined it with vernacular language in his "Seven Moments of Love: An Un-Sonnet Sequence in Blues" (1940), he found in the sonnet a space where these seemingly disparate sources could be synthesized. Chapter 4 traces the emergence of what Matthew Hart calls a "synthetic vernacular" aesthetic in the sonnets of Hughes, Brooks, and Hayden. It suggests that the sonnet became a crucial, if overlooked, laboratory for the Afro-modernist project that shaped African American literature in the post-war period.

The sonnet sustained this creative potential during the Black Arts movement, but in a very different environment. While much of this study argues for the centrality of the sonnet to the development of African American poetry,

Chapter 5 traces the subsistence of the form at the margins of the Black Arts movement. The black cultural nationalists of the 1960s and 1970s regarded the sonnet as a paradigmatic "white" form that constrained black self-expression and had to be excluded from the black nation. The chapter shows how the demand for an oral, authentic, collective poetry led poets to dismantle the traditional sonnet structure and adapt the form to cultural nationalist demands. In providing evidence that the Black Arts movement exerted both a confining and a creative influence on poets of the time, these transformations of the sonnet confirm the nuanced view of the movement that has emerged in recent scholarly discussion.

Subsisting in enclaves of the black nation, the sonnet remained an unruly presence that troubled the aesthetic and ideological boundaries of the Black Arts movement's cultural nationalism. When the movement's influence began to recede the sonnet returned to the center of African American poetry. From the late 1980s onward, an unprecedented number of sonnets appeared and the sonnet sequence entered African American literature as a distinct phenomenon. Chapter 6 argues that its dissident role within the Black Arts movement made the sonnet a preferred site for negotiating and revising the legacy of that movement. Poets like Ed Roberson, Wanda Coleman, and Rita Dove experimented with the sonnet to transgress rather than maintain boundaries of form, meaning, culture, and nation. The chapter argues that their work confirms the revalorization of deconstructive experimental poetry in recent criticism, but at the same time questions the tendency among scholars to privilege temporality as the site of innovation and resistance. The contemporary African American sonnet sequence combines temporal and spatial strategies to subvert conventional notions of blackness and the limitations they impose on black life and identity.

Each of these chapters addresses historically specific assumptions about African American literature that a closer look at the uses of the sonnet questions or complicates. The study as a whole also negotiates two broader assumptions that recur throughout the history of the African American sonnet and help explain its neglect in scholarly debate. One is the notion that poetic forms with a European provenance are "veils" or "masks" that black writers don to hide their true thoughts. This notion comes out of a long tradition of theorizing black identity ranging from Thomas Jefferson, who regarded blackness itself as a "veil" that impoverished African American subjectivity (130–50), to W. E. B. Du Bois's *The Souls of Black Folk* (1903) and Frantz Fanon's *Black Skin, White Masks* (1952), both of which stressed the agency and psychological complexity black people sustained by veiling or masking themselves in a racist society.

Literary writers occasionally used these metaphors as well—most famously Dunbar in "We Wear the Mask" (1896)—and pioneering scholarly studies such as Robert Stepto's *From Behind the Veil* (1979) employed them to draw attention to the depth and richness of the African American literary tradition.

The poetic mask Dunbar wanted to shed was not traditional form, however, but the dialect verse his white readers and publishers expected him to write. His example indicates that the use of mask and veil metaphors to describe African American literary writing, which continues to the present day, is not without risk. These metaphors can easily reinforce binary conceptions of black and white, authentic and false, that the literature itself complicates. Moreover, the static images of the mask and the veil fail to capture the transformative influence black writers have exerted on white forms and vice versa. These mutual transformations have begun to be discussed in scholarship, most importantly in Keith Leonard's *Fettered Genius: The African American Bardic Poet From Slavery to Civil Rights* (2006).[7] The following chapters continue this examination in that they demonstrate how African American poets have transformed the sonnet form and the traditions associated with it from the beginning.

A second overarching assumption that a closer look at the sonnet challenges is that African American writing has primarily been rural and parochial in scope. Implicitly or explicitly, we will see, this assumption pervaded debates around African American poetry from the nineteenth-century interest in dialect verse to the romanticization of folk expression in the modernist period. Traces of it can be found in the Black Arts movement, which defined the purpose of black art with reference to the political situation in the United States and framed even its interest in the African origins of black culture in nationalist terms. The limitations of parochial conceptions of black writing have widely been discussed following the appearance of Paul Gilroy's *The Black Atlantic* (1993). Brent Hayes Edwards, John Cullen Gruesser, and many others have since documented the transnational scope of African American literature.[8] The following chapters add to this discussion in examining one of the most consistently transnational forms of African American expression. Albery Allson Whitman's "Sonnet: The Montenegrin" indicates that the sonnet, with its transnational connotations and genre history, served from the very beginning to question and transgress the boundaries imposed on black writing in the United States. The sonnet was invented at the court of Frederick II in medieval Sicily, where different cultural spheres—Arabian, Italian, Germanic, Norman, and African—overlapped. After its early absorption in Italian and Hebrew poetry, the form went on to inspire poets all over the world, from Bengal, where a sonnet tradition has existed since the early nineteenth century, to Cuba, where a sonnet written by a slave initiated the abolition movement.[9] African American poets have consistently evoked this transnational history in their sonnets, often as a counterforce to the spatial boundaries implied by the Wordsworthian conception of the form. By participating in a tradition that preceded and transcended the limitations they encountered in the United States, this study shows, African American poets have troubled conventional notions of blackness, nationality, and literary expression—often all at the same time.

Chapter 1

THE GENTEEL TRADITION AND THE EMERGENCE OF THE AFRICAN AMERICAN SONNET

In 1889 the *A.M.E. Church Review,* a widely read organ of the emerging black middle class, carried an essay on "The Province of Poetry" by society leader and occasional poet Josephine Turpin Washington. The main purpose of poetry, Washington wrote, was to improve the reader through refined ideas and sentiments. While "the cultivation of an inner, a soul life, does not directly contribute to the breadwinning process," she argued, "it sweetens and strengthens man's whole nature, and so fits him for the better performance of any duty . . . Poetry is allied to our best affections. Home, wife, mother, country, are themes ever dear to the poet" (quoted in Bruce, *Black American* 21). For Washington as for many of her contemporaries, the province of poetry had clear boundaries. It was circumscribed by the nation and the domestic sphere, bounded off from the base self-interest of "the breadwinning process," from politics and business. Yet, in spite or because of these boundaries, poetry enabled flights of fancy, emotional refinement, and intellectual insight. It was both fundamental and superior to the life outside.

Her idealism, domesticity, and penchant for self-improvement situate Washington in the social and aesthetic sphere that historians have come to call the genteel tradition. Coined by George Santayana in 1911, the term refers to a set of norms and values that shaped American middle-class culture from the mid-nineteenth century into the early twentieth. The genteel tradition as characterized by Santayana and later historians was conservative, elitist, and idealistic in outlook. Its aesthetic values were modeled on an idealized European tradition and favored romanticized settings, moral edification, and allegorical interpretation. Most genteel readers and critics believed that these values found their purest manifestation in poetry, and that poetry was therefore the highest of literary genres. As Franklin Frazier, Dickson Bruce, and others have shown, the black middle class largely embraced these genteel preferences in its quest for social recognition in a racially segregated society. For educated African Americans, refined taste and behavior became a means of deflecting racist insults, asserting intellectual capability, and contesting legalized discrimination.[1]

In the twentieth century the genteel conception of literature fell out of favor with African American critics. Against the background of the New Negro and Black Arts movements, critics tended to prefer writing that had an openly political purpose and was inspired by such sources of cultural authenticity as folk expression, popular music, and African traditions. Even Saunders Redding, in many ways a genteel figure, dismissed most poetry of the postbellum period as "dilettantism," "conventional," and "without substance" (85–92). Under the influence of the Black Arts movement, some critics went further and accused poets like Paul Laurence Dunbar and William Stanley Braithwaite, along with the black genteel tradition as a whole, of subordination to white racism.[2]

As a result of this shift in critical opinion, studies of postbellum African American poetry tend to neglect the generative, politically empowering dimension of genteel conventions. Some scholars have identified cases of subversive or empowering appropriation in the work of individual poets, especially Dunbar and Albery Allson Whitman, and discussions of the genteel interest in classical subjects occasionally hint at this dimension. The only detailed study of the subject is Keith Leonard's *Fettered Genius: The African American Bardic Poet from Slavery to Civil Rights* (2006), which explores the "middle ground" Dunbar and other black genteel poets inhabited between the boundaries conventionally ascribed to the black and the white literary traditions. Rather than imitating or rejecting genteel aesthetics, Leonard points out, these poets brought it into a mutually transformative interplay with African American concerns and traditions.[3]

The sonnet is not only an outstanding example of this mutual transformation, this chapter argues, but it offers unique insights into the productive appropriation of the genteel tradition by African American poets between Reconstruction and the Harlem Renaissance. The sonnet was a favorite genre in the genteel tradition, so much so that Edwin Arlington Robinson derided his fellow poets as "little sonnet-men" by the end of the nineteenth century (93). African American poets drew on its authority to negotiate and revise the themes Josephine Turpin Washington calls "ever dear to the poet": love, interiority, patriotism. For technically accomplished poets the sonnet provided various opportunities to signify on racial prejudice in a covert manner. Mastery of one of the oldest and most demanding forms in the Western canon alone made a compelling case against allegations of black intellectual inferiority. In exploring the technical intricacies of the sonnet form, the most innovative poets of the time became remarkably adept at turning genteel conventions against the racial prejudice these conventions implied.

After exemplifying these signifying strategies in sonnets by Braithwaite and James Weldon Johnson, the chapter focuses on two conventions of the genteel sonnet that poets appropriated for purposes of self-assertion. One is the Romantic notion of the sonnet as a key to the poet's heart, which African American poets adapted to express what they were not supposed to acknowledge or even possess: emotions, desires, and generally a complex inner life. The other is the fashion for tribute sonnets, which African American poets appropriated to defend the legacy of Reconstruction by celebrating abolitionists and anti-slavery fighters. The concluding section of the chapter demonstrates how, in commenting on and engaging with respected public figures, these poets troubled traditional hierarchies of expression and contributed to the new poetic subjectivity by shifting the focus from the (often white) addressee to the black speaker.

William Stanley Braithwaite, James Weldon Johnson, and Genteel Signifying

The outstanding representative of genteel values in African American poetry, many contemporary and later observers agreed, was William Stanley Braithwaite. A self-made man whose light skin opened the doors of New England's intellectual elite to him, Braithwaite gained a position of influence and authority in the literary field unimaginable for previous writers of African descent. His anthologies of English poetry and his regular column in the *Boston Evening Transcript* (from 1905) made Braithwaite the country's most influential poetry critic by the beginning of the twentieth century. Some later commentators accused him of disavowing his race in the process, and indeed Braithwaite avoided categorization as a black writer, which would have reduced him to dialect work in public perception.[4] Yet he did use his influence to promote individual African American writers, and his own poetry, which has been neglected in critical debate, casts further doubt on the notion that he was an apolitical figure.

Inspired by the English Romantics and fin-de-siècle aestheticism, Braithwaite's poetry epitomizes genteel tastes and values. It includes a considerable proportion of sonnets, most of which are Keatsian in attitude and center on the feelings of the lyrical I. In his second collection, *The House of Falling Leaves* (1908), however, Braithwaite begins to use genteel conventions to signify on racial stereotypes, for example in the sonnet "This is My Life":

> To feed my soul with beauty till I die;
> To give my hands a pleasant task to do;
> To keep my heart forever filled anew
> With dreams and wonders which the days supply;
> To love all conscious living, and thereby
> Respect the brute who renders up its due,
> And know the world as planned is good and true—
> And thus—because there chanced to be an *I*!
> This is my life since things are as they are:
> One half akin to flowers and the grass:
> The rest a law unto the changeless star.
> And I believe when I shall come to pass
> Within the Door His hand shall hold ajar
> I'll leave no echoing whisper of *Alas!* (101)

The poem is an amalgam of stock devices from the genteel archive. A softened Romanticism, devout Christian morality, fin-de-siècle languishing, and aestheticist egocentrism all flow into this vague, complacent self-conception. What saves the poem from redundancy is its strict focus on the lyrical I. The ostentatious title imbues the abstract statements of the poem with autobiographical significance and the unusual syntax reinforces this referentiality. The entire octave consists of a subordinate clause that leads up to the italicized "*I*" and the repetition of the title at the beginning of the sestet. The suspension of this eponymous reference creates a vanishing line that puts the I of the nodal passage firmly at the center of perception and leads up to its first apotheosis. The second apotheosis comes in the sestet: the reader's gaze is directed from the earth to the sky and the I enters heaven, where he holds divine judgment over himself after God has awaited him at the door like an obliging Negro Servant. Under the disguise of conventional diction and perfectly mastered form, Braithwaite sketches a spiritual autobiography in the grandest terms available to white Christian gentility. His work in the sonnet here parallels his biographical trajectory in that it revises the covert racial hierarchies of the genteel tradition simply by inserting a black subject in an otherwise conventional framework.

The next step for genteel signifying was to extend this revisionary dynamic to the formal framework itself. Braithwaite did not take that step, but the other outstanding figure of black genteel poetry did. James Weldon Johnson published the sonnet "Mother Night" in the February 1910 issue of *Century* magazine, a respectable middle-class outlet. Arguably the most accomplished sonnet by an African American before the Harlem Renaissance, "Mother Night" signifies on the formal conventions of genteel poetry to articulate a message of black racial empowerment in the innocuous guise of an allegorical lament.[5]

> Eternities before the first-born day,
> Or ere the first sun fledged his wings of flame,
> Calm Night, the everlasting and the same,
> A brooding mother over chaos lay.
> And whirling suns shall blaze and then decay,
> Shall run their fiery courses and then claim
> The haven of the darkness whence they came;
> Back to Nirvanic peace shall grope their way.
> So when my feeble sun of life burns out,
> And sounded is the hour for my long sleep,
> I shall, full weary of the feverish light,
> Welcome the darkness without fear or doubt,
> And heavy-lidded, I shall softly creep
> Into the quiet bosom of the Night.

Beneath its placid tone and apparently genteel imagery, the poem inverts and revalorizes a number of oppositions inscribed into the Western poetic canon: day and night, aspiration and resignation, light and dark, creation and chaos, linearity and cyclicality, male and female. Against the traditional emphasis on day as the period of life, clarity, and lucidity, Johnson makes night the all-encompassing ground of his poem. Night frames not only the poem itself, appearing in the title and as its last word; it also frames day and human life in general. On an individual level, the speaker experiences it as a refuge from the physical and emotional strains caused by daily life, as a sphere of peace and quietude associated with the nurturing principle of motherhood. Johnson's modification of the sonnet structure emphasizes this stance. Instead of developing a countermovement, the sestet endorses the initial argument and draws the speaker into the scene he has described in the octave. Even as night becomes death the speaker continues to welcome the quietness and peace it offers: creeping into its bosom is his only active movement in the entire poem.

Whereas the traditional love sonnet put a strong emphasis on the speaker's aspiration toward his beloved and the ideals associated with her, the speaker of "Mother Night" has no aspirations at all, except a vague yearning for death. Along with its preference for night and sleep over day and life, the poem valorizes resignation as the more appealing form of aspiration. It adopts the aestheticist posture of languishing world-weariness, yet complements it with a revised version of the "uplift" idea of individual aspiration prominent in contemporary race discourse (Gaines 1–17; 67–99). Avoiding mere escapism, this move invests the conventional aestheticist posture with new meaning and new assurance as it comes to express the poem's dark ontology. Johnson lends new depth to the sentimental yearning for otherworldly peace and moves beyond other genteel poets, white and black, in his subtle use of allegory and his revision of conventional symbolism.

"Mother Night" makes a sustained argument for the superiority of darkness and radicalizes this argument through various social and political allusions. The poem describes darkness as the complete absence of light, and thus as blackness. In the context of contemporary debates over the origins of human culture, the "dark place" from which all life originates might be Africa, and contemporary black readers would likely associate the "blaze" and "flame" that characterize day(light) in the poem with the lynchings and Klan bonfires that had been regular newspaper features for decades and that appear in several of Johnson's poems from the period. A more sustained and explicit layer of allusions is established by the religious references. Trigger words like "eternity" and "chaos" link the poem to the Christian narrative of creation and resurrection that dominated both genteel and African American spirituality at the time. In the octave, the focus is on creation and on life in general ("darkness was upon the face of the deep," Gen 1:2); in the sestet, on death and on individual lives (death as a "long sleep," Eccles 46:19). In both cases the Christian version is subordinated to the poem's revisionist ontology. The Biblical genesis is reduced to an insignificant flicker in the eternities of night, and the afterlife becomes a cyclical return to night rather than an ascent to the light of heaven. The linear, teleological worldview of Western culture is superseded by the cyclical worldview and mythical time of the African tradition. The Christian Father is replaced by the dark, archaic Mother Night.

The shift from the male to the female principle supports not just the religious argument, but also Johnson's negotiation of the genteel tradition. The intellectual avant-garde of the 1910s regarded the genteel tradition as the outcome of a fundamental division of American society into a practical, progressive, male sphere and an abstract, nostalgic, female one. In the lecture that gave the genteel tradition its name, Santayana described "the sphere . . . of the American woman" as that "half of the American mind . . . not occupied intensely in practical affairs" (128–29). Around the turn of the century the influential critic and novelist William Dean Howells had written repeatedly and ambivalently about the "tradition of decency" in American literature, which he had endorsed on the grounds that "the vast majority" of the American reading public "are ladies, and that very many, if not most, of these ladies are young girls" (149–50). In the first half of the twentieth century many modernist writers and critics, including some members of the Harlem Renaissance, took up the gender argument to emphasize their masculine, progressive stance. One of the most notorious examples is Saunders Redding's description of Countee Cullen as "a gentle poet" whose "vision of life is interestingly distorted . . . as if he saw life through the eyes of a woman who is at once shrinking and bold, sweet and bitter" (110).

The conspicuously gendered "Mother Night" engages and complicates this debate in several ways. In some respects it reiterates genteel notions of gender: the female principle (night) is associated with passivity, fecundity, and motherhood, while the male principle (sun) is described as active and powerful. In the sestet the male role is smoothly conferred from the sun to the speaker ("when my feeble sun of life burns out") but the return-to-the-womb scene that follows affirms the gender opposition. At the same time, however, the poem inverts the hierarchy implicit in the genteel active/passive dichotomy as it assumes that night will outlast not just one but many suns, and that night is the primary ground from which the suns, and the speaker, originate and to which they return. In a complete reversal of the Biblical genesis narrative evoked elsewhere in the poem, Johnson thus accords ontological primacy to the female principle. And while the sonnet form he chooses for his address to Mother Night recalls the idealizing tendencies of courtly love poetry, this beloved has nothing ethereal about her. If anything, it is the sun with his "feverish light" who seems to be less real than he pretends, and the dreamy, half-asleep speaker seems hardly qualified to judge the reality of things. Johnson's replacement of the mainstream American narrative of linear progress with an African American narrative of spiritual nurturing is thus at the same time an ambivalent position-taking on the gender conventions of the genteel tradition.

The Biblical references indicate that Johnson's signifying on genteel conventions extends to the transnational literary canon that earlier African American sonneteers uncritically adopted for their articulation of a poetic interiority. The most prominent instance of this strategy is the poem's title. The phrase "Mother Night" has a rather conventional ring to it, but its only noteworthy antecedent in literature is Goethe's *Faust* (1808). In the standard translation of the period published by genteel idol Bayard Taylor in 1872, Mephistopheles introduces himself as "Part of the Darkness which brought forth the Light, / The haughty Light, which now disputes the space, / And claims of Mother Night her ancient place" (48). The argument Mephistopheles makes in this notorious scene is remarkably similar to Johnson's in "Mother Night": light is short-lived and "fettered . . . unto bodies" (48); bodily death is a return to darkness; darkness is therefore the superior and the "primal" sphere. While it is not certain that Johnson had read *Faust*, his wide reading, his knowledge of German, and his drama studies with Brander Matthews suggest that he was familiar with this set text of the nineteenth-century canon. Casting the speaker of the poem as a Mephistophelian figure, this intertextual allusion reinforces the poem's confident stance and lends additional poignancy to its religious and ontological revisionism. In extending his signifying to a European classic at the core of the genteel canon, Johnson demonstrates his mastery not only of the sonnet but also of the transnational literary conversation that was an important source of identity and cultural authority for the genteel tradition.

THE GENTEEL SONNET AND AFRICAN AMERICAN POETIC INTERIORITY

The main points of reference in this transnational conversation were the English Romantics and Victorians, who had revalorized the sonnet as a medium of authentic self-expression. Drawing on August Wilhelm Schlegel and German Romanticism in general, Wordsworth had famously celebrated the sonnet as the "key" with which "Shakespeare unlocked his heart" (*Last Poems* 82) and Keats had proven that the Shakespearean variant could still inspire outstanding poetic achievement. Largely because of their influence, a majority of critics ranked Shakespeare's sonnets with Milton's by mid-century, and the demand for authenticity and emotion in the sonnet was kept alive by influential publications like Charles Armitage Brown's *Shakespeare's Autobiographical Poems* (1838) and Leigh Hunt's *Book of the Sonnet* (1867).[6] The sensational success of Elizabeth Barrett Browning's *Sonnets From the Portuguese* (1850) further contributed to the revival of the self-expressive sonnet. It started a fashion for revelatory love sonnets that Elizabeth's husband, Robert Browning, would later deride together with the entire Shakespeare/Wordsworth argument in his poem "House" (1876). While they seemed blandly conventional to avant-garde writers like Browning, the innocuous gentility of these sonnets allowed African American poets to express interior dimensions of their lives and personalities that had remained hidden up to this point.

The notion that the speaker of a poem had a complex inner life to reveal was slow to emerge in African American writing. Black public figures in the eighteenth and nineteenth centuries were lone representatives in a public sphere dominated by whites. Under double pressure from racist hostility and their responsibilities as representatives of their race, their main concern was to present a favorable public persona rather than an ambivalent subjectivity. This concern pervaded even genres that were explicitly marketed as "authentic," such as slave narratives and dialect verse. While titles such as Du Bois's *The Souls of Black Folk* (1903) and James Weldon Johnson's *Autobiography of an Ex-Colored Man* (1912) evoked the promise of interiority, recent scholarship has shown that these books too offer carefully constructed performances of black identity rather than personal self-expression.[7] The preponderance of public over private speaking would continue to shape perceptions of African American literature far beyond the postbellum period. Not until the twenty-first century did critics begin to examine what the poets Elizabeth Alexander and Gregory Pardlo have conceptualized as the "black interior": a realm of black self-expression that eludes the familiar paradigms of oppression and resistance.

In her 2004 study of that title, Alexander explores the overlapping of spatial and psychological interiority in African American literature and art. Interior spaces, she claims, offer a more authentic rendering of black life than public ones. She points out that the sonnet, which she calls a "little room" in continuation of the spatial conception of the form (see the introduction), has functioned as a private space in which black poets have permitted readers access to both their homes and their inner lives. Pardlo too emphasizes the psychological dimension and revalorizes "poems of the interior" as a preserve of black identity and a means of communicating across racial and other boundaries. Following up on these insights, Kevin Quashie recuperates the interior for political purposes in *The Sovereignty of Quiet* (2012), where he seeks to overcome the limiting notion that African American writing must be "public," "dramatic," and resistant. The new critical attention to interiority has revealed pervasive strategies of self-inscription in early African American literature.[8] The following discussion suggests that the soul-searching of genteel poetry, however constrained and artificial it may seem in retrospect, was one such strategy. The bounded space of the genteel sonnet offered African American poets a sanctuary from the public pressures that had prevented them from exploring their subjectivity.

Given that the love sonnet was a particularly effective genre for the expression of intricate emotions, surprisingly few poets of the period explored its possibilities. Only a handful of writers, including Braithwaite and Dunbar, published sonnets whose psychological insights can be attributed to the poet. The vilification of black desire in American society might have been a cause of this restraint, as was the discouragement of female desire in genteel circles. The few female writers who published sonnets before Alice Dunbar-Nelson and Anne Spencer avoided the merest hint of autobiographical reference. Regardless of their gender, outright self-revelation was hardly an option for African American poets of the post-Reconstruction period, whom renewed racial oppression had taught to keep their inner lives, and especially their desires, to themselves. Rather than a mouthpiece for unrestrained subjectivity, the sonnet became for African American poets an ambivalent matrix whose innocuous appearance allowed for some degree of self-expression, and sometimes covert self-celebration, without openly confronting the racial taboos of American society.

The evolution of black poetic interiority from the late nineteenth century to the eve of the Harlem Renaissance is illustrated by two pioneering sonnet sequences: Samuel A. Beadle's "Sonnets to My Love" (1899) and Joseph S. Cotter Jr.'s "Out of the Shadows" (1920). Beadle, a slave-born lawyer from Mississippi, has the distinction of being the first African American who published a sonnet sequence. The 17 poems of "Sonnets to My Love" are badly written and badly organized. Only a few of them actually feature a beloved: the sequence opens with reflections on the death of the speaker's mother, and more than half of the poems are devoted to his dreams and nightly musings. The language of these sonnets switches continually between the artificial and the simple, often several times within the same poem. Together with Beadle's complete disregard for rhythm and scansion, this stylistic volatility results in a curious mixture of stilted doggerel and bursts of rough spontaneity that read almost like free verse. In its frequent shifts between convention and frankness, his sequence exemplifies the tension between the genteel and the subjective in the early African American sonnet.

What makes the sequence remarkable in historical perspective is its disregard of the ubiquitous constraints on black subjectivity. Writing in a time and place—the Deep South at the nadir of race relations—where any expression of black desire in public was likely to meet with abhorrence and worse, Beadle openly invites his beloved to share "the delicious joys young lovers steal / While making love beneath the verdant trees" (V.10). For him the sonnet is not a mask but a conduit for his many-faceted emotions and desires—a function that had previously been reserved for white poets. Beadle was not the only African American to write poetry of the interior in the 1890s: many of Dunbar's poems belong into this category, and there are sonnets by George McClellan and Charles Henry Shoeman that center on the feelings of the lyrical I. But Beadle went furthest in emphasizing the blackness of his lyrical I and in giving it a bodily dimension. Whether or not he was familiar with similar efforts by European avant-garde poets like John Addington Symonds, it is remarkable that a modestly talented amateur from Mississippi chose to express this bodily dimension in the venerable form of the sonnet.

That Beadle consciously inscribes his black subjectivity into a white tradition becomes obvious in the concluding poem of the sequence, which takes its cues from an exemplar of authentic love poetry notable for its subversive play with color: Shakespeare's sonnet 130, "My mistress' eyes are nothing like the sun."

XVII

Who is the queen of my fancy? Well,
My friend would you really like to know?
She is not yellow, white nor gray, and so
Must be something else. I'm afraid to tell,
Since all that's mean between heaven and hell,
Abhor the color black. She's cherub, though,
And all the fair and the impartial know,
She is a beautiful, beautiful angel.
I care not what your prejudice, you'll love
Her in your heart, when the light of her dark eyes
Beam [sic] on you, like the flash of stars above
A dark and rolling cloud; her form complies
With all the art the Grecian sculptors prove;
"Her voice?" A chord escaped from paradise.

While not exactly a beacon of aesthetic achievement, this is the first African American love sonnet explicitly devoted to a black person. The speaker is clearly aware of transgressing accepted boundaries in disclosing his beloved's color. After much playful prevaricating he brings the subject up in a strikingly pejorative manner. Once he has come out with it his mood shifts, his "fancy" takes wings, and the rest of the poem is all adoration and praise. In expressing these moods, the poem engages both the Shakespearean and the Petrarchan traditions. The Shakespearean tradition makes itself felt in the playful wit that underlies the first quatrain (is the speaker abasing himself or is he just teasing the ignorant reader?). It also informs the structure of the poem: like

Shakespeare's sonnet 130, Beadle's sonnet moves from an apologetic description of the beloved's unconventional looks—especially her dark skin—to a celebration of the speaker's love. The African features of Shakespeare's beloved were rarely acknowledged by nineteenth-century genteel readers, but for Beadle they provide an important precedent that serves to legitimize his articulation of black love in a traditionally white form.

Beadle's resurrection of the racial element in Shakespeare's sonnets suggests an alternative reading not only of these texts but of the entire canon of white love poetry and its tendency to occlude other ethnicities. The shift to the Petrarchan mode in the second part of the sonnet extends this dynamic to another major figure in the canon. Here Beadle's strategy is based not on continuity but on revision. He now employs the traditional Petrarchan patterns and devices that Shakespeare ridiculed—the beloved as angel, her eyes like stars, her voice like music from paradise—but modifies them with the adjective "dark." The awkward, paradoxical constructions that ensue signify on the racial exclusiveness of traditional love imagery, which is predicated on lightness not darkness. A phrase like "the light of her dark eyes" is comical rather than celebratory, and no matter whether Beadle is continuing the Shakespearean wordplay or simply writing thoughtless poetry, he exposes the limitations of the traditional love sonnet by forcing it to accommodate black subjects. This makes him one of the first African American poets to question the racial epistemology associated with love poetry and the sonnet form in the European tradition.

The nexus of poetic subjectivity and racial signifying reappears with conspicuous variations in Joseph S. Cotter Jr.'s "Out of the Shadows" (53–75), which dates from 1918 and was published in 1920, a year after the poet's early death. Though unfinished, Cotter's sequence has an accomplished, at times intricate structure and is written in a polished if derivative genteel style. Its overall conception is modeled on the Elizabethan sequences; its language on the Romantics,' especially on Keats's. Cotter's craftsmanship shows in his sophisticated style and, most clearly, in the way the sequence holds together as a whole. Its blend of physical and religious love, of adoration and self-reflection, might easily have diluted the narrative structure and overall impact, but Cotter's adept use of leitmotifs and his smooth transitions between individual sonnets create a sense of continuity and make the sequence a unified whole. The authentic feel of these sonnets derives not from rough simplicity but from romantic soul-searching, not from style but from content. It is most palpable when Cotter juxtaposes his worldly, physical love with his anxieties about his impending death.

This tension appears at the beginning of the third sonnet ("'What of the old love?' cries my heart to me; / Ah let it die, I say; ah let it die."), where it remains tentative and is superseded by a discussion of remembered love. It comes to the fore in sonnets V and VI, which record the speaker's flight from a world of mortality and pain to a higher interior vision.

> Here where men, weeping, spend a passing day,
> See one grand sun-set and its after-glow,
> Feel a brief passion, then the heart's decay,
> God rest me as I stand beneath the blow. (V, 5–8)

> All but the vision of thy loveliness
> That dwells within my heart and will not down,
> All must I give for fate is merciless
> And garbs my youth in age's sable gown.
> Though wreathed in tears and deep in sorrow laid,
> I have the vision and it shall not fade. (VI, 9–14)

The transient outer world is described in terms familiar from Keats ("Here, where men sit and hear each other groan"; 370), and the speaker's wistful appeal to the never-fading vision is on one level a conventional topos of genteel romanticism. What makes Cotter's sequence appear more authentic than the usual aestheticist staple is the autobiographical subtext such passages consistently evoke. Like Keats, Cotter died of tuberculosis in his twenties, and by the time he was writing "Out of the Shadows" he knew his death was near. Following the model of such Keatsian classics as "To Autumn," he loads his poems with autobiographical allusions to create an impression of urgency and sincerity despite the highly poeticized language. Cotter's father, who became his literary executor, made sure that these allusions would not be lost, and the handful of scholars who have discussed Cotter's poetry all follow his lead. In James Robert Payne's edition of the *Complete Poems,* for example, Cotter's poetic allusions to his "numbered years" (63) blend seamlessly into the editor's Keatsian musings about "the final autumn of the young poet's life" and the "special poignancy" the sonnets acquire against this background (14–15).

Drawing on the Keats legend to enhance his own renown as a poet, Cotter is effectively signifying on his illustrious precursor. In keeping with the polished genteel style of his sonnets, Cotter's signifying remains a covert suggestion rather than a political statement, but on this covert level it does extend to racial questions, for example through the frequent leitmotifs. The very first sentence of the sequence—"The starlight crowns thee when thou standest there"—already indicates the conflation of profane and religious elements in the leitmotifs "stars," "light," and "crown," which are joined by "child" and "wreath" in the second poem. Later on, the light/dark imagery serves to link the beloved's appearance to the speaker's inner life: the dark in her eyes reminds him of the darkness in his soul; his vision, in the passage quoted above, is "wreathed in tears." Many of the leitmotifs can be read in a racial sense. Almost every poem in which the beloved is described mentions her "dark eyes," which sometimes become "darkling eyes" in the speaker's imagination. Cotter also uses the trigger word "veil" and links it with fin-de-siècle "twilight visions" in a poem that suggests both a conventional and a racial reading (XII, 1–2, 10–14). Of course the title of the sequence, "Out of the Shadows," easily lends itself to a racial reading as well: though Cotter hesitates to link the "shadows" with the situation of black Americans, the title alone was likely to suggest such a reading in the transition to the Harlem Renaissance.

Published in 1899 and 1920, respectively, the sequences by Beadle and Cotter frame the period leading up to that movement, not just chronologically but also in their very different ways of developing psychological interiority in the sonnet form. Beadle's sonnets are simple, blunt, rough; Cotter's are sophisticated, eloquent, and smooth. Both sequences seem to be modeled on Shakespeare, but where Beadle adopts the outspoken sincerity of Shakespeare's sonnets Cotter focuses on their structure, wit, and wordplay. What both poets have in common is their assured subjectivity and their use of the love sonnet as an innocuous venue for self-expression in spite of the restrictions placed on blacks at the time. Their signifying points a way out of the dilemma Johnson was to identify in his *Book of American Negro Poetry* (which incidentally does not include work by either Beadle or Cotter): the dialect white readers and publishers expected from African American poets effectively restricted their range to "humor and pathos" (22); it barred them from formulating complex ideas and subjectivities without sounding pretentious or burlesque. The sonnet liberated poets from this dilemma in that it conferred dignity rather than ridicule on the expression of black feeling. The troubling self-inscriptions of Beadle and Cotter show how the narrow room of the sonnet became both a sanctuary and an operational base for a politicized black interior.

Paying Tribute: The African American Praise Sonnet

After the Reconstruction period, when many Northerners lost interest in the black cause and the old Southern elites were reasserting their influence, African

American writers found their options for political intervention severely curtailed. Poets seeking publication in the widely read quality magazines were expected to offer dialect verse or apolitical genteel poetry. The genteel tradition did champion one genre, however, that lent itself to effective political intervention: poetic tributes to public figures, which were a staple of the leading magazines. Alongside poems dedicated to canonic writers and artists, these magazines continued to accept tributes to abolitionists and Civil War heroes, especially if these tributes followed genteel conventions. One of these conventions was the sonnet form, which had been popularized as a vehicle for politicized praise by the household gods of the genteel intelligentsia, Milton and Wordsworth. The praise sonnet supported African American poets' claims to intellectual equality with canonic white figures and enabled them to articulate racial concerns in a widely accepted form.

Scholars such as Josephine Milnes have argued that American poetry was a poetry of praise from the beginning: praise of the new land and its inhabitants, expressed in eighteenth-century forms of public tribute such as the ode, which persisted in the United States long after the leading British poets had dropped them. While this genealogy is debatable on several counts, it draws attention to a strand of American writing in which African Americans played an important role from an early point. The earliest known poem by an African American, Lucy Terry's "Bars Fight" (c. 1746), praises settlers for repelling an Indian attack, and Phillis Wheatley's widely discussed *Poems on Various Subjects* (1773) largely consist of tributes. Since these tributes were addressed to whites, including slaveholders, they were neglected by generations of literary historians. Recent scholarship has shown, however, that Wheatley used many of her praise poems for subtle criticism or covert political exhortation (Willard 234–43).

On the whole, her successors in the antebellum period did not continue this legacy. Openly political tributes such as Joseph C. Holly's "Freedom's Champions" (1853), a roll call of abolitionist heroes, remained exceptions to the rule. This changed during the Civil War, which inspired a host of partisan tributes to public figures from white and black poets alike. Though neglected by many histories of Civil War writing, these tributes fulfilled important functions in contemporary political discourse. Beside strengthening patriotic feelings on either side, they often called on volunteers to join the battle. The most frequent subject of poetic tributes was Abraham Lincoln, who came to embody the virtues of freedom, moral integrity, and upward mobility to which Northern writers laid claim.[9] Many African American writers, for example John Willis Menard, caught on to the trend and published tributes to political figures that contained explicit political demands (3–4; 50; 66–67). Its most important legacy was the inclusion of African Americans such as Phillis Wheatley and Frederick Douglass among the circle of addressees. Given that "American Negroes as heroes form no part of white America's concept of the race," as James Weldon Johnson was to note several decades later ("Dilemma" 479), these tributes exerted a subtle but persistent revisionary force on the collective imagination.

Interest in the political demands of African American poets receded with the demise of Reconstruction, but poetic tributes remained a vehicle for covert revisionary strategies. On the one hand, poetic tributes played an important role in the struggle over the emancipatory legacy of the Civil War, which white supremacists in the South were busy rescinding. By the end of the century, Daniel Aaron points out, an uneasy mixture of guilt, nostalgia for the antebellum period, and "oblique sympathy for the beaten South" pervaded public discourse (*Unwritten War* 92). African Americans, by contrast, had a specific set of achievements to defend and of political goals to reach. The genteel bourgeoisie was the very group they needed to win over in order to revive the struggle for civil rights. On the other hand, the praise sonnet afforded a means of self-expression and self-assertion, especially if the speaker was foregrounded or put on an equal footing with the addressee. With the exception of Martin Griffin's *Ashes of the Mind* (2008) and James Smethurst's *The African American Roots of Modernism* (2011), which feature discussions of Dunbar's praise sonnets, the political uses of this form in the postbellum period have escaped scholarly attention. The remainder of this chapter shows that several other poets worked alongside Dunbar to turn the praise sonnet into a vehicle for political demands and for the new black subjectivity.

The importance and the political ambivalence of the African American praise sonnet are illustrated by the work of H. Cordelia Ray, the most prolific poet in the genre. Her first sonnet appeared in a biography of her father, the clergyman and abolitionist Charles B. Ray, that she published with her sister Florence in 1887. Cordelia's sonnet, "To Our Father," introduces the biography and announces the sisters' genteel approach. It opens with a mythological adoration scene and closes with the father's death and divine approval; in between it refers vaguely to the "captive brother" and the "bondman's need" he encountered in his service to Freedom (lines 5; 7). Since these allusions remain abstract, the poem can easily be read as an allegory. It makes no explicit mention of race or slavery, and the general tone is one of benign retrospection. Much the same can be said of the sonnets to abolitionist leaders Cordelia collected in her second volume, *Poems* (1910). The racial or political message of these sonnets is always framed by at least four lines of abstract, idealist apostrophe at the beginning of the poem and several lines of serene glorification at the end. The composition of these sonnets mirrors the publication strategies of many contemporary collections of poetry: potentially controversial statements are couched in thick layers of innocuous gentility.

Despite these limitations, Cordelia's sonnets are of historical interest in that they anticipate the twofold aim of the African American praise sonnet: intervening in political debate while troubling restrictive boundaries of expression. As James Phelan has shown, genteel poets and critics widely regarded the formal constraints of the sonnet as an analogue of the Miltonic values of strictness and propriety (4). While Cordelia published sonnets in praise of both Shakespeare and Milton, her adoption of genteel ideals is signaled by the fact that both of these sonnets are legitimate in form. In the same vein, she locates the achievement of her artist figures not in their personal growth or individual genius but in transcendent determination: "the sight divine" (Milton), "planets . . . in unique arrangement" (Shakespeare), "Celestial forms" (Raphael). Unlike Longfellow's "Chaucer" (1875), for example, Cordelia's artists seem to exist in an abstract, idealistic sphere far removed from any concrete environment, and their art is praiseworthy because it emerges in subordination to higher principles.

While Cordelia does not question the genteel poetics of restraint, her choice of addressees indicates her increasing awareness of a very different force operative in the contemporary praise sonnet: the opportunities it provided for intervening in political debate by celebrating individuals who stood for specific causes such as abolitionism and racial equality. These opportunities were more fully realized as the leading African American poets of the day turned to the form. Paul Laurence Dunbar and Joseph Cotter Sr. published sonnets to Frederick Douglass, Robert Gould Shaw, Harriet Beecher Stowe, Booker T. Washington, and the bishop Charles Woodcock around the turn of the century. Henry Davis Middleton wrote one to W. E. B. Du Bois in 1908, two years before Cordelia Ray reissued her tribute to her father at the head of a group of praise sonnets entitled "Champions of Freedom" that featured addresses to leading abolitionists and to Romantic heroes like Shaw and Toussaint L'Ouverture. The increasing number of black addressees reflected a general trend in the African American intellectual community, where influential figures like the historian William Wells Brown and the journalist Pauline Hopkins sought to instill race pride through portraits of outstanding black figures. As editor of the widely circulating *Colored American Magazine,* Hopkins wrote a series of articles on "Famous Men of the Negro Race" that included pieces on Douglass, L'Ouverture, and many others. She stressed the didactic value of portraying "the deeds of men who have been the models and patterns for the great mass of humanity" and favored stories of individuals who had overcome poverty and discrimination.[10]

The strategic complexity of the praise sonnet in this context is illustrated by the work of the most popular and accomplished African American poet of the time. Paul Laurence Dunbar wrote four praise sonnets, all of them to public figures involved in the struggle against slavery and racism. While he has often been faulted for a lack of racial awareness, his praise sonnets confirm the argument of scholars like Daniel Black and Margaret Ronda that Dunbar's work in traditional European forms had a subversive political dimension. The heroes of his sonnets are clearly situated in the struggle and are judged by the impact they made in it. The concluding lines of "Harriet Beecher Stowe" (1898), for example, draw on the religious, idealistic vocabulary of the genteel tradition to reframe the Civil War as a cleansing experience of racial unity, and they implicitly challenge genteel readers to keep alive its legacy:

> Around two peoples swelled a fiery wave,
> But both came forth transfigured from the flame.
> Blest be the hand that dared be strong to save,
> And blest be she who in our weakness came—
> Prophet and priestess! At one stroke she gave
> A race to freedom and herself to fame. (191; lines 9–14)

The ambiguously subjective voice of these lines capitalizes on the speaker-addressee dynamic inherent to the praise sonnet that acquires political implications when tribute is paid in public. Dunbar was the first African American poet to realize and exploit the interpretive authority that the praise sonnet afforded its speaker. Where the octave of "Harriet Beecher Stowe" conventionally praises the heroine for her service to "Freedom" (line 5), the sestet abruptly shifts to a personal level as the speaker identifies with those who were saved in their "weakness." He leaves it open whether it was American society as a whole that was weak or—the more obvious reading—whether he is a member of the "race" that was led out of its weakness by the prophet-priestess. The same ambiguous subjectivity informs the concluding lines, where Dunbar interweaves the heroic mode with a delayed erotic subtext: the quasi-divine gesture of the priestess giving the race to freedom is conflated with the physical act of the female writer giving herself to fame. At the end of the sonnet, the Harriet Beecher Stowe of the popular imagination turns into a vision of Dunbar's, whose subjective voice marks his claim to a special understanding of his heroine. The political dimension of this vision is not limited to the internal dynamics of the praise sonnet. Dunbar inscribes it into a public debate revived by new editions of *Uncle Tom's Cabin* in the 1890s and the continuing protest the novel incited from white Southerners. Besides taking a stand against Southern revisionism, its formal strategies associate his sonnet with the genteel establishment that was increasingly claiming Stowe as one of its own.[11]

In foregrounding the speaker's thoughts and emotions, Dunbar contributes to the emergence of black poetic interiority discussed earlier in this chapter, but he goes a step further than his contemporaries in that he turns the sonnet into a site of struggle between speaker and addressee. This empowering strategy is best illustrated by a comparison with Cordelia Ray's sonnets to European artists, where the supremacy of the addressee remains unquestioned. Ray largely effaces her speaking voice from these sonnets and leaves the stage to the heroes and the divine forces inspiring them. Her sonnets may foreshadow the defining power of the praise mode, but on the whole they reflect the unfavorable position in which African Americans of the period found themselves when interacting with whites. The sonnet tradition provided influential models for such skewed interaction, but what many genteel poets failed to realize was the subversive power these very models offered.

European poets had explored the dynamics of the speaker-addressee relationship from an early point, as the love sonnets of Petrarch and his epigones indicate. In situating the beloved in an ideal sphere beyond his reach, the speaker of the Petrarchan sonnet opens himself up to his beloved in full knowledge that real communication and physical interaction are unattainable. The very act of verbalizing this abject posture gives the speaker an important advantage over the beloved: it is he who speaks, and thus has the power to define both the beloved and his relationship to her. The Petrarchan hierarchy was never strictly adopted in the English sonnet nor, for that matter, in the sonnets of Michelangelo, which educated African Americans were likely to have read in Longfellow's popular translations.[12] As a theoretical perspective, however, it captures quite succinctly the position of early African American praise sonneteers. Like Petrarch, these poets had little hope of meeting their heroes on an equal footing. Death or celebrity put most addressees beyond their reach; the segregationist ideology of the period discouraged unrestrained communication between black and white; and African Americans were barred from the sort of cultural and political stature that would have provided a counterweight to the hero's. A sonnet like William Cullen Bryant's "To Cole, the Painter, Departing for Europe" (1829), whose speaker praises and advises the illustrious addressee not just as a friend but with the authority of a whole continent behind him, was inconceivable in nineteenth-century African American poetry.

Despite these limitations, the ambivalent address of the praise sonnet provided black poets with the same opportunities Petrarch had gained from it. Dunbar made use of these opportunities to explore strategies of indirect self-assertion and subjective reinscription. In the sonnet to Harriet Beecher Stowe, for example, he brings his defining power to bear on the addressee's achievement and inflects the commanding, authoritative voice of the Miltonic-Wordsworthian tradition with a distinctly African American individuality. Another striking example for such self-assertion is his attempt to position himself among the most revered poets of the genteel canon. His 1903 sonnet to Frederick Douglass, the critic Marcellus Blount notes, ostentatiously fore-grounds the hero by depicting him as a god-like father figure whose return to this world would amount to a Second Coming ("Caged Birds" 232). Such exalta-tion notwithstanding, the opening lines of the poem indicate that Dunbar's focus is not on praising Douglass. It is on investing his own voice with the sort of authority Bryant had deployed in his sonnet to Cole:

> Ah, Douglass, we have fall'n on evil days,
> Such days as thou, not even thou didst know,
> When thee, the eyes of that harsh long ago
> Saw, salient, at the cross of devious ways,
> And all the country heard thee with amaze. (339; lines 1–5)

This opening is at once deeply personal and consciously public. It can be read either as an intimate conversation between two leaders of the race or as an appeal of (black) America to a past that was "harsh" but still preferable to the present. Dunbar was keenly aware of the representative role accorded to him by whites and blacks alike, a role that brought enormous expectations to weigh on his work. His sonnet to Douglass first appeared in an issue of the influential magazine *Outlook,* for example, alongside the first installment of Booker T. Washington's *Up from Slavery* and a story by Charles Chesnutt. It takes to new heights the self-assertion of the speaker, who claims to represent "all the country" and signifies on the opening lines of Wordsworth's "London, 1802" ("Milton, thou should'st be living at this hour! / England hath need of thee"; *Poems* 185) to position himself as the new Wordsworth to Douglass' Milton.

Through its many-layered voice Dunbar's sonnet unsettles much of the racial certainty on which mainstream America based its culture and self-conception. Not only does it elevate an African American into the ranks of universally acclaimed leaders, but the Wordsworth intertext posthumously establishes a veritable genealogy of black achievement and authority. Pivoted on the ambiguous "we" of the first line, this authority no longer confines itself to the black sphere but may be read as expanding onto America as a whole. It hints at the reversal of fortune for blacks after Reconstruction in forceful but general imagery that might just as well refer to the entire country, the ship of state: "Not ended then the passionate ebb and flow"; "the waves of swift dissension swarm"; "Honour, the strong pilot, lieth stark" (lines 6–10). The fate of African Americans is conflated and tied up with the fate of America as a whole, and the boundaries between the two begin to blur.

There is a similar pattern in "Robert Gould Shaw" (1900), whose initial publication in *Atlantic Monthly* and subsequent reprints across the nation are a measure of Dunbar's mastery of genteel aesthetics. Shaw, a Civil War officer who agreed to command the all-black Massachusetts 54th Regiment and fell in battle, had quickly become a hero among Northerners and especially among African Americans, who regarded him as a martyr to the cause. Among the several dozen poems written about him in the aftermath of the war, Dunbar's is unique because of its pessimistic stance. Like many of these poems, including one by Cordelia Ray (*Poems* 88), it opens with the stock devices of genteel praise as Shaw is envisioned studying the military arts in an idealized, mythological setting. This has led some scholars to conclude that it exemplifies the contemporary preference for elegiac, depoliticized tributes, but the implications of Dunbar's poem point beyond the genteel tradition in several respects.[13]

Instead of the rhetorical questions familiar from genteel poetry, for example, the poem opens with an uneasy interrogation into the motives that impelled Shaw to replace military school with the fateful commission. The conventions of the sonnet genre suggest that these questions will be answered in the sestet, but Dunbar goes on to reinforce his doubts about Shaw's decision instead of sublating them:

> Far better the slow blaze of Learning's light,
> The cool and quiet of her dearer fane,
> Than this hot terror of a hopeless fight,
> This cold endurance of the final pain,—
> Since thou and those who with thee died for right
> Have died, the Present teaches, but in vain! (360; lines 9–14)

Rather than celebrate the historic hero, he relates the hero's deeds to the present time and uses the idyllic setting of the octave as a foil against which the bleak reality of post-Reconstruction racial conflict stands out the more forcefully. Dunbar has been called "the first pessimistic poet in the black literary tradition"

(Bruce, *Black American Writing* 78), and the imagery of lines 11 and 12 in particular foreshadows protest sonnets like Claude McKay's "If We Must Die" (1919) in its embittered starkness (see Chapter 2). At the end of the poem the speaker's situation and feelings overshadow the hero's deeds—a new development in the African American praise sonnet, and one that recalls the shift from the Miltonic to the Wordsworthian mode in the English sonnet. Dunbar's ambiguity, pessimism, and focus on current problems contradict Griffin's claim that by this time "the evocation of the Civil War had . . . been cleansed of any emancipatory dynamic" (*Ashes* 27). Dunbar's praise sonnets announce a shift that would lead away from assimilation and the Bookerite celebration of race achievements toward the protest of the Harlem Renaissance.

The effects of this shift were slow in making themselves felt among Dunbar's contemporaries. Dunbar was enormously influential as a dialect poet and a representative of his race, but the praise sonnets that emerged in the decade or so after his death were conventional or even retrogressive in voice and style—including one sonnet to Dunbar himself by James D. Corrothers.[14] The hierarchy of speaker and addressee was rarely questioned in these sonnets, nor did the speaker assert his individuality in any way. There are two exceptions to this rule: two contemporaries of Dunbar's who did use the praise sonnet to carve out positions for themselves, albeit in a more restrained manner than their famous peer. The first of these is T. Thomas Fortune, a radical journalist and agitator whom John Hope Franklin ranks "preeminent among the secular black leaders of his time" (vii). While Fortune seems to have regarded poetry more as a filler for newspapers than as a vocation in itself, his radical beliefs occasionally led him beyond the confines of genteel taste. In a distinctly Keatsian sonnet to Edgar Allan Poe, Fortune opens not with an apostrophe to the hero but with a statement by and about the speaker:[15]

> I know not why, but it is true—it may,
> In some way, be because he was a child
> Of the fierce sun where I first wept and smiled—
> I love the dark-browed Poe. (lines 1–4)

The autobiographical references in these lines underline that the speaker is not a generic 'lyrical I' but T. Thomas Fortune, a black man born in the Old South. The ostensible hero of the sonnet, Poe, does not appear until the fourth line, by which point he has been defined in terms of his likeness to Fortune. The heroes' shared biography is presented in a remarkably racialized vocabulary. Fortune's contemporaries were likely to stumble over the phrase "a child / Of the fierce sun"—not so much because it misstates Poe's biography (born in Boston, he was widely regarded as a Southerner in the nineteenth century) but because in a racial context it connoted African rather than Southern origins. Speculating about the "mixed blood" of celebrated artists was a favorite pastime among the emerging black intelligentsia. Beside obvious cases like Pushkin and Dumas, popular candidates included Robert Browning, Leigh Hunt, and Ludwig van Beethoven, whom Cordelia Ray had praised in rather unsuspicious terms (Brawley, "Elizabeth" 28). Against this background Fortune's description of "dark-browed Poe" suggests a bond that goes deeper than intellectual or geographical proximity. Together with the poem's general focus on interior kinship, the suggestion lays claim to a much closer relationship between speaker and hero than in most other praise sonnets of the time, including Dunbar's.

The other African American poet of the period to modify the hierarchies of the praise sonnet was William Stanley Braithwaite, who wrote in a style similar to Fortune's but, as we have seen, stood for a decidedly individualist conception of black achievement. His elevated social position made Braithwaite the first black poet who could address well-known white figures on a basis of personal acquaintance and mutual esteem, the way the Boston Brahmins of the nineteenth century had acknowledged each other in their verse. Braithwaite was invited to the centenary celebration of Whittier's birth in 1907, to which he contributed an ode, and most of his praise sonnets are occasional poems of this kind. Beside several tributes to his idol Keats, he wrote sonnets on the deaths of Arthur Upson and Thomas Bailey Aldrich and a birthday sonnet to his friend and benefactor Thomas Wentworth Higginson (*House* 23–26; 82). These sonnets emphasize the genteel, aristocratic environment in which speaker and addressee interact, and they develop a voice that is at once confidential and representative. Braithwaite circumvents the degradation implicit in earlier African American tributes by directing his praise not to major figures like Shakespeare and Lincoln but to acquaintances from his own social environment. Speaking from a secure position within this environment guarantees his praise a certain reciprocity, and the rhetoric of his poems reinforces this claim.

The contrast to previous African American praise sonnets is most palpable in Braithwaite's sonnet to Higginson. A noted abolitionist, Higginson commanded the all-black Massachusetts 55th Regiment in the Civil War. Unlike Robert Gould Shaw, the commander of the 54th, Higginson did not die in battle but went on to become a respected member of the liberal Boston elite. While the sonnets to Shaw praise a legendary martyr, Braithwaite praises the venerable honoree at a birthday party, and where the other poets look up to their hero in Elysian heights, Braithwaite is a member of the party and addresses a friend (*House* 82):

> Beneath the bare-boughed Cambridge elms to-day
> Time takes no flight in his unwintered heart;
> Where fourscore years and three came to depart,
> The vision shines that cannot burn away. (lines 1–4)

In this aristocratic setting Braithwaite speaks for the assembled New England elite. He deploys a "we" very different from that of earlier African American poets, and even among this illustrious gathering his laudatory role grants him a prominent position. Rather than bow before the addressee, he brings the full authority of his representative role to bear on Higginson when he crowns him in the name of the entire party: "O reverend head, take this our crown of praise, / On his, thy birthday, hallowed by our love" (lines 9–10). The status of near-equality Braithwaite achieved and articulated through his poetry distinguishes him from other African American poets of the time, but it came with the price of complete assimilation: assimilation to a white literary field that was always ready to play the race card against him (Szefel, "Beauty" 575), and assimilation to a genteel tradition that discouraged poets from innovative, political, let alone race-conscious approaches.

While none of the poets discussed in this chapter went so far as to articulate open protest, it has become clear that the sonnet form served a variety of political ends in the late nineteenth century. The praise sonnets of Dunbar, Fortune, and Braithwaite challenged the conciliatory narrative of the Civil War that was helping suppress black people and black perspectives. They laid claim to a position in the literary and social fields for the author and appropriated a venerable genteel form for the purpose. Much the same can be said about Beadle's and Cotter's sonnets of interiority, which challenged racial prejudice in various contexts. All of these sonnets are examples for what Houston Baker calls the "mastery of form" (*Modernism* 24–27), but they go beyond the mere demonstration of intellectual ability. In addressing specific areas of racial discrimination and developing formal strategies to articulate their concerns, they point forward to the ethnic and cultural self-confidence that would characterize the Harlem Renaissance.

Chapter 2

NEW NEGRO AND GENTEEL PROTEST
The Sonnet during the Harlem Renaissance

Historians have suggested various starting points for the Harlem Renaissance: the Silent Protest Parade of 1917, for example, which saw some 10,000 African Americans marching down Fifth Avenue to protest racist violence, or its more audible counterpart, the return parade of the Harlem Hellfighters from World War I (Gill 220; Jobs 55). While these parades contributed to the emerging Harlem Renaissance by troubling the geographical and discursive boundaries of racial segregation and discrimination, another troubling event took place in the bounded space of the sonnet. The publication of Claude McKay's "If We Must Die" (1919), possibly the best-known sonnet by a black writer, spread a message of radical protest among a mass audience. Reprinted and recited across the country, its memorable message quickly spread beyond the narrow, genteel readership of previous African American poetry and came to include many Americans who could not even read. From contemporaries such as Arna Bontemps, Sterling Brown, and James Weldon Johnson all the way to recent scholars like Ann Douglass and Cameron McWhirter, it has been viewed as a key contribution to the unprecedented cultural self-confidence that came to characterize the Harlem Renaissance.[1]

In more strictly literary terms, "If We Must Die" asserted the confrontational attitude toward the white tradition that Houston A. Baker has identified as characteristic of African American modernism. In *Modernism and the Harlem Renaissance* (1987), Baker claims that earlier African American writers were predominantly concerned with "mastery of form": the attempt to participate in the white literary tradition by adopting and perfecting its forms of expression. While mastery of form held considerable potential for subversion from within, Baker argues, it limited black self-expression by restricting writers to predefined rules. The early twentieth century marks the historical point when mastery of form was superseded by its counterpart, "deformation of mastery." Baker characterizes deformation of mastery as a "phaneric" attitude in that it resembles the "display" of animals defending their territory (56; 91).

A statement of vigorous, uncompromising protest like "If We Must Die" epitomizes this deformative approach—one would think. In Baker's view, however, McKay's poem is an attempt at mastery of form because it relies on the predefined form of the sonnet (85). This paradoxical classification raises a question central to the conjuncture of politics and poetics in the Harlem Renaissance: Why were so many black writers adopting the conventional form of the sonnet to attack white racism at a time when the white avant-garde was already dismantling that form? By 1920, George Hutchinson points out, black writers no longer needed to adopt traditional forms to get published in avant-garde magazines (255–57). American poetry was being reshaped by iconoclasts like E. E. Cummings, who made his mark by stripping the sonnet of all recognizable rules, and William Carlos Williams, who believed that the sonnet and other conventional forms needed to be "de-formed" because they lacked originality. If Williams thought that the sonnet "stultifies" the liberatory impulse of modernist experimental writing (18), why did African American writers, for whom the liberatory project had far greater urgency, take the trouble to express radically deformative protest within its boundaries?

This chapter traces several possible reasons for their choice, all of which suggest that the search for a starting point of the Harlem Renaissance risks obscuring the continuities at work in African American writing of the 1910s and 1920s. For one thing, "If We Must Die" was not a singular or unprecedented manifestation of black protest in the sonnet form. Drawing on a much broader archival basis than previous scholarship on African American sonnets from the period, the chapter traces a gradual, cautious shift toward political radicalism in the protest sonnet of the 1910s—a heritage McKay adapted once he began to publish in progressive magazines later in the decade. The protest sonnets of the period are characterized by a tension between individual and collective assertion that found its most poignant expression in McKay's oeuvre but was shared by a number of other African American poets. The structural and historical characteristics of the sonnet seem to have made it a preferred venue for dramatizing this tension.

Another continuity that helps explain poets' interest in the sonnet is the persistence of the genteel conventions that had encouraged the adoption of the form in the late nineteenth century (see Chapter 1). A survey of leading journals of the Harlem Renaissance, especially *The Crisis, The Messenger,* and *Opportunity,* shows that literary and political writers alike were used to articulating protest in ways compatible with genteel sensibilities. In literary criticism, the frequent use of the sonnet form was largely taken as a matter of course. One of the few skeptical comments came from Wallace Thurman, a champion of experimental and vernacular writing, who argued that McKay's "message was too alive and too big" for the boundaries of the form (34). For most other critics, schooled as they were in the European literary tradition, it was hardly surprising that a Renaissance would produce sonnets. Alain Locke even welcomed these sonnets as a promise of Dantesque achievements to come. If "the Umbrian stiffness is still upon us," he wrote, "the Florentine ease and urbanity looms just ahead" (115). William Stanley Braithwaite tempered his praise of McKay's sonnets by noting that "If We Must Die" "hovers . . . over the race problem" despite its "admirable spirit of courage and defiance" ("Negro" 40). There was nothing remarkable, it seems, about the notion of voicing defiance in a sonnet: for genteel critics the only surprise was that a gifted poet like McKay would choose to voice defiance at all.

Scholars including Nathan Huggins and Barbara Foley have pointed out that the focus on cultural achievement that came to characterize the decade was the result of a successful attempt by middle-class intellectuals to steer the New Negro movement away from leftist radicalism. While the genteel leanings of influential figures such as James Weldon Johnson, W. E. B. Du Bois, and Alain Locke are often noted, scholars tend to foreground the politically and aesthetically progressive aspects of the period.[2] Even studies of the continuities between nineteenth-century and Harlem Renaissance literature, most importantly James Smethurst's *The African American Roots of Modernism* (2011), foreground the modernism of earlier writers rather than the gentility of later ones. As a result, the pervasive influence of genteel conventions on the Harlem Renaissance has rarely been examined in any depth.

The second section of the chapter offers such an examination. Its survey of the sonnets published from the mid-twenties onward confirms the shift from radical to genteel politics and identifies the sonnet as a space in which genteel and protest traditions came together. The aesthetically accomplished sonnets of Countee Cullen, Sterling Brown, and Helene Johnson articulate political protest much less directly than McKay did some years earlier. Instead of voicing an explicit, confrontational message, they signify on racial prejudice in a manner comparable to the genteel poets of the late nineteenth and early twentieth centuries. These sonnets largely heed the boundaries of bourgeois taste and often require academic background knowledge for their protest message to become readable in the first place. They too challenge Baker's distinction between mastery of form and deformation of mastery: they are unquestionably concerned with aesthetic achievement but assert their superiority over most readers, including whites, on the grounds of this very achievement. The deeply ambivalent sonnets of the Harlem Renaissance, this chapter argues, do not so much attempt to deform the white literary tradition as to *re*form it.

THE SONNET AND THE EMERGENCE OF BLACK RADICAL PROTEST

When McKay entered the African American poetic scene in the mid-1910s, he arrived in time to witness the transformation of the nineteenth-century uplift sonnet into a vehicle for political agitation. While uplift sonnets like James D. Corrothers' "The Negro Singer" (1912) were still appearing in genteel quality magazines, the emergence of the black protest sonnet took place in the pages of *The Crisis,* which McKay must have known from an early point. Sociologists define protest as a collective, often emotional political attempt to transform certain aspects of society that uses language as one of its tools (Melucci 332–34; Opp 45–57). The sonnet is conducive to such intervention because its tight shape, metric pattern, and regular rhyme scheme allow for poignant messages and make it easy to memorize. The rhetoric of persuasion that shaped the history of the genre provides ample material for protest poets. In traditional love and praise sonnets, however, persuasion had been an intimate matter that took place between speaker and addressee. The previous chapter has shown that the genteel sonneteers of the postbellum period tended to retain this intimate setting.

The tension between the generic individualism of the sonnet and the collective demands of New Negro protest can be found in many sonnets from the period, including Leslie Pinckney Hill's "Vision of a Lyncher." Published in the January 1912 issue of *The Crisis,* this was the first African American sonnet that openly protested against racial injustice:

VISION OF A LYNCHER

(Written for The Crisis and dedicated to His Excellency, the Governor of South Carolina.)

Once looked I into hell—'twas in a trance
Throughout a horrid night of soul-wrought pain;
Down through the pit I saw the burning plain,

Where writhed the tortured swarm, without one glance
Upward to earth or God. There in advance
Of all the rest was one with lips profane
And murderous, bloody hands, marked to be slain
By peers that would not bear him countenance.
"God," cried I in my dream, "what soul is he
Doomed thus to drain the utmost cup of fate,
That even the cursed of Tartarus expel?"
And the great Voice replied: "The chastity
Of dear, confiding Law he raped; now Hate
His own begotten, drives him forth from hell."

The sonnet's political thrust is established as early as the dedication, which marks it as a concrete intervention in the lynching debate. Like many of Hill's poems it proceeds didactically, by means of a deterrent example. The neat syntactic division of the Petrarchan sestet into two tercets focuses the reader's attention on the moral lesson of the last three lines. The religious framing allows Hill to announce his lesson in the voice of God and to posit an indisputable divine Law that overrules whatever human laws the governor of South Carolina might invoke or pervert to condone lynching. The most remarkable aspect of the sonnet is the hierarchy established by the speaker's gaze at the beginning: where the highest possible position envisioned by the black genteel sonneteers like William Stanley Braithwaite was equality with whites (see Chapter 1), Hill emphatically looks "down" on the lyncher from a position of topographical and moral superiority.

Arthur Tunnell's "On Segregation" (1914) is another early manifestation of direct protest in the African American sonnet. Like "Vision of a Lyncher," it was published in *The Crisis,* is marked as a direct political intervention by its subtitle ("Inspired by the Washington protest meeting"), and draws on religious arguments to claim moral superiority for African Americans. Tunnell's sonnet is less effective than Hill's because it recommends propaganda ("Sing . . . the truth") instead of action and ends on a rather weak note of Christian conciliation. But its opening foreshadows some of the strategies McKay would later adopt for his protest sonnets, in particular the direct appeal to his readers and the use of the plural voice to establish a communality of the oppressed:

Strong spirits must awaken! for the time,
Unhealthy with a bitter sick unrest
That ne'er relaxes in our fevered breast,

Bids that we, Godlike, rise above the crime
That sullies the still beauty of our time . . . (lines 1–5)

Tunnell goes beyond the analogies of "Vision of a Lyncher" in that he is not content to claim divine authority but actually equates oppressed blacks with God. The transcendent principle has an ambivalent role, however, since the sonnet builds its claim for black superiority on a Christian attitude of endurance and forgiveness that ultimately weakens the political effectiveness of its protest message. This ambivalence would lead many black protest writers of the twentieth century to shed the religious framework, as John Stauffer has noted (xiii–xv). Tunnell, who passed for white to join a Canadian regiment in World War I and read Dunbar to his comrades without revealing the poet's racial identity ("Notes"), foreshadows this radicalization but remains safely within traditional boundaries. He generally confines himself to formal mastery in this sonnet, even while he tests its limits by including potentially revolutionary appeals.

It was McKay who overstepped these limits and radicalized the protest sonnet following his introduction into radical circles in the mid-1910s. The first of his protest sonnets to reach a wider audience, "To the White Fiends," had been rejected by *The Crisis* before it was published in *Pearson's Magazine* in 1918 and reprinted in the more radical *Liberator* the following year. Like Tunnell's "On Segregation" it opens with a direct appeal, but this appeal is directed at the oppressors, who are confronted with a series of confrontational questions:

Think ye I am not fiend and savage too?
Think ye I could not arm me with a gun
And shoot down ten of you for every one
Of my black brothers murdered, burnt by you?
Be not deceived, for every deed ye do
I could match—out-match: am I not Afric's son,
Black of that black land where black deeds are done? (*Complete Poems* 132–33,
    lines 1–7)

One does not need to contrast these lines with Tunnell's laborious hypotaxis to see that the immediate effect of these questions is phaneric: they confront whites with a frightening display of physical and mental strength. McKay achieves this effect by signifying on the racist associations of blackness with evil, the animalistic, and the unfathomable. Unlike the animal behavior Baker cites as an example for phaneric display, however, McKay's performance is neither instinctual nor unintelligible. It is directed at a specific opponent and uses the opponent's sub-conscious prejudices and fears to stage an impressive confrontation.

The phaneric performance comes to an abrupt end halfway through the poem, however, when the mood shifts toward Christian self-control not much different from Tunnell or genteel uplift ("But the Almighty from the darkness drew / My soul"). A pivotal text in the history of the black protest sonnet, "To the White Fiends" shows that radical protest did not suddenly replace genteel rhetoric but emerged alongside it and slowly began to supersede it at this historical point. Also, the unusual structure of "To the White Fiends" asserts that McKay's choice of the sonnet form is an autonomous act rather than an imitative one. By placing the volta after the seventh line, earlier than his European-trained readership would expect, McKay follows his phaneric performance with yet another display of autonomy. Emphatically placed at a point chosen by himself, McKay's return to placid imitation might be intended to demonstrate his ultimate disregard for the rules and conventions he is imitating. Adopting the white form is no longer a forced concession or a matter of laborious mastery but an off-hand exercise.

McKay's most effective protest sonnet, "If We Must Die," continues the phaneric performance but develops a more specific message: a unifying appeal to the speaker's own community to resist oppression on all levels and by all means.[3]

> If we must die, let it not be like hogs
> Hunted and penned in an inglorious spot,
> While round us bark the mad and hungry dogs,
> Making their mock at our accursed lot.
> If we must die, O let us nobly die,
> So that our precious blood may not be shed
> In vain; then even the monsters we defy
> Shall be constrained to honor us though dead!
> O kinsmen! we must meet the common foe!
> Though far outnumbered let us show us brave,
> And for their thousand blows deal one deathblow!
> What though before us lies the open grave?
> Like men we'll face the murderous, cowardly pack,
> Pressed to the wall, dying, but fighting back!

"If We Must Die" does away with a number of mediating layers that temper the earlier interventions of Hill and Tunnell: the religious framework, the appeal to a common humanity, the focus on the opponent, and the indirect address.

The speaker of "If We Must Die" does not need divine justification to attack injustice: his standard is the well-being of his people. He no longer cares for the oppressors' point of view but focuses on expressing his own. And where the previous sonnets looked to the next world, to their own community, or into the speaker's mind, McKay's speaker is emphatically in this world, his back to the wall, gazing steadily and fearlessly at the enemy. From beginning to end this sonnet is a phaneric confrontation, and no distracting considerations are allowed into it.

What makes "If We Must Die" singular is its appropriation of the sonnet space for a message not previously conceivable in that space. It resolves the tension between the individual and the collective voice by introducing the speaker as part of a clearly defined community—the "kinsmen" who are "hunted" and "outnumbered" by the oppressor. In addition, it signals a fierce willingness on the part of this collective to defend its geographical and discursive space. In retrospect, McKay was too much of an individualist to identify with any community for long, and he rightly pointed out that the collective voice of his best-known poem is not defined along racial lines. Nevertheless, "If We Must Die" helped engender the collective confidence of the Harlem Renaissance and inspired a surge of protest sonnets that were among the earliest literary documents of this new attitude. Volumes such as Raymond Garfield Dandridge's *The Poet* (1920), Leslie Pinckney Hill's *The Wings of Oppression* (1921), Georgia Douglas Johnson's *Bronze* (1922), Carrie Clifford's *The Widening Light* (1922), and McKay's own *Harlem Shadows* (1922) carried numerous sonnets that directly challenged whites and the racial discrimination from which they profited.[4]

These interventions arguably appropriate the sonnet's traditional suitability for articulating desire: first to create a black collective identity, and in a second step to project this collectivity into the public domain, which up to this point had been defined and controlled exclusively by whites. Since they conceive this project in both collective and confrontational terms, however, they contradict Baker's implication that the sonnet cannot be used for deformative purposes by black poets (85). The sonnets discussed so far are more accurately described as combining mastery of form and deformation of mastery. They go well beyond Dunbar and Du Bois, whom Baker regards as precursors of the deformative approach, in their expansive claims for political self-expression. At the same time, they show that the protest sonnet was one of the few forms of African American expression to blend both approaches into a symbiotic whole.

A closer look at the politics underlying the early African American protest sonnet indicates that this symbiosis was made possible by a shared third, a discursive node that linked and held in place the strategies of formal mastery and deformation: the desire to "re-form." Baker's only use of this term in *Modernism and the Harlem Renaissance* comes in a statement on Southern black culture around the turn of the century, which he says "knew it had to re-form a slave world created by the West's willful transformation of Africans into chattel" (47). This statement draws on two meanings of the word 'reform': as a political program and as a redefinition of the discursive and performative spaces Baker calls "forms" (16). We can thus conceptualize re-form as a strategy that employs formal mastery but turns it toward a more aggressive goal: a fundamental redefinition of the rules of behavior and enunciation in American society (cf. Wagers). This aggressive attitude in turn is what re-form shares with the deformation of mastery. In Baker's argument, deformation of mastery requires the discursive construction of a homogeneous original space that can be defended and, ideally, extended onto other spaces. Re-form does not entail such binary, inside-out aggression. Instead it envisions a recharting of the entire enunciative and behavioral sphere that is American society, including those spaces inhabited or contested by African Americans. This inclusive component defies narrow conceptions of black collectivity.

Its visionary outlook notwithstanding, Harlem Renaissance protest was hardly more successful than earlier periods when it came to the short-term, practical effects of re-form. In the discursive space, however, it laid the foundations for later African American achievements by reversing the direction of its re-formative efforts. Instead of imposing mainstream views on black culture, it sought to extend the influence of African Americans' views about race and society. McKay's intellectual background illuminates the scope, strategy, and ambivalence of early Harlem Renaissance re-form efforts. In Jamaica, where his family was well off and held positions of political responsibility, McKay had been introduced to the Fabian movement. The Fabians envisioned a socialist, "collectivist" restructuring of English society.[5] What distinguished them from other left-wing groups was their emphasis on constitutionality and freedom of thought: their goal was change within the system, through political agitation and constructive debate. Even in the most tumultuous periods of the labor struggle in late nineteenth-century England, its co-founder Edward Pease recalled, the Fabian Society "was altogether constitutional in its outlook; political parties of Socialists and Anarchists combining progress with stability were the features of the future we foresaw" (54).

The same combination arguably characterizes the protest sonnets of McKay and his contemporaries: they combine the stability of the sonnet with a progressive call for racial equality. The sonnets McKay published in left-wing journals like *Seven Arts* and *The Liberator* from 1917 onward reflect both his

Fabian leanings and the suitability of the sonnet for such a project of constitutional re-form. The heavily intertextual "J'Accuse" (1919), for example, presents a speaker both scandalized and dejected by reports of yet another lynching. The brutal torture inflicted on the victim is described in visceral detail, yet this powerful message is framed by the conventional sonnet form and embedded in allusions to Zola, Shakespeare, and the Bible. Rather than accusing society as a whole, the poem invites readers to join the speaker in a sphere of civilized interaction opposed to the savagery of racist violence. One of McKay's best known sonnets, "America" (1921), sustains a similar tension between protest and restraint. Here too a radical message of defiance and doom is bounded by the sonnet, whose formal requirements are paralleled with the exigencies of American society: they test McKay's ability at the same time to control his hate and to express it as forcefully as is possible "within [its] walls" (line 9). The poem's emphasis on disciplining boundaries recalls the ambivalent politics of Wordsworth's "scanty plot of ground" (see the introduction) and reflects McKay's own situation in the United States, where his marginal position left him unable to put his re-form ideas into practice—a desire indicated by his initial plan to study agricultural science in order to improve conditions in his homeland. Stripped of the power and resources necessary to re-form society as a whole, McKay and other African American intellectuals turned to phaneric protest as the only remaining way of articulating their re-form ideas.

Ambivalences of Genteel Protest

The younger poets who emerged in the mid-twenties had not experienced the stultifying effects of racial discrimination to the same degree as their predecessors. Born in the early years of the century and raised in aspiring middle-class households, poets like Countee Cullen, Sterling Brown, and Helene Johnson were too young to have lived through the nadir of racial oppression. They were able to acquire a formal education and entered black letters at a point when the emerging literary field of the Harlem Renaissance was establishing a network of intellectual and institutional support. In this congenial atmosphere their focus was on erudition and craftsmanship more than on political combat; on subversive irony more than on phaneric rebellion. In many ways they took up the project of formal mastery begun by the genteel poets around the turn of the century (see Chapter 1). Instead of uplift efforts and pleas for equality, however, they assumed a position of intellectual superiority that allowed them to signify on blacks and whites alike. James Weldon Johnson pointed to the political dimension of this approach when he wrote, in "The Dilemma of the Negro Author" (1928), that "white America does not welcome seeing the Negro competing with the white man on what it considers the white man's own ground" (479). While the sonnets of Cullen, Brown, and Johnson remain within the bounds of received taste, they construct a speaking position from which the white tradition, and especially the absurdities of racism and social segregation, can be exposed to ridicule. The genteel protest sonnet continues the project of re-forming discursive and social structures, but it does so by means of formal mastery and revision rather than phaneric display.

Perhaps because of the general reluctance to emphasize the genteel dimensions of African American writing, the political thrust of this poetry was long undervalued in scholarship on the Harlem Renaissance. Helene Johnson's work was all but ignored until the publication of Verner D. Mitchell's edition of her poetry, *This Waiting for Love*, in 2000. Scholarly discussion of Brown's poetry has focused on his explorations of the vernacular and often bypassed the substantial body of formal poems—including several sonnets—he published in outlets like *The Crisis* and included in his signature collection *Southern Road* (1932).[6] Cullen received ample attention from the beginning but was cast as weakly imitative by early commentators on the grounds that he used conventional forms and European traditions. His declaration that he was going to be a "poet and not Negro poet" became a lightning rod for writers and critics who regarded his work, and by extension most formal and European-influenced poetry, as weak and insufficiently racial. Following Baker's reappraisal of Cullen in *A Many-Colored Coat of Dreams* (1974), critics have tended to acknowledge his artistic achievement but continue to associate his formal choices with a conservative outlook.[7] A few scholars, most notably Jeremy Braddock, have begun to question this association, arguing that Cullen subverts conventional readings of the European intertexts he evokes, and thus revises limiting assumptions about black and formal writing alike.

The sonnet remained a haven for genteel poets throughout the Harlem Renaissance. In quantitative terms, a wide majority of the several hundred sonnets written by African Americans in the 1920s and 1930s are genteel in content, language, and perspective. They revolve around the conventional themes of love, nature, self-awareness, and religion; employ old-fashioned, imitative phrasing; and adopt an apolitical view often directly indebted to uplift principles. Even in collections by outspoken protest poets like Dandridge and Hill, political sonnets are outnumbered by blandly conventional ones. In the 1920s, however, some poets began to signify on the ideological implications of the form. Anne Spencer's "Life-Long, Poor Browning" (1927) playfully commiserates Robert Browning for never having known the beauties of Virginia but does not expand this attitude into a challenge to the authority of the European tradition. Jean Toomer's "November Cotton Flower," on the other hand, celebrates African American liberation and empowerment—"Brown eyes that loved without a trace of fear" (24, line 13)—in the guise of a simple nature story. It proceeds in rhymed couplets, but once the rhyme scheme has been safely established Toomer makes it accommodate the black vernacular by rhyming "saw" with "before" (lines 11–12). Since the poem appeared in Toomer's widely praised book *Cane* (1923), it must have been known to most poets of the Harlem Renaissance and certainly to core figures like Cullen, Brown, and Johnson. It might have taught them that even a finely wrought, genteel sonnet could carry a subversive political message.

Cullen was the first to put this idea into practice. His pervasive engagement with European poetic forms is signaled by the prominence of sonnets in his poetry collections. His first two collections open with a sonnet—*Color* (1925) with "Yet Do I Marvel" and *Copper Sun* (1927) with "From the Dark Tower"— and feature a number of additional sonnets, as do his later volumes *The Black Christ and Other Poems* (1929) and *The Medea and Some Other Poems* (1935). It was in the sonnet that Cullen honed his strategies of formal and discursive revision. In 1925 he inaugurated the genteel protest sonnet with its best-known specimen: "Yet Do I Marvel."

> I doubt not God is good, well-meaning, kind
> And did He stoop to quibble could tell why
> The little buried mole continues blind,
> Why flesh that mirrors Him must some day die,
> Make plain the reason tortured Tantalus
> Is baited by the fickle fruit, declare
> If merely brute caprice dooms Sisyphus
> To struggle up a never-ending stair.
> Inscrutable His ways are, and immune
> To catechism by a mind too strewn
> With petty cares to slightly understand
> What awful brain compels His awful hand.
> Yet do I marvel at this curious thing:
> To make a poet black, and bid him sing! (*Color* 3)

Paradigmatically for genteel protest, the sonnet makes its point indirectly and in a somewhat aloof manner. The speaker introduces himself as an eloquent, educated man familiar with Christian religion and classical myth, two of the main discursive resources of genteel poetry (see Chapter 1). The first line signals agreement with the core values of the genteel tradition and its assimilation to mainstream opinions, but the introductory phrase "I doubt not" already performs a fine act of double-voiced ambivalence. It emphasizes the speaker's compliance, yet through this very emphasis indicates a residuum of non-compliance, just as his negation of doubt centers on the very word "doubt." The phrasing of the first line suggests that it will be followed by a qualifying clause ("but . . .") and thus subjects all the assurances that follow to an elusive qualification. The new type of protest manifest in this sonnet is based not on confrontation but on doubt, ambiguity, and questioning. In the same vein, Cullen disrupts the Petrarchan proportionality of statement and reflection by devoting a third quatrain to his already qualified assurances, thus building up suspense and bringing to its full force the subversive exclamation in the concluding couplet. Like McKay's sonnets, "Yet Do I Marvel" feeds on the tension between the stable boundaries of the sonnet form and the unsettling ambiguity of the message. But where McKay adopts the form wholesale and makes it the conduit of his phaneric message, Cullen revises the form so as to occupy the space of the sonnet and the tradition it represents.

"Yet Do I Marvel" takes up the notion that the very phenomenon of the African American sonnet signifies on the white tradition associated with the form, but it radicalizes this notion by means of irony and parody. This opens the sonnet space up to a strategy that Henry Louis Gates calls "motivated" signifying: the attempt to "redress an imbalance of power, to clear a space, rhetorically," which exemplifies the nexus of formal and political revisionism (*Signifying* 124). These qualities are particularly noticeable in Cullen's signifying on religion and on Greek myth. "Yet Do I Marvel" starts as an argument about God's unqualified power but then, in the concluding twist, makes his empowerment of the black poet the only positive ground for God's greatness. The allusions to Tantalus and Sisyphus do not signify on Greek myth itself but on the readers, whom Cullen challenges to keep up with his erudition (Cueva 25–26). On yet another layer, "Yet Do I Marvel" even signifies on the sonnet form itself. As in the genteel praise sonnet, the sonnet form serves to camouflage the racial protest message. Cullen takes this a step further, however: in a metapoetic twist, he challenges the very association of the sonnet form with white intellectual accomplishment. The racial prejudice implied by marveling at the phenomenon of the black poet is reduplicated by the fact that this black poet is singing in one of the most venerable forms of the European poetic tradition.

All of these signifying devices rely on irony and ambivalence so that the message of the poem is more equivocal than that of earlier protest sonnets. The varied critical response to "Yet Do I Marvel" and similar poems shows that many readers do not notice or appreciate their subversive thrust and instead categorize them as "pathetic," "tragic," or otherwise non-empowering. On the other hand, the variety of potential readings secured such poems a broad audience across the racial divide. White magazines kept publishing Cullen's work, and many black preachers read his poems to their congregations. It is a measure of Cullen's stature among his contemporaries that he was the only Harlem Renaissance poet to inspire numerous poetic tributes from his peers.[8] The allusions to "Yet Do I Marvel" in a number of contemporary African American sonnets attests to the influence of his signifying strategies.

These allusions take very different forms, ranging from heartfelt but inept restatements like Gladys Hayford's "A Poem" (1929) to sonnets that can be seen as signifying on Cullen in their turn. Jonathan Henderson Brooks's "Still Am I Marveling" (1928), for example, identifies itself as a direct response to "Yet Do I Marvel" in the subtitle and matches the original, if not in technical execution, then certainly in ambivalent engagement and political thrust. Brooks begins by explaining that he is "moved to supplement" Cullen's "marvel" (37, lines 1–3), and this supplement turns out to be just as ambiguous as the poststructuralists later claimed when they adopted the term. Brooks initially underscores his precursor's argument but gradually clarifies that he is marveling not so much at the mythical and religious ramifications of poetic vocation but at its concrete, material conditions. What he wonders about, he explains in the concluding couplet, is "How one black poet ploughs the whole day long / And burns the oil of midnight for a song" (lines 13–14). Hinting at the propitious influence of Cullen's genteel upbringing, Brooks toys with the suggestion that his own achievement is even more marvelous since it took place in less favorable circumstances; at the very least he prods the reader to question Cullen's favorable self-description. In effect, Brooks takes over the role of the signifying monkey and casts his famous colleague as the poetic lion outwitted by a seeming inferior. A look at contemporary African American sonnets also shows, however, that irony and parody were not the only signifying strategies explored by Cullen's peers.

Sterling Brown is now primarily known for his literary criticism and his folk poetry of the 1930s, but like Du Bois, Garvey, and other black leaders he wrote and admired conventionally genteel poetry (Glaser; M. Thompson). Brown's best-known sonnet might be "Salutamus" (1927), which echoes Cullen's "From the Dark Tower" in its somber evocation of "bitterness," "despair" and "disappointment."

SALUTAMUS

O Gentlemen the time of Life is short.
Henry IV, Part 1

The bitterness of days like these we know;
Much, much we know, yet cannot understand
What was our crime that such a searing brand
Not of our choosing, keeps us hated so.
Despair and disappointment only grow,
Whatever seeds are planted from our hand,
What though some road wind through a gladsome land?
It is a gloomy path that we must go.

And yet we know relief will come some day
For these seared breasts; and lads as brave again
Will plant and find a fairer crop than ours.
It must be due our hearts, our minds, our powers;
These are the beacons to blaze out the way.
We must plunge onward; onward, gentlemen. . . . (*Collected Poems* 106; lines 1, 5)

While Brown's phrasing is somewhat less archaic than Cullen's, his road allegories, passive conclusions ("relief will come some day"), abstract diction, and omission of race as an explicit theme align "Salutamus" with the genteel tradition rather than New Negro protest. The poem acquires a political dimension through its epigraph, which Brown takes from Shakespeare and revises in order to signify on American racism and the white literary tradition. "O Gentlemen the time of Life is short" is a line from Hotspur's speech before he leads his troops into desperate battle against the king at the end of *1 Henry IV*. Paralleling Cullen's use of Greek myth in "Yet Do I Marvel," Brown appropriates this literary and historical centerpiece of the English tradition for a subtle if fateful expression of black rebelliousness. The poem thus unsettles—at least potentially—the complacency of its white readership and undermines racial hierarchies by claiming for contemporary African American concerns the rebelliousness, urgency, and stature that the cultural mainstream reserved for the heroes of white history.

Brown reiterates this claim on a metapoetic level by italicizing the last line of the poem to match the epigraph, even though it is his own: "*We must plunge onward; onward, gentlemen*" (line 14). This double-voiced pastiche undermines the hierarchy separating Shakespeare and Brown, and it blurs the distinction between Hotspur's exhortations and Brown's. In effect it turns the sonnet into a racial, textual, and linguistic hybrid, lending its message a universal touch at the expense of political topicality. It should be noted, however, that Brown added to the poem's immediate relevance some years later when he republished the poem at the beginning of the "Vestiges" section of *Southern Road*. By aligning it directly with the folk poetry that precedes it in this collection, he suggests that both the road allegories and the agricultural imagery ("plant and find a fairer crop than ours," line 11) of "Salutamus" might be grounded in a black folk tradition. With this retrospective reinterpretation, Brown effectively signifies on his own poem.[9]

While Brown voices subtle protest through agricultural imagery, the work of Helene Johnson demonstrates that the urban spaces of 1920s Harlem could be used to the same effect. While recent scholarship by Katherine Lynes and Rebecca Walsh (88–89) has drawn attention to the environmental dimension of Johnson's poetry, her much-anthologized "Sonnet to a Negro in Harlem" negotiates black identity in an urban setting.

> You are disdainful and magnificent—
> Your perfect body and your pompous gait,
> Your dark eyes flashing solemnly with hate,
> Small wonder that you are incompetent
> To imitate those whom you so despise—
> Your shoulders towering high above the throng,
> Your head thrown back in rich, barbaric song,
> Palm trees and mangoes stretched before your eyes.
> Let others toil and sweat for labor's sake
> And wring from grasping hands their meed of gold.
> Why urge ahead your supercilious feet?
> Scorn will efface each footprint that you make.
> I love your laughter arrogant and bold.
> You are too splendid for this city street!

The sonnet does not clarify whether the protagonist is to be taken seriously, or, for that matter, whether the speaker takes him seriously. He is described with a host of adjectives, many of them ambivalent and paired in opposites: disdainful/magnificent, perfect/pompous, rich/barbaric, arrogant/bold. The very first of these adjectives already announces his individualism, which is then traced in his psychology (non-imitative), physiognomy (height), background (foreign), and above all his refusal of Western materialism and competitiveness.

While this attitude distinguishes the protagonist from the disenchanted masses of the modern "city street," it also prevents him from making an impact and instigating any kind of progress either for himself or for his race. Even though the poem can be read as celebrating the protagonist's attitude in a black nationalist spirit, the trope of the vanishing footprint also emphasizes the transience of his territorial gains in both the geographical and the discursive sense of the term. The erasure of his footprint can of course be read as a critique of his supercilious unconcern, but the celebratory tone of the poem also implies a critique of the "best foot forward" camp and its overly instrumental conceptions of racial representation, which threaten to exclude the unconventional, affirmative individuality embodied by the protagonist.

The poem links its spatial imagery with the sonnet form on several levels. The trope of the footprint might be read as alluding to a notion that pervades the major sonnet sequences of the English Renaissance: that mortal humans could be "eternized" by the poet's verse, in the words of a Spenser sonnet about vanishing traces in the sand (645, line 11). At the same time, it illustrates the poem's ambivalent take on its protagonist and the type of African American he represents. Moreover, the discourse on imitation and (verse) feet worked into the poem opens up a metapoetic layer on which the protagonist transcends the very limitations of the form Johnson chooses to celebrate him (Wheeler). In this reading the poem enacts a claim similar to that of McKay's "If We Must Die." It announces a radical break with the rules of a white-dominated society in a form defined by white poets and perfectly obedient to their rules. In contrast to McKay's phaneric attitude, however, Johnson camouflages this announcement in several ironic twists and reversals.

This indirect approach combined with an undeniable mastery of the form gained the second generation of protest poets a wider and more influential audience than their immediate precursors. Yet the second generation fell behind the first as it abandoned the deformative, phaneric attitude from which the early protest sonnets derived much of their force. The emphasis on mastery of form in the second phase opened up new possibilities in terms of range and subversiveness but, divested of the accompanying strategy of deformation, it set narrow limits to the project of re-forming the discursive and behavioral boundaries of American society. And indeed, genteel protest failed to exert significant historical influence despite its aesthetic superiority. Its elitist stance epitomized the African American self-confidence that defined the high period of the Harlem Renaissance but fell out of fashion when the Great Depression shifted the focus to social realism, the folk, and the working class. Neither McKay's individualism nor Cullen's gentility had much to contribute to the collective spirit of social realism. In the years around 1930, McKay, Cullen, and others increasingly turned their attention to the transnational dimension of African American identity and the sonnet became one of their preferred means of exploring the new spaces this turn opened up to them.

Chapter 3

The Sonnet and Black Transnationalism in the 1930s

One of the most influential statements of Harlem Renaissance poetics, W. E. B. Du Bois's "Criteria of Negro Art" (1926), begins with an anecdote about travel. While black Americans understandably demand full citizenship, Du Bois notes, there are moments that make them question the desirability of joining the American mainstream. For him, one such moment was a visit to the Scottish Highlands.

> In the high school where I studied we learned most of Scott's "Lady of the Lake" by heart. In after life once it was my privilege to see the lake. It was Sunday. It was quiet. You could glimpse the deer wandering in unbroken forests; you could hear the soft ripple of romance on the waters. . . . A new day broke and with it came a sudden rush of excursionists. They were mostly Americans and they were loud and strident. They poured upon the little pleasure boat,—men with their hats a little on one side and drooping cigars in the wet corners of their mouths; women who shared their conversation with the world. They all tried to get everywhere first. They pushed other people out of the way. They made all sorts of incoherent noises and gestures so that the quiet home folk and the visitors from other lands silently and half-wonderingly gave way before them. (290)

While Du Bois frames his anecdote in terms of race ("We who are dark can see America in a way that white Americans can not"), he arrives at its central insight by way of travel—the leisurely, cultivated travel of the gentleman abroad. The Americans appear vulgar to him because they disturb the tranquility of his first solitary exploration, because their noisy competitiveness disturbs his own cultured interest in the scenery, and above all because they compare unfavorably to the Europeans who populate the area. "Criteria of Negro Art" thus opens with a nod to genteel transnationalism but radicalizes its political implications. The outside perspective afforded by travel, in Du Bois's view, allows African Americans to recognize and overcome white America's attempt to universalize its own worldview. Instead of aspiring to white standards, he suggests, the cultivated black traveler will bring a variety of experiences and perspectives to bear on the struggle against racial oppression at home. This is what Du Bois did from the 1930s onward, when he turned first to communism and then to Pan-Africanism as means of black liberation. His comments in "Criteria of Negro Art," published at the height of the Harlem Renaissance, highlight the continuity of transnational perspectives in African American culture.

Following the seminal work of James De Jongh, Ann Douglass, and R. Baxter Miller, scholars have widely acknowledged the transnationality of the Harlem Renaissance. Throughout the twenties Harlem was transformed by an unprecedented influx of migrants from the rest of African America and the Caribbean. Artists working in Harlem interacted with other ethnicities, cultures, and nationalities as a matter of course, and those working elsewhere contributed ideas and innovations from around the Atlantic.[1] The popularity of the sonnet is one indicator of this transnationality. Claude McKay and Countee Cullen were among the first to explore the potential of the form for negotiating their relationship to Europe and Africa. Many histories of African American literature suggest, however, that the transnational reach of the Harlem Renaissance faltered in 1929, when the economic crash drained the resources available to African American literati. With few exceptions, scholarship on the African American 1930s focuses on national concerns and regards social activism and folk expression as the shaping forces of literary production. Sterling Brown, Zora Neale Hurston, and Richard Wright are central figures of this narrative, while transatlantic travelers like Cullen and McKay are cast aside as remnants of an earlier period.[2] There is much to be said for the productivity of social and folk poetry, but a closer look at the sonnets from the period shows that transatlantic exchange remained an important factor in African American literature throughout the 1930s. The only area of transatlantic exchange that has received sustained scholarly attention is the communist movement, but the sonnets direct attention to two other areas in which transnational concerns shaped African American writing: travel and Pan-Africanism.

Both travel writing and Pan-Africanism had a longer tradition in African American culture, one that can be traced back as far as the first slave narratives and the emigration societies for freed slaves in the mid-nineteenth century. Both were prominent during the Harlem Renaissance, whose leading representatives frequently traveled to Europe and Africa while the masses were attracted to Marcus Garvey's "Back to Africa" rhetoric. In his study *Artistic Ambassadors: Literary and International Representation of the New Negro Era* (2013), Brian Russell Roberts shows that considerable effort went toward securing ambassadorships for African Americans, and that literary travelers negotiated the ambivalences of being regarded as unofficial ambassadors for a country that denied them full citizenship at home. The social turmoil of the 1930s added further dimensions to black transnationalism: travelers faced the charge of escapism and social irresponsibility while at the same time the communist movement put African Americans into contact with a supposedly global struggle against exploitation, racism, and colonialism.

Despite its frequent theoretical critiques of nationalism, the communist movement drew liberally on national symbolism and strove for a fraternity of workers' republics conceived along national lines. Yet the influence communism exerted on American writers was transnationalizing in more ways than one.[3] The ideal of solidarity among workers undermined the sovereignty of the nation state, as governments around the world were quick to realize. It also motivated intellectuals to look beyond national boundaries, and communism became a main impulse behind African Americans' engagement in debates over international politics and anti-imperialism. Many African Americans on the left also engaged communist policy itself, in the shape of directives from the Moscow-based Communist International. Scholars including Barbara Foley, Gerald Horne, and William J. Maxwell have pointed out that African Americans were no mere recipients of Comintern directives; on the contrary, they subjected such directives to critical discussion at home and sometimes even in Moscow. While these debates were often one-sided and ideologically narrow, they did much to uncover the arbitrariness of American racism and its role in perpetuating social inequality. From the mid-thirties, moreover, the communists appropriated Pan-Africanist positions to broaden their appeal with African Americans, which provided another impulse to look beyond national boundaries.[4]

Whereas travel and Pan-Africanist poets of the thirties found in the sonnet a genre congenial to their transnationalism, communist writers showed little interest in the form. McKay occasionally references communism in his travel sonnets, as we will see, but he had severed his ties with the movement by that time. Cullen's sonnet on the Scottsboro Boys is titled "Not Sacco and Vanzetti" but makes no further reference to the communists although they were instrumental in organizing legal defense for the defendants.[5] Only the regional poets Marcus Bruce Christian and Octave Lilly published a handful of sonnets protesting social inequality that echo communist ideas. Christian's "McDonough Day in New Orleans" (1934), the strongest of these sonnets, details the privations that go into a black girl's festive dress and protests racial as much as social oppression. Lilly's "Saint Charles Avenue" (1938) draws on many of the strategies McKay explored two decades earlier to fault readers for tolerating the lethal effects of social inequality. While both of these poems were published in *Opportunity* magazine, they remained isolated specimens of social protest in the African American sonnet of the period.

The many communist sonnets published by white writers at the time raise the question of why communism and the sonnet did not come together in African American literature. One answer might be that the Comintern tended to conceive African Americans as peasants bound to the local soil, whereas the sonnet, as we have seen, emphasized mobility and intellectual recognition. A related factor was the Black Belt thesis, which held that blacks in the American South constituted an oppressed nation of peasants under white feudal rule. While the Black Belt thesis stressed black self-determination, it effectively bounded African American identity within a conventional territorial nationalism. This ambivalence was particularly noticeable in the literary scene. The communists were early champions of African American literature, as Henry Louis Gates and others have noted, but only when that literature could be read as "social" or "folk" art. Langston Hughes, Sterling Brown, and Richard Wright became the exemplars of such writing, and their prominence ensured that African American literature of the 1930s is still largely perceived in these categories.[6]

For the marginalized transnationalists among black writers, the sonnet offered a means of resisting the limiting implications of folk and social art. While the form was not regarded as incompatible with a leftist agenda, the communist tendency to equate African American writing and folk expression put black poets in a special position. In their hands, the sonnet asserted a degree of mobility and cultivation that the racialized expectations of leftist critics tended to discourage or occlude. It was thus a resistant form but not an escapist one, as Jon Woodson notes in *Anthems, Sonnets, and Chants: Recovering the African American Poetry of the 1930s* (2011), the only extended discussion of the African American sonnet of the period. While Woodson rightly emphasizes the tension between the collective framework of leftist politics and the individualism enacted in the sonnet, his reduction of this individualism to romantic subjectivity is problematic on several counts. The notion that a romantic subjective voice was in itself subversive at this late point in African American literary history is anachronistic (see Chapter 1) and occludes the range of individualities explored not least in the travel sonnet, whose existence seems to have escaped Woodson.[7] The following discussion expands on his and other accounts of African American writing in the 1930s in that it highlights the importance of the travel sonnet and the Pan-African protest sonnet. Poets used both forms to negotiate the collectivist demands of social and folk writing, and to explore geographical, intellectual, and poetic alternatives to national constraints.

TRAVEL, MIGRATION, AND THE SONNET

Some historians of African American writing have drawn a direct line from the slave narrative to twentieth-century travel writing in order to posit mobility as a constitutive category of the African American experience. This broad claim elides the differences between the enforced mobility of slavery and the leisurely connotations of modern travel, and it disregards the fact that before the late twentieth century few black Americans had the time and opportunity to travel outside the United States. The leading writers of the 1920s and 1930s were a privileged minority in this respect, and their reports from abroad were read with interest in *The Crisis* and other publications. Yet the slave narrative genealogy points to an important feature of African American travel writing: such writing complicates the hierarchy of privileged traveler-observer and objectified local population that scholars of travel writing have identified as a template of the genre.[8]

It was the emergence of postcolonial studies that drew attention to this hierarchy and revived scholarship on travel writing in the process. Scholars like Steve Clark, Patrick Holland, and Graham Huggan have pointed out, however, that early postcolonial approaches tended to view the encounter between the traveling colonizer and the local population in binary oppositions such as active/passive and mobile/static, thus effectively reinscribing the power structures they were exposing.[9] This binary model was complicated when travelers from the colonies began to visit the metropolis. The genre-specific power structure of travel writing (the observer defining the observed) now unfolded against the larger, racialized power structure of the colonial system. The writings of African Americans traveling to Europe further complicate this constellation. Marked as racially other yet often perceived as representatives of an economically and politically dominant nation, African American travelers needed to negotiate a variety of subject positions from which to write. They found themselves thrust in shifting self/other constellations as they crossed national, ethnic, and social boundaries. Studies and anthologies of African American travel writing illustrate the variety of ideological currents underlying such writing, which often congeal in the question of race. One example is Langston Hughes's autobiography *The Big Sea* (1945), which ironically chronicles the various races locals ascribed to him in the United States, Mexico, and Western Africa.[10]

The sonnet, like poetry in general, is seldom discussed by scholars of travel writing even though its history is marked by travel. After originating in medieval Sicily, the form spread to country after country, accommodated new languages, and assimilated to regional and national cultures. It acquired a mediating function similar to that of human travelers, with whom it shared the strategy of reporting new observations in a familiar cultural framework. Joachim du Bellay's travel sonnets in *Regrets* and *Les Antiquités de Rome* (1558), the latter translated fairly literally by Spenser as *Ruins of Rome* (1591), inspired a long tradition of brief poetic sketches recording a picturesque scenery and the speaker's response to it. The travel sonnet heightens the tensions between subject and object and between individual and community that characterize travel writing in general. By putting the observing speaker in a privileged position it foregrounds his power of definition while at the same time emphasizing his distance to the observed scene. When the African American writers Alpheus Butler, Countee Cullen, and Claude McKay turned to the travel sonnet, they enacted a many-faceted black transnationalism and explored a broad range of subject positions, from Butler's leisurely gentleman-observer to McKay's unruly vagabondage.

Butler's "Travel Sonnets," a section of his collection *Make Way for Happiness* (1932), are the first sequence of travel sonnets published by an African American. Butler writes in the genteel tradition and assumes the persona of the aloof connoisseur familiar from colonial travel and postcolonial tourism.[11] Despite their broad geographical range—the sequence covers locations in the United States, Cuba, Europe, and Asia—his sonnets remain distant from the places he describes rather than engaging them. Here is Butler's response to a "Castle in Spain":

> A modern youth, while looking at these walls,
> Recalls quaint pictures from a merry past.
> These come to live again. Soon romance calls
> Within this house built then to stay and last. (lines 9–12)

The sonnet draws on several distancing devices. The speaker's personal response is routed through that of a generic "modern youth," which turns the travel experience into an allegory. The historical scene in the speaker's imagination is presented as more interesting than the scenery he actually encounters. This impression is underscored by descriptors such as "quaint" and "exotic," which recur throughout the sequence and suggest that an otherwise unassuming scenery only becomes worthy of interest because of the associations the cultivated traveler brings to it. While Butler succeeds at times in gauging the cultural diversity he encounters in such places in Paris and Havana, his aloofness prevents the kind of engagement with the foreign from which travel poems usually draw their energy. He typically projects the "romance" of his own imagination on the scene he finds before himself, which leaves the hierarchies of conventional travel writing intact. This might have been the reason why Cullen, who traveled in a similar style and with a similar outlook, abandoned the travel sonnet after a few initial attempts.

Cullen's first trip to Europe was part of a pilgrimage to Jerusalem with his father, a pastor and devout Christian. The places Cullen most wanted to see on the way were Paris and Rome, cities that epitomized the European cultural heritage and were associated with some of his favorite poets. Two of the earliest African American travel sonnets, "At the Wailing Wall in Jerusalem" and "To Endymion" (subtitled "Rome, August 1926, after a visit to the grave of Keats"), were inspired by this trip and appeared on adjacent pages in his 1927 collection *Copper Sun* (75–76). In subsequent years Cullen spent most of his summers in France, immersing himself in the language and literature he was teaching in New York. He rarely referred to these experiences in his poetry, however, and even the Jerusalem and Rome sonnets transmit little information about their locations beyond the references in the paratext. They are poetic meditations on endurance in the flow of history, a quality Cullen finds both in the ancient wall and in Keats's poetic legacy. Like Butler, Cullen keeps his distance from the scenes he describes by foregrounding his own reflections and associations.

It was McKay who explored the full complexity of the black traveler's encounter with the foreign, and turned the sonnet into a congenial medium for these explorations. In a way, Harlem was already a part of the transnational experience for McKay since he had moved there from the Caribbean and never fully settled in the United States. In Harlem he found his way into the urban counterculture and associated with communist circles as well as the Caribbean diaspora. His first trip to Europe was to Russia on an invitation from the new communist government, and when the United States government denied him re-entry because of his communist ties he became a self-styled "vagabond."[12] His travels in Europe and Northern Africa were thus involuntary to a considerable degree, and they were rarely undertaken on the kind of financial basis that would have allowed him to remain aloof of local ways.

The sonnets inspired by these travels, known as the Cities sonnets, date from the mid-1930s but remained unpublished in McKay's lifetime. They have recently been recovered amid a general surge of interest in his transnational experience. While some scholars have tried to recuperate this experience into a national agenda by describing his travels as "tragic" or as motivated by an "obsession" to find a "place he could call 'home,'" McKay's life and work are now widely taken to exemplify the trajectories, challenges, and opportunities of the twentieth-century black migrant experience.[13] Since scholarly discussion has focused on his prose writings and his Jamaican poetry, the crucial role of the Cities sonnets in his evolving transnationalism has not yet come under scrutiny. These sonnets, we will see in the following, correct and extend some of the claims made about McKay's transnationalism by previous scholarship.

The Cities sonnets record McKay's attempts to come to terms with the unadulterated experience of new places and cultures. A sensitive traveler, he immerses himself in the atmosphere of each city but remains aware of his inability fully to understand and participate in the foreign culture. Where Butler's sonnets are overly refined, McKay's are raw, unfinished, and often unsuccessful from an aesthetic point of view. They present his immediate impression of a city from the privileged perspective of the educated traveler, but at the same time they reflect on this perspective, drawing attention to the traveler's outside status. While the cities are often described as communities that take the traveler into their fold, McKay remains a misfit, a self-conscious outsider who is only traveling through. His refusal to commit to any form of organized collectivity stands in sharp contrast to the implicit demands of most of the cities he visits. In their different ways, the contested spaces of Northern Africa as well as the European capitals of imperialism (London, Paris) and totalitarianism (Berlin, Moscow) require the visitor to position himself within or toward bounded communities. While he does not systematically challenge these boundaries, McKay uses the travel sonnet to question and resist them in various ways.

McKay's tendency to conceive the indigenous community as "folk" suggests that he is negotiating the tensions between individuality and collectivity against the background of contemporary debates among leftist and African American critics. Like these critics, he regards the folk as a homogeneous, collective entity defined by its rural simplicity. In "Barcelona," a triple sonnet, he describes a festival where the "folk" come "together / From pueblo, barrio, in families" (I.4). In "Fez," the locals appear to him as a "folk so strangely sad": a community unfathomable in its shared sensuality that leaves the traveling observer "haunted" by the glimpses it affords him (8, 5). As in his encounters with communism and the African American bourgeoisie, McKay distances himself from these collective entities. He emphasizes his individuality by foregrounding his own perception of the local "folk."

Since his perception relies primarily on the visual dimension, the sonnets can be read as manifesting the 'imperial gaze' of the colonial traveler (Spurr 13–27). "Fez" is marked as a visual appropriation of the city by its opening words, "Mine eyes saw Fez"; in "Barcelona" the traveler locates himself on the city's "natural towers," watches its "blue carpet spreading to their feet" (lines 2–3), and generally establishes the visual as a leitmotif of the poem. In both poems McKay contrasts the superiority of the appropriative gaze with the thrilling experience of abandoning ratio and control in the city's sexualized underworld. In "Barcelona" the traveler descends from the mountains "Down—to your bottoms sinister and strange: / The nights eccentric of the Barrio Chino" (II.8–9); in "Fez" he glances at the "hood[ed] beauty" of virgins in the "dim passages" of the city (lines 4, 6); in "Marrakesh" his gaze travels from the "high ramparts" of the city walls to the "Salome-sensual dance of jeweled boys" in Berber tents (lines 1, 13). By foregrounding this subjective response, McKay dramatizes the ambivalence of his own position in between national and cultural communities. He is torn between identifying with the local folk and distancing himself through a sexualized, imperial gaze.

Both of these strategies open his sonnets up to charges of Africanism. As John Cullen Gruesser shows in *White on Black: Contemporary Literature about Africa* (1992), Africanism often manifests in the tendency to perceive the continent as a "blank slate" on which various preconceptions and stereotypes can be projected (3–8). McKay's emphatic subjectivity and reliance on the imperial gaze veers into such projection at several points. Arguably, however, his Cities sonnets document no facile Africanism but rather the poet's attempts to understand the foreign without resorting to reductive collective templates. The second sonnet on "Tanger," for example, opens with a critique of colonial exploitation that highlights the stranded vagabond's affinities with the city. Tanger is described as an "iron pirate fettered now," forced to watch the ships go by with their "golden cargo" (II.1–5). The octave concludes with an unanswered question—"What thoughts are hid behind your lowered brow?"—that sounds the note of Africa as a blank slate. Instead of projecting his thoughts on that slate, however, the speaker transfers this role to present-day tourists who "stop to gaze at you in chains / And purchase from the souks a souvenir" (II.9–10). Distancing himself from the touristic gaze, the speaker turns to the countryside, the bled or bilad, where he senses the true soul of this community:

But in the bled the rugged mountaineer,
Invoking God in fierce fanatic pride,
Lives by the shattered glory that still remains. (II.12–14)

Both the tourists and the folk are contrasted with the traveler, who communicates with each sphere but remains individualized and apart. This triangular setup complicates the conventional opposition between colonial traveler and colonized locals, and it highlights the ambivalent position of the traveler, who is more observant than the tourists yet unable to explain the folk spirit he fathoms in the countryside. On the basis of McKay's prose texts, the scholars Joel Nickels and Robert Philipson have argued that McKay sought to replace fixed communities like those of class and nation by a more flexible vagabond community of spiritual kinship. The Cities sonnets complicate that reading as well. Instead of developing a vagabond community like "The Ditch" in *Banjo* (1929), they dramatize the individual traveler's encounter with local communities that are bounded, rooted in the land, and ultimately inaccessible. Rather than promising easy identification with the foreign, McKay's sonnets seem oriented toward a transnational ethos of empathetic communication. The traveler cannot fully understand the African communities—cannot know the "thoughts" behind their "lowered brow." He can avoid being a mere tourist, however: by resisting Africanist projection, by empathizing with his environment, and by responding to a city's populace, street life, history, and architecture in a manner that combines the intellectual and the sensual. It is this ethos that McKay underscores when he repeatedly casts the traveler as a lover praising the beloved city.

One of the forms of transnational solidarity that scholars have identified in McKay's oeuvre is communism. While McKay had rejected communism by the late 1920s, the movement and its underlying ideas seem to have been on his mind when he was composing the Cities sonnets. The increasing communist activity in the United States would have worked to that effect, as did the controversial discussion of Stalinism among Western communists.[14] McKay's negotiation of communism in the Cities sonnets reflects his general stance on bounded communities: he recognizes the strength they exert but ultimately remains skeptical of the claims they make on the individual. In "Moscow," for example, McKay nostalgically recalls his visit to the city ten years earlier and praises the "human" communism of Lenin he encountered there (line 14). Ultimately, however, the poem undercuts the collective ethos of the movement by alluding to Stalin's inhuman rule and emphasizing the speaker's sensual response to the buildings, ornaments, and sounds of the city. McKay's reservations about strategies of collective empowerment such as communism and cultural nationalism are palpable throughout the Cities sequence, even where he indicts racist and colonial oppression.

The uneasy relationship between McKay's anti-colonialism and his individualist transnationalism manifests in the first "Tanger" sonnet. The sonnet evokes an atmosphere of "hate" and warfare between the cultures and religions that come together in the city. It suggests that this atmosphere is sustained, if not caused, by arbitrary colonial power:

> Morocco's severed head is Europe's ball
> Kicked from goal to goal and all around—
> In the African game of the European (I.9–11)

The fact that these sonnets were never published might explain the inferior quality of the last line and the prosaic diction McKay slips into whenever he wants to drive home a point. Nevertheless, the passage illustrates the continuities between his earlier protest poetry and the political perspective he brings to his travel sonnets. The unremitting, visceral imagery recalls the protest of "If We Must Die" and "A Roman Holiday" (see Chapter 2), and the international outlook adumbrated in his early socialist sonnets comes to fruition in the confidently judgmental conclusion of the first "Tanger" sonnet. Kicked around between the colonial powers, McKay ironically notes, Morocco is "desolate and helpless from intrigue / And aptly christened International!" (lines 13–14). His redefinition of "International" strips the word of its associations with grand affairs and aloof cosmopolitanism; instead, the capital letter emphasizes its communist overtones.

On a more literal level, the word draws attention to the powerlessness and silence of those in between the established nations. They become mere footballs, or indeed "game" (an earlier, better version of line 11 read "African game of Europe's little league"), for the dominant nation-states of the time. McKay proves himself aware of and sympathetic with these in-between communities, but at the same time he remains unaffected by their fate. Neither silent nor powerless, he assumes a position of superior insight into their situation that enables him to voice their plight in the language of the cosmopolitan educated elite. McKay occasionally called himself an internationalist (*A Long Way* 300), but the "Tanger" sonnets signal that he is not inter-national in this debasing sense. Using vocabulary not yet available at the time, his position and outlook can be described as *trans*national in that he remains independent of national struggles and their debilitating effects. This transnationalism is empowering but at the same time limited in its reach. It relies on individualism—on one's readiness and ability to leave a place behind when things get unpleasant. It combines the liberating transgression of vagabondage with its social irresponsibility.

As these examples show, the travel sonnet of the thirties negotiates the dynamics at the core of black transnationalism: the relationship between home and abroad, roots and routes, identity and mobility. The sonnets of Butler, Cullen, and McKay are susceptible to charges of stereotyping and projection, and some enact the privileged role of the observing traveler. Yet the very phenomenon of African Americans traveling and publishing their impressions undercut some of the structuring oppositions of Western travel writing. McKay explored this subversive quality more radically than his contemporaries, highlighting the black traveler's uneasy subject position in between communities variously defined by race, nationality, or geography. In his Cities sequence, both the observing traveler and the observed locals emerge as composite identities that cannot be adequately understood in binary terms such as oppressor/oppressed or mobile/static. The sonnet becomes a testing ground and an emblem of this troubling transnationalism. Traditionally structured by the opposition between observer and observed, it offers a means of dramatizing, examining, and questioning this opposition. In its exploration of flexible conceptions of self and other, home and foreign, the African American travel sonnet of the 1930s presciently addresses concerns that would come to shape debates around African American identity from the late twentieth century onward.

The Italo-Ethiopian War, the Protest Sonnet, and Transatlantic Pan-Africanism

While the travel accounts of black writers reached a limited number of contemporaries, questions of black transnationalism returned to center stage in 1935. As fascist Italy prepared to invade on the country then known as Abyssinia, the last African nation free from colonial rule, African Americans took a strong interest in the fate of Emperor Haile Selassie and his people. During the lengthy lead-up to the invasion both parties struggled for the support of international public opinion. Since the United States government's doctrine of neutrality left black Americans with few options for material support, writers and journalists felt it their duty to raise consciousness and strengthen solidarity with the Ethiopian cause. While their interest waned rather quickly, the Italo-Ethiopian War of 1935/36 captured the imagination and the emotions of more African Americans than any other international event of the time. It inspired an outpouring of literature not only on the war itself but on Abyssinia, Africa, and Pan-African brotherhood.[15]

Scholarship on the literary response to the Italo-Ethiopian crisis has remained scant. John Cullen Gruesser and Ichiro Takayoshi have examined prose writing on the crisis and identified the transnational struggle against colonialism as a main impetus. The only sustained discussion of the poetic response, Woodson's *Anthems, Sonnets, and Chants,* notes that the use of "archaic" devices like the sonnet might be a reason for the scholarly neglect of poets such as J. Harvey L. Baxter, Marcus Bruce Christian, Owen Dodson, and P. J. White. Woodson further suggests that these poets helped create an imagined community between blacks in Ethiopia and the United States, thus blurring the boundary between individual and collective identities and between the local and the global.[16] The sonnet was particularly suited for negotiating these categories, as the travel poets of the period had demonstrated. A closer look at the Pan-Africanist sonnets published in response to the Italo-Ethiopian crisis confirms both the pervasiveness of transnational concerns in African American writing of the thirties and the continuing tension between genteel conventions and radical political protest.

Pan-Africanism had taken various shapes since its inception as an organized movement. Initially associated with the project of settling free blacks in the self-governed African nation of Liberia, it acquired a wider agenda in a series of international conventions from 1900 onward. The Pan-African Congresses propagated the cultural and spiritual unity of all people of African descent, defended the sovereignty of the free black nations (Haiti, Liberia, Abyssinia), and envisioned a unified Africa governed by blacks. Their activities were complemented, and sometimes contradicted, by grassroots efforts like Marcus Garvey's "Back to Africa" movement, which kept the idea of African American emigration to the mother continent alive well into the twentieth century. Garvey regarded black people as a community lateral to established nation states but like many Pan-Africanists used nationalist tropes to imagine unity among black people and propagate joint political action. Pan-Africanism is therefore often equated or conflated with black nationalism, itself a highly ambiguous term whose connotations range from the communist Black Belt thesis to the Black Power movement and the anticolonial struggles after World War II (see Chapter 5). The continental strand of Pan-Africanism, which propagated a united African nation from which whites and their culture were to be excluded, can indeed be called nationalist in the conventional sense. In the thirties, however, the Pan-Africanist movement was dominated by its transatlantic strand, whose idea of transnational black solidarity challenged geographical and discursive boundaries across the Black Atlantic.[17]

The sonnet, which had traveled from the Mediterranean through Europe to the Americas and back across the Black Atlantic, epitomized this boundary-crossing impulse. While the protest sonnet had been a formative element of the Harlem Renaissance, it had fallen into disuse in the 1930s—presumably because protest was now associated with the communist movement, which as we have seen discouraged the use of conventional poetic form by African American poets. The outstanding poets to adopt the Ethiopian cause in the United States, Langston Hughes and Melvin Tolson, disregarded the form and drew on social and folk poetry to voice protest.[18] The minor poets might have looked to McKay, however, for models of effective protest in the sonnet form. McKay had published a number of international protest sonnets early in his American career, which led the Pan-Africanist movement to claim him as one of its own. He encouraged this reading when he claimed that his most famous work, the sonnet "If We Must Die," was written for the "abused, outraged and murdered, whether they are minorities or nations," all over the world. St. Clair Drake, another writer of sonnets and traveler of the Black Atlantic, liked to conclude his Pan-Africanist speeches and essays by quoting from McKay's "Like a Strong Tree," and the historian Colin Legum cited the sonnet "Outcast" as an epitomic manifestation of the movement. The sonnet thus gained Pan-Africanist credentials, while its European ancestry remained an insurance against the primitivism that the African American middle-class tended to suspect in all things African.[19]

This double function made the sonnet a fitting medium for literary interventions on the Italo-Ethiopian crisis. Since the political debate around the crisis largely took place in Europe, culminating in the emperor Haile Selassie's speech before the League of Nations at Geneva, these interventions could not simply collapse the idea of black solidarity into Back-to-Africa rhetoric. Instead they negotiated the shifting political, cultural, and emotional alliances at play around the Black Atlantic. Tropes of Africa as the motherland or root of black culture remained in wide use, as did the civilizationist notion that much of Western culture could be traced to ancient Africa. The main challenge for writers on the crisis was to address an African country that had long stood synecdochally for the entire continent in a spirit of admiration and solidarity without reiterating outmoded essentialisms.[20]

The sonnets of Baxter and Christian indicate the range of possible responses to this challenge since they approach poetry and the Ethiopian conflict from very different vantage points. Baxter was an aspiring member of the black bourgeoisie whose provincial background and genteel values left him out of touch with the cultural and aesthetic developments of the preceding decades. Christian was a socialist who corresponded with leading Harlem Renaissance poets, published in black news media from *The Crisis* to the *Pittsburgh Courier,* and researched black folk life for the WPA's Negro Writers Project. Both took up the most widespread motif of Ethiopian protest: the contrast between the exiled emperor's passionate struggle for support and the world powers' hypocritical neutrality, which was brought out most starkly by Selassie's Geneva speech.

Baxter's sonnet on the speech, "Oh, Hang Your Heads, a Voice Accusing Cries," adopts the emperor's voice and compresses his speech into a series of metaphorical images that rather gratuitously evoke such commonplaces as the sufferings of Christ, the assassination of Julius Caesar, and the lynching of African Americans. As Woodson points out in his discussion of this sonnet, Baxter's rendition stands in unfortunate contrast to the emperor's actual speech, which was delivered in quiet dignity and impressed the horrors of Italian chemical warfare on the audience through mere factual retelling. The "exaggerated histrionics" of Baxter's sonnet, which opens with an image of the emperor pointing "a finger shaking in your face" (line 2), rob the speech of both dignity and effect (Woodson 182–85). The conclusion, "God will remember, time will not forget" (line 14), is taken almost verbatim from the speech but sounds curiously deflated after this parade of over-dramatized images.

Christian's "Selassie at Geneva" (1938) is a more controlled rendition of the same event. It uses the Petrarchan volta to keep apart the theatricality of international politics and the tragic potential of Selassie's struggle. The octave recounts Ethiopia's desertion by the Western powers in bitter tones. The sestet identifies the emperor's speech as "the closing scene" of this disingenuous performance and builds toward an impressive, dramatic conclusion:

> Pile lies upon wrongs, ring the curtain down
> Upon the closing scene of this last act;
> The King of Kings now yields his ancient crown
> To those who signed the Non-Aggression Pact,
> As weaker nations vanish, one by one . . .
> Blow, bugles! Armageddon has begun! (*High Ground* 34; lines 9–14)

Both Baxter and Christian cite the trope of the King of Kings, blending the emperor's official designation with the Biblical reference to Jesus Christ (1 Tim 6:15; Rev 17:14, 19:16). While Baxter ineffectively mixes his allusions, Christian uses the trope as a structuring device, a pivot on which the poem swings from disillusioned political commentary to the apocalyptic threat of the conclusion.

Christian generally succeeds in avoiding primitivist overtones by focusing on realpolitik and on the specific lessons to be learned from the Ethiopian failure. Baxter's 1936 collection *Sonnets to the Ethiopians*, by contrast, remains caught up in paternalistic stereotypes about Africa that tend to undermine his calls for action. The opening sonnet, for example, uses the plural "we" to identify with the Ethiopians and establish a transnational fraternity of oppressed peoples. Instead of citing instances and perpetrators of oppression, however, it foregrounds the victimhood of the oppressed: "The world's a mummery of groggy lies, / And we are victims of its undertow" (3, lines 1–2). This passive attitude carries over into the following sonnets, which are addressed to Africa or Ethiopia but read more like a catalogue of clichés about the continent than a negotiation of the contemporary crisis. The poet announces himself as "a singer, yet a champion / Of the undone, benighted folk," a vengeful Zeus whose poem is a "thunder-bolt to blast around / Each chain and pillory" (4, lines 3–6). He addresses the continent as "natal Mother" and reiterates the civilizationist notion that the continent preceded the Western empires in history and deserves esteem because its people have "Fought oft with Jew and Nomad Bible races" (4, lines 9, 14). Baxter does realize the new topicality of this notion. He mentions that "*Italia*" was among the cultures preceded and influenced by this primeval Africa, but in his clumsy sermonizing fails to derive any political leverage from such observations (5, line 12).

The artificiality of Baxter's protest may be most evident in those poems that borrow the vocabulary of McKay's "If We Must Die" and "America." Lines like "My hate is one indignant world of fire, / My anger is the madness of a tide" become implausible when they succeed one of his metaphor-laden reflections on the woes of "crafty Romans" and "France and England's tardy hand and pulse" (12). Nevertheless, these sonnets are of historical interest in that they provide insight into the range of Pan-Africanisms at play in black transatlantic discourse at the time. They foreshadow the tensions between universalism and black nationalism that would erupt in the 1960s, and they contain one of the first explicit formulations of a political transnationalism in African American literature. Moreover, they epitomize the dilemma that prevented most poets from taking the sonnet beyond the confines of the genteel tradition. When Baxter apologizes in his preface that "my meager and somewhat artless philippics bristle with too much ardor, and my temper of style fails to show the appropriate poise that should be apparent in a work of this kind" (xiii), he betrays the universalist presuppositions that were so firmly associated with traditional poetic forms in the bourgeois imagination. His project of drawing on the cultural authority of such forms for the black cause follows in the steps of the genteel praise sonnets of the nineteenth century, but his clichéd notions and archaic phrasing fall behind even early figures like Dunbar and Braithwaite. Most African American sonneteers of the thirties were facing these problems, which might explain the comparative poverty of their efforts in the form. It was Langston Hughes, by then an undisputed eminence of African American letters, who would understand these problems and find a way to revive the form as the decade came to a close.

Chapter 4

The Vernacular Sonnet and the Afro-Modernist Project

The period framed by the spectacular success of Richard Wright's *Native Son* (1940) and the awarding of the Pulitzer Prize for Gwendolyn Brooks's *Annie Allen* (1949/50) brought momentous reorientations for African American literature. Whereas Wright promoted social realism and open political protest, the Pulitzer signaled mainstream recognition for writers who negotiated racial concerns in a modernist poetic framework. And while Wright and the social realists could connect seamlessly to the post-Depression aesthetic of the 1930s, the resurgence of Afro-modernism after World War II is part of a more complicated lineage. The branch of scholarship sometimes called New Modernist Studies has shown that the writings of Pound, Eliot, and their circle were not the only kind of modernism pursued by writers in the first half of the twentieth century. The experimental approach to language and form propagated by these influential writers made its way into African American literature at an early point, via the work of Jean Toomer, Langston Hughes, and Sterling Brown. The African American sonnet of the 1920s and 1930s, by contrast, pursued modernist concerns such as the relationship between the individual artist and the literary tradition, but usually did so in the poetic diction and conventional form of earlier periods. Moreover, the experimental poets who had emerged in the Harlem Renaissance either faded from view (Toomer) or turned to folk and vernacular writing in the following decade (Hughes, Brown).[1]

When the next generation around Gwendolyn Brooks, Robert Hayden, and Melvin Tolson took up the Afro-modernist project from the 1940s onward, they did not have a unified tradition to extend or reject. They drew on a variety of sources and traditions, particularly high-modernist formal experimentation and black vernacular speech, which they brought together into an idiom

Matthew Hart calls a 'synthetic vernacular' (7–9). Hart points out that the modernist ideal of combining material from different cultural sources into an organic work of art recalls the Hegelian concept of synthesis, while the vernacular idiom created by the poetic avant-garde of the time can be called synthetic in that it was artistically fabricated and sometimes self-consciously artificial. For Afro-modernist poets the synthetic vernacular provided an opportunity to subvert racially essentialist readings of black speech.

The subversive, destabilizing effect of the vernacular has been stressed by many of its theorists. To "vernacularize is to 'dialectize' as a process," Homi Bhabha writes: "it is not simply *to be* in a dialogic relation with the native or the domestic, but it is to be on the border, *in between,*" and thus to "displace . . . the domestic. But such resistance is not a 'negation' of the rule of the universal . . . it is to take your position at the point in space and time of the 'unexpected trans-formation'" ("Unsatisfied" 202). Larry Scanlon points out that "incompletion is the sign of the vernacular, and incompleteness it embraces and proclaims. Moreover, vernacular subversion depends on this incompleteness, for it is precisely the vernacular's self-proclaimed incompleteness that gives it the syn-cretic power to appropriate and redefine other traditions, whether dominant or not" ("Poets Laureate" 222–23). The critical establishment at mid-century had a different conception of the vernacular, however, associating it with the primitivist aesthetic embraced by some modernists but decidedly rejected by the black middle-class.[2] The new generation of poets around Brooks and Hayden needed a more acceptable framework in which to explore modernist vernacular poetics.

This chapter argues that the sonnet provided such a framework and that Langston Hughes, a highly regarded precursor figure among these poets, was the first to recognize its potential. Hughes's now-forgotten sequence "Seven Moments of Love: An Un-Sonnet Sequence in Blues" (1940) was a nodal point in this process. It sketched out a synthetic vernacular that was then adopted and transformed in the sonnets of Brooks and Hayden. Poets who employ a synthetic vernacular, Hart argues, "embrace the formal and ideological complications between the universal and the particular" and navigate these complications in a language whose "materiality . . . refuses to disappear in the moment of overcoming" (8–9). Much the same can be said of modernist experimentation with the sonnet, a form that has often been associated with Hegelian dialectic argumentation (Borgstedt 466–75). Many avant-garde writ-ers in the post-war period, from the confessional poets to the Afro-modernists, explored the tension between the polished completeness of the traditional son-net and its modernist disruption. In the course of these explorations the formal composition of the African American sonnet underwent a fundamental change for the first time. The sonnet became an instable but productive synthetic space that allowed poets to negotiate the relationship between modernism and the vernacular, between individual and collective achievement, between a universalist poetics and black cultural specificity, between its European genre tradition and its black vernacular language and setting. In the two decades following the war, a form many white modernists had dismissed as outdated thus became a hub of the Afro-modernist project.

LANGSTON HUGHES AND THE BLUES SONNET

Hughes's critical writing indicates the poetological differences between his synthetic vernacular poetics and contemporary work that privileged either the African American or the European traditions. Hughes was never interested in simply transcribing vernacular speech in the manner of nineteenth-century dialect poets, and he conceived neither blues music nor vernacular expression in the terms of black-soil writers like Brown. "I'm not a Southerner," Hughes explained. "I never worked on a levee. I hardly ever saw a cottonfield except from the highway.... Life is as hard on Broadway as it is in Blues-originating land. The Brill Building Blues is just as hungry as the Mississippi Levee Blues" ("Jazz" 492). Hughes much preferred the blues he heard in Manhattan vaudeville theaters, an urban blues responsive not so much to the Southern cotton field as to the expectations of an ethnically mixed, culturally educated audience. His favorite male singer was Lonnie Johnson, whose versatility and adaptability reflected Hughes's own conception of the blues. As for himself, Hughes made it clear that he was primarily a poet, not a musician, and that the blues was only one of the sources he tapped for inspiration.[3]

When he decided to place "Seven Moments of Love: An Un-Sonnet Sequence in Blues" at the beginning of his collection *Shakespeare in Harlem* (1942), Hughes emphasized the pivotal role of the vernacular sonnet in his return from the social activism of the thirties to the experimental blues poetry that had made his name. Given the prominence of this signal, it is remarkable that neither his reviewers nor later critics picked up on its significance. The main studies of blues and the vernacular in Hughes's work ignore the sequence, while Onwuchekwa Jemie in his introduction to Hughes's poetry only mentions it to reject the designation "love sonnets" in favor of "love blues" (43–44). In the only critical discussion of the sequence to date, James Edward Smethurst is palpably concerned with foregrounding its deviations from the sonnet form, presumably to sustain his broader argument for continuity between African American poetry of the 1930s and the 1940s.[4] A closer look at the sequence suggests, however, that the interplay of European form and the black vernacular engenders a distinctly Afro-modernist poetics.

The brief prefatory statement in *Shakespeare in Harlem* announces Hughes's strategy of managing this interplay: he intends to draw on the flexible oral expressivity of the blues to play around the unfinished edges.

> A book of light verse. Afro-Americana in the blues mood. Poems syncopated and variegated in the colors of Harlem, Beale Street, West Dallas, and Chicago's South Side.
>
> Blues, ballads, and reels to be read aloud, crooned, shouted, recited, and sung. Some with gestures, some not—as you like. None with a far-away voice. (19)

Rather than glossing over the divergent cultural sources from which he is drawing, Hughes admits all of them into his poetry. It is from the encounter between tradition and innovation, high culture and popular culture, white form and black sound, that the collection gains its creative force. The subtitle "An Un-Sonnet Sequence in Blues" exemplifies this strategy in that it playfully proclaims both its investment in and its disregard of the sonnet form.

Beside the obvious differences, this encounter reveals surprising analogies. Both the blues and the "little song" (*sonetto*) emerged as an oral practice and later inspired a legacy of written poetry. Both came to prominence as laments for lost or unfulfilled love, laments addressed to the beloved but often more concerned with the despondent lover and his attempt "to draw from others a reaction of sympathy" (Odum and Johnson 20–21). And both take care to create a sense of spontaneous, emotional self-expression in language that most often has been carefully crafted with a view to audience response, so that they ultimately celebrate, as Larry Neal once said of the blues, "the ability of man to control and shape his destiny."[5] With its play on the divergent connotations of fusion and craftsmanship, dialectical sublation and artificially fabricated material, Hart's concept of synthetic vernacular writing captures both the productivity and the artifice of Hughes's strategy. The vernacular sonnets of the 1940s and beyond aspire to a high-modernist aesthetic of organic unity but at the same time jeopardize this unity by exposing it to the black idiom. Or, seen from the opposite angle, they draw on the authenticity of the vernacular but inevitably question that authenticity by adapting it to the requirements of a predetermined formal framework.

The synthetic quality of Hughes's blues sonnets is tangible in their oscillation between spontaneity and artifice, spoken and written language, laughter and lamentation. Thematically, they position themselves in the blues tradition through characteristic leitmotifs: music; loneliness; the basic human needs of sleep, food, and love; the overarching theme of disappointed affection. The speaker has been left by his wife—a plight Hughes regarded as the archetypal blues situation ("Jazz" 492)—and responds with a show of buoyant independence that disintegrates into loneliness and desire as the sequence progresses. The individual poem titles indicate temporal progression and evoke the typical settings of the blues: "Twilight Reverie," "Supper Time," "Bed Time," "Pay Day." The most productive technique Hughes adopts from the blues is repetition. He replaces the traditional rhyme schemes of the sonnet with pair rhymes and occasional triplets, a technique that recalls the structural simplicity of common blues stanzas (AAA, AAB, AABB) and came to inspire a certain legacy among the Black Arts poets.

The second poem of the sequence, "Supper Time" (24), illustrates both the new approach to rhyme and the frequent repetition of lines, words, and phrases in identical or slightly altered form. It is structured by repetitions on several levels. Repetitions within lines—for example in the opening line, "I look in the kettle, the kettle is dry"—create a musical rhythm that carries over into the following lines. Anaphoric repetitions like "Listen at my heartbeats trying to think / Listen at my footprints walking on the floor" (lines 6–7) connect different rhyme pairs and draw attention to important motifs, such as the silence and loneliness suggested by the speaker's ability to hear his heartbeats and thoughts. On a macrostructural level the poem consists of three sections. The expository description of material deprivation (lines 1–5) is linked by a pair rhyme to its causal source, the emotional deprivation that is the main theme of the poem (lines 6–10). Lastly, a conclusion repeats the initial description—the motif, in blues terminology—of material deprivation (lines 11–14), indicating that the speaker, maybe representing black folk in general, is forced to deal with material problems before he can indulge in emotional ones.

The broader significance of Hughes's repetitions is usefully captured by Tony Bolden's concept of epistrophy. Coined by Thelonious Monk to name one of his jazz standards, the term 'epistrophy' signifies on the classical rhetorical device of epistrophe, the repetition of the end of a line or phrase for additional emphasis. Bolden draws on this etymology to argue that formal repetition, especially the allusive reference to genre conventions, is both subversive and affirmative: subversive because it demonstrates the iterability of supposedly authentic or essential conventions, for example by riffing on the blues tradition;

affirmative because in the very act of simulating such conventions the poet revitalizes the "cultural (re)memory" associated with the "larger poetic tapestry" they represent (Bolden 58–59; 100).

Epistrophy can be traced on various levels in Hughes's sonnets. His use of pair rhymes, for example, can be read as an oblique, allusive form of epistrophy in that it suggests the repetitive structure of the blues and signifies on the more intricate stanzaic structure of the sonnet through ostentatious simplification. Hughes also incorporates traditional types of epistrophe and inflects them with the black vernacular voice and the themes and structures of the blues. In the last poem, for example, the speaker assures his beloved, "if you think I been mean before, / I'll try not to be that mean no more" (27, lines 12–13). In a larger perspective, such instances of epistrophy point to Hughes's appropriation of both the blues and the sonnet traditions, neither of which enters his sequence in its pure form. The very act of combining them signifies on the values and worldviews they are conventionally assumed to represent. The synthetic construct of the blues sonnet disallows easy essentialisms like high culture vs. low culture or artifice vs. earthiness; it results in a "double-voiced utterance," as Bolden argues via Mikhail Bakhtin and Henry Louis Gates, that draws attention to the simulatedness of genre conventions and the cultural memories they convey (58).

Having identified the most pertinent blues structures in "Seven Moments of Love," we can now shift perspective and examine its transformation of the sonnet tradition. A first indicator comes in the ambivalent subtitle, "An Un-Sonnet Sequence in Blues," which establishes the chronological order and causal relatedness of the traditional sonnet sequence while at the same time signaling its dissolution. The sequentiality is confirmed by the titles of the individual sonnets, which outline the progression from evening to night to morning and from workday to Sunday to payday. While this overarching frame and the many cross-references within the poems produce a tightly knit texture, the structure of the individual sonnets unravels in the course of the sequence. The first poem, which begins in sets of neat pair rhymes but ends with a triplet, thus adding a disruptive fifteenth line, announces the direction the sequence will take: both the rhyme scheme and the fourteen-line pattern will loosen as the sequence progresses. The fifth poem is the first not to start with a pair rhyme, and the last two poems considerably exceed the prescribed length, running to 20 and 21 lines respectively. The seventh poem has several rhyme pairs, however, suggesting a cyclical return to coherence as the speaker's hopes for his marriage revive. In the world of Hughes's blues sonnets, unity is a possibility but remains under permanent threat from outside forces and is never entirely fulfilled.

More effectively than most earlier attempts, Hughes's synthetic experiments turn the sonnet into a vehicle for African American voices and concerns. In the tradition of the blues, the speaker relates his personal experience and gives his narrative an oral quality by imagining spoken dialogues in every single poem. He talks to himself, to his feelings, to his alarm clock, and most importantly to the absent woman. The sequence is thus a "speakerly text," in Gates's term from *The Signifying Monkey,* "oriented toward imitating one of the numerous forms of oral narration to be found in . . . Afro-American vernacular literature" (191). This vernacular heritage enters the sequence through the speaker's syntax, vocabulary, and pronunciation. In stark contrast to the predetermined structures of the traditional sonnet, Hughes derives the blues rhythms of his sequence from syntactic inversions and reductions ("I got to find me"), and he is careful to signal the oral layer of vernacular communication by transcribing typical pronunciation patterns ("Lawd").

This latter strategy inspires a momentous innovation in the African American sonnet: the systematic use of slant rhyme, which breaks through the formal strictness of traditional rhyme schemes to admit the flexibility of the vernacular. Hughes used slant rhyme in many of his blues poems and was promptly criticized for it in the first major study of his work, James A. Emanuel's volume in the Twayne series. Recent commentators have generally recognized its aptness for vernacular poetry, a judgment confirmed by comparison with conventional black sonneteers of the time. Many of Hughes's contemporaries were careful to avoid any trace of the vernacular in their sonnets. Where they used pair rhymes it was not to evoke black oral traditions but for juvenile versifying along the lines of "Farmers in shirt sleeves and jeans proudly walk, / The cardinal perched on last year's corn stalk"—the beginning of Estelle Eaton's "Spring-Time Scenes for the Painter" (1959). Hughes, by contrast, made the slanted rhyme pair an integral element of his blues sonnets and, arguably, the most consequential manifestation of epistrophy in his poetry. He found it highly suitable for reflecting the "tensions between repetition and improvisation" that characterize both the blues and the black oral tradition.[6]

"Seven Moments of Love" does not succeed entirely in managing these tensions. Hughes's departure from the stanzaic patterns of the blues takes away much of its musical quality, especially in comparison with the more traditional blues poems in *Shakespeare in Harlem.* The concluding couplets are not always effective, and the lines are too varied in length and content to establish the metrical and semantic rhythms that characterize the blues. It is indicative of these problems that the sonnets of "Seven Moments of Love" covertly rely on the oral voice to achieve their musicality. Instead of speaking for themselves, they need to be "read aloud, crooned, shouted, recited, and sung," as Hughes admits in his preface. In modernist terms, this is also a shortcoming in crafts-manship, a charge leveled most forcefully by Owen Dodson in his *Phylon* review of *Shakespeare in Harlem*. "Because verse is 'light,'" Dodson admonishes, "it doesn't therefore follow that anything goes." He calls the book "a careless surface job" hampered by the author's lack of "discipline" (337–38). And indeed, there is a striking difference between the blues experiments in the early sections of the volume, which read more like song lyrics than like poems in their own right, and the more carefully crafted pieces further back that recall Hughes's pioneering blues poetry from the 1920s. This does not diminish the historical significance of his experiments. In exploring the synthetic vernacular, they take on the challenge of striking a balance between the orality of the black vernacular and the exigencies of the high-cultural sonnet tradition.

Gwendolyn Brooks, Robert Hayden, and Synthetic Afro-Modernism

The most innovative poets of the post-war generation, Gwendolyn Brooks and Robert Hayden, grappled with the same challenge. In their work the tension between literary and vernacular elements intertwines with the tension between the individual and the collective voice. Brooks, who gained public notice before Hayden, was in regular communication with Hughes from her late teens and continued to acknowledge his influence throughout her career. She shares with the older poet a concern with black daily life, a focus on the deferred dreams of the lower classes, and a pioneering role in establishing modernist techniques in African American poetry. Brooks also admired Hughes as an innovative craftsman and, particularly after her 1967 conversion to the Black Arts movement, as a critic of racial injustice.[7] The interplay of integrationism and radicalism, and also that of high modernism and vernacular realism, situ-ate her poetry in a direct line from Hughes's sonnets.

Not only does Brooks resort to the sonnet form with remarkable consistency in her early work, but she dialectizes the form in both senses of the term, just as Hughes had.[8] Like the soldiers in the opening sonnet of her 1945 sequence "Gay Chaps at the Bar," she "knew white speech," which allowed her to claim the cultural authority of modernist avant-garde poetry (*World* 48). At the same time, she connected with the black tradition by inflecting this "white speech" with vernacular elements: characteristic words and phrases, racially charged images, allusions to black popular culture, and most importantly, slant rhyme.

In the opening poem of the sequence, slant rhyme expresses the soldiers' disconcerting war experience. The ruptures in the pure, harmonic rhymes of the traditional sonnet reflect the cacophony of frontline battle and its devastating effect on the mental stability of the soldiers, who have been trained in the very tradition of "gaiety in good taste" and "smart, athletic language" that the poem discards. While the artificiality of rhymes like "islands"/"talents" seems to preclude a vernacular reading, there are also rhymes that evoke the sort of orality we find in Hughes. The characteristic pronunciations indicated by "dash"/"lush" and "women"/"omen" blend with other allusions to the black vernacular, such as the imagery of "The summer spread, the tropics, of our love" and the racially charged vocabulary of "white speech," "holler," and "lions."

All of these references remain oblique, and the overall reading experience is dominated by the convoluted, image-laden style of Western high modernism. But their presence, unobtrusive as it is, suffices to launch a dialectical and dialectizing interchange between black and white speech—between the soldiers' residual cultural identities and the dominant societal narratives that occlude such identities. This latter aspect is underscored by the poem's evasiveness about the speaker's race. The generic title "gay chaps at the bar" (Brooks uses small capital for individual poems) suggests a transracial experience, and it is not until halfway through the poem that the speaker's blackness is confirmed. The irony of this inverted confirmation—it is his claim to knowing "white speech" that marks him as black—points to the relationality of both cultural and linguistic categories.

Not only does Brooks use slant rhyme more widely than Hughes, but she consistently deploys the classic rhetorical patterning of the sonnet. "Each sonnet articulates a desire," Ann Stanford suggests in her reading of the sequence, "and an oppositional reality, a pull toward the truth" (202). This dialectical setup, which Petrarch and Shakespeare had used for some of their love sonnets, contributes to Brooks's realistic description of lower-class life and suggests a demystifying conception of love reminiscent of Hughes's blues poetry. The novelty of her approach is particularly striking in comparison with the love sonnets of earlier African American poets such as Countee Cullen, Alice Dunbar-Nelson, and Helene Johnson (not to mention the sequences discussed in Chapter 1). Brooks combines the unsparing social realism of Wright's *Native Son* and the scientific approach of two other fellow Chicago intellectuals, St. Clair Drake and Horace Cayton, whose landmark study of black urban life, *Black Metropolis,* appeared in the same year as "Gay Chaps at the Bar."[9] There is no trace of genteel sentimentality or uplift optimism in her sonnets, but neither is there anger or protest openly directed at a white readership.

The synthetic vernacular of the *Bronzeville* sonnets serves several purposes. It infuses a supposedly non-racial form with a racial message. In terms borrowed from the first and last lines of "gay chaps at the bar," it disrupts the "order" of the sonnet with the "holler" of the black speakers. It also links the two main tenets of Brooks's aesthetic: social-realist description and modernist experimentation. Signaling both authenticity and innovation, the synthetic vernacular allows Brooks to study black life with no apparent concern for the white reader's response and to discard the prescribed length and meter of the traditional sonnet, thus disentangling her poetry from restrictive expectations on either side.

If Hughes laid the groundwork for these transformative strategies by introducing post-war poets to the possibilities of the synthetic vernacular, then Brooks continues his legacy but tries to avoid some of the problems he had encountered, especially the problem of artificiality. While she adopts aesthetically innovative elements such as slant rhyme, she uses the vernacular more sparingly than Hughes. Her firm commitment to modernist aesthetics at the time led her to regard the vernacular as a technical device rather than a rivaling cultural force. But her attempt to reconcile modernist aesthetics with the African American everyday experience held pitfalls of its own, and the "Gay Chaps at the Bar" sequence shows a certain unevenness in voice and style. It has been faulted for overly intricate and "archaic" diction (Gray 183), and while some of this criticism might simply reflect contemporary black critics' wariness of experimental poetry, it does indicate how precarious the balance between vernacular realism and modernist aesthetics remains in Brooks's sonnets. In our context the most striking problem of the sequence is its failure to sustain the style, and thus the vernacular-inflected voice, established in the beginning. The two "love notes" sonnets toward the end of the sequence, for example, sound very much like Brooks herself, as opposed to the soldiers whose voice they ostensibly record. They discard the black vernacular altogether in favor of a refracted, alienated voice reminiscent of Cummings. Yet they fail to evoke the visceral emotionality of Cummings' more successful poems, which leaves them indistinguishable at times from the sentimental outpourings of contemporary amateur poets. It seems that the vernacular remained indispensable to the new poetics, and those of Brooks's sonnets that make use of its dialectizing effect became signal achievements of Afro-modernist poetry.

Brooks's difficulties in sustaining the vernacular voice of the soldiers might be indicative of her struggles with the demands of the collective. Critics like to contrast the humanist valorization of individuality in her early work with the collectivist black aesthetic she adopted from the mid-1960s onward.[10] The fact that she dropped, and indeed vilified, the sonnet after her conversion to the

Black Arts movement suggests that she associated the form with the individual rather than the collective voice. Her best-known sonnets focus on individuals, and even in "Gay Chaps at the Bar" she is at her most convincing when she zooms out to render the soldiers' experience from an overarching observer's perspective. In the opening poem of "Gay Chaps at the Bar," the universalizing implications of this perspective are counteracted by the vernacular, which synthesizes the soldiers' voice with that of the overarching observer. In some of the other sonnets, Brooks discards the vernacular and explores other synthetic devices that primarily work on the semantic level.

The most successful of these is metonymy, which informs the widely anthologized "the white troops had their orders but the Negroes looked like men" (54). The sonnet describes the integration of the military during and after World War II from the perspective of the white troops—a strategy indicative of the integrationist endeavor to educate white America from within rather than confront it from the outisde. James Baldwin went so far as referring to African Americans as "they" in his essays, but where he brashly adopted the "we" of mainstream America (27), Brooks keeps an ironic distance to the white troops by rendering their impressions in free indirect speech. This technical choice has several advantages. It makes the punch line of the poem, "These Negroes looked like men," more surprising and thus more effective. It exposes the contradictions of white racism through a faithful rendering of its paradoxes. The white soldiers find it inconvenient, for example, "to remember those / Congenital iniquities that cause / Disfavor of the darkness" (lines 5–8). And it allows Brooks to articulate the moral of the poem—integration is a natural process without negative consequences for either race—in an unassuming but authoritative voice that can be read as either the white troops' or that of an objective commentator.

The sonnet bears traces of vernacular speech ("Who really gave two figs"), but the vernacular is that of the white troops. It breaks through the association of non-literary language and social realism with the African American lower classes in the rest of the sequence. More prominent than the vernacular is the stylistic device of metonymy, which here and in later sonnets such as "First fight. Then fiddle" develops into an instrument of political synthetization.[11] Like free indirect speech, metonymy thus serves to articulate racial concerns in the framework of a universalist agenda. The community of soldiers can be read as a metonymy for the peaceful coexistence of all humankind, a vision Brooks underlines by humanizing the white troops in the course of the poem: from the "hooded gaze" and formal rigidity of the first lines, they develop to the collegial and colloquial relaxation of "Who really gave two figs?" in the sestet.

In a more specific metonymical allusion, the sonnet draws on the notion of the army as a microcosm of society to suggest that racial integration can and should be achieved in all areas of American life—an unobtrusive but consequential expansion of its political message. Throughout her sonnets, Brooks draws on various synthesizing devices, both formal and political, to criticize racism in the terms of a humanist individualism. She synthesizes vernacular realism and experimental modernism into a poetics of organic unity, of which the vernacular sonnet is both a medium and an epitome.

While the importance of the sonnet to Brooks's emergence as a poet has been widely recognized, it is little known that the other outstanding poet of the period, Robert Hayden, began experimenting with the form at the very same time. Though four years older than Brooks, Hayden was still an obscure figure in the late 1940s. His only collection to date was *Heart-Shape in the Dust* (1940), a volume of juvenilia that Hughes judged derivative and immature. Like Brooks, Hayden had approached Hughes for comment and later acknowledged his influence. A closer look at Hayden's work of the 1940s shows him refining his technique while at the same time incorporating vernacular elements as a way of developing a style unmistakably his own.[12] The synthetic vernacular of Hughes's *Shakespeare in Harlem,* which appeared shortly after his critical comments on Hayden, seems to have provided a model for this new strategy and pointed Hayden to the sonnet as a formal option.

Hayden's best-known sonnet is "Frederick Douglass," which he chose as the concluding poem of all three collections that made his name: *A Ballad of Remembrance* (1962), *Selected Poems* (1966), and *Angle of Ascent* (1975). Few readers of these collections are aware that "Frederick Douglass" is a product of the 1940s. Hayden initially wrote it for "Five Americans" (1945), a sequence of educational praise sonnets to nineteenth-century abolitionists presumably modeled on Walter Snow's "Five Portraits of Liberators," which had appeared in the summer 1942 issue of *The Liberator.* The sonnets of "Five Americans" are apprentice work, but as Robert Chrisman points out they mark the beginning of Hayden's transition toward modernist techniques (134). Hayden soon discarded the rest of the sequence, but he revised "Frederick Douglass" and published a second version, almost identical with the poem we know today, in the February 1947 issue of *Atlantic Monthly.* The genesis of "Frederick Douglass," I suggest, allows us to trace Hayden's development toward a vernacular modernist poetics and to examine the role of the sonnet in this development.

Like all of Hayden's early sonnets, the first version of "Frederick Douglass" is written in conventional standard English and, though unrhymed, follows a traditional Petrarchan pattern.

Such men are timeless, and their lives are levers
that lift the crushing dark away like boulders.
Death cannot silence them, nor history,
suborned or purchased like the harlot's crass
endearments, expatriate them. Like negatives
held to the light, their weaknesses reveal
our possible strength. Their power proves us godly,
and by their stripes are we made whole in purpose.

Douglass, O colossus of our wish
and allegory of us all, one thinks
of you as shipwrecked voyagers think of
an island. Breasting waters mined with doubt
and error, we struggle toward your dream of man
unchained, of man permitted to be man. (quoted in Chrisman 135)

The germs of the later versions are already visible here: Douglass is praised in terms of his achievement for the black community as a whole, and the concluding lines gesture toward the pulsating rhythm and soaring rhetoric for which the later versions would be known. As it stands, however, this early version suffers from its overly formal language. Some of its imagery is random ("waters mined with doubt") or derivative ("shipwrecked voyagers"); it spells out what it ought to express ("allegory of us all"); it is bogged down by far-fetched similes; and the line breaks interrupt rather than accentuate its flow. Aside from these technical problems, the poem narrows its scope by retaining the individualist focus familiar from genteel praise sonnets (see Chapter 1). The focus is on the heroic figure himself, whose achievement is contextualized not in the experience of his people but in a traditional pantheon of "timeless" men. The poem never arrives at a convincing collective voice: the "we" of the octave is overly general to the point of abstraction, while the sestet initially switches to a rather stilted "one" and then harnesses the "we" into an image that suggests an individual rather than a group ("Breasting waters . . ."). Thus the concluding "dream of man / unchained" becomes a Promethean image of individual achievement more than a political image of black liberation. Similarly, "man permitted to be man" takes on a sense of individual entitlement not unlike Countee Cullen's "poet and not Negro poet," which Hayden would later echo in his controversial self-description as "a poet who happens to be Negro" (Llorens 62).

Hayden seems to have found the solution to these problems in the vernacular—not in the sense of dialect or signifying, but as a rhythmic, stylistic, and semantic principle synthesizing the contradictions at work in his poetry: individualism and communality, humanist universalism and the specific-ity of the black experience. In the later versions of the poem he retains the elevated diction and vocabulary characteristic of his style but embeds them in a chant-like rhythm and oral voice reminiscent of the folk sermons James Weldon Johnson had identified as models for a black vernacular poetry in *God's Trombones* (1927). These changes make both the language and the speaking voice more accessible. Whereas the first version, with its technical vocabulary, was spoken by a poet, the later versions are palpably spoken by the people.

> When it is finally ours, this freedom, this liberty, this beautiful
> and terrible thing, needful to man as air,
> usable as earth; when it belongs at last to all,
> when it is truly instinct, brain matter, diastole, systole,
> reflex action; when it is finally won; when it is more
> than the gaudy mumbo jumbo of politicians:
> this man, this Douglass, this former slave, this Negro
> beaten to his knees, exiled, visioning a world
> where none is lonely, none hunted, alien,
> this man, superb in love and logic, this man
> shall be remembered. Oh, not with statues' rhetoric,
> not with legends and poems and wreaths of bronze alone,
> but with the lives grown out of his life, the lives
> fleshing his dream of the beautiful, needful thing.[13]

As the emphasis shifts from the hero to his people, from abstraction to lived reality, from declamation to expressivity, the vernacular becomes a semantic principle of the poem as well. The new "Frederick Douglass" is still a praise sonnet, but one that reverses the conventions of poetic tributes along with the order of octave and sestet. It opens not with the hero but with the hopes and aspirations of his people, the collective "we," and it claims that the hero's central goal of freedom is the natural right of the people rather than a gift handed them by the hero. It emphasizes from the beginning that the hero has not fully accomplished his goal and that freedom is not "finally won." The very first word of the poem transfers the celebratory impulse into the future and into the con-ditional, so that the hero's status remains dependent on the fate of his people: if they truly achieve freedom he will be remembered; if not, he will have failed.

These reversals underscore the political message Hayden brings to fruition in the poem. They dissolve the hierarchies of hero-worship into a celebration

of the humanity that Douglass shares with all African Americans. They empha-
size a progressive outlook by focusing on an ideal to be reached in the future
rather than on the deeds of the past. And they strike a balance between the
individual and the collective by foregrounding the collective and delaying the
very mention of Douglass' name to the second part of the poem. The individual
is introduced as part of the community but, given that his appearance defines
the sestet-octave division, also as a defining force within that community.
This problematizes the accusation of excessive individualism that the Black
Arts movement brought against Hayden. Most scholars continue to take this
accusation at face value, which leads those who want to recuperate Hayden's
work to argue that his individualism has a broader communal significance. Yet
a closer look at his sonnets, and especially his revision of "Frederick Douglass,"
suggests that Hayden achieves a synthesis of individualist and communal prin-
ciples rather than subordinating one to the other. A broader look at American
poetry of the time seems to support this reading. Surveys of American poetry
tend to place Hayden, and also Brooks, in the communal camp as distinct
from the much more radical individualism of white avant-garde poetry in
the 1950s and 1960s.[14]

In foregrounding the self-expression of the black community, the new ver-
sion of "Frederick Douglass" balances the high-modernist artifice of the first
version against the flowing rhythm, engaging style, and collective voice of the
black vernacular. The flexible accentual meter of the new version, an important
innovation in the African American sonnet, is reminiscent of experimental
poets like Gerard Manley Hopkins (whom Hayden cited as an influence) and
also of blues poetry in the vein of Hughes's vernacular sonnets. The idiom
of "Frederick Douglass"—as of other classic Hayden poems such as "Middle
Passage" (1962) and the sonnet-variant "Those Winter Sundays" (1966)—is thus
a synthetic vernacular in several senses of the term. It derives its energy from
the dialectic interplay between Western and African American traditions, and
it self-reflexively enacts this dialectic, thus showing awareness of its artificial
quality. Yet it pursues the aesthetic and political ideal of synthesizing the black
people, in its past, present, and future dimensions, into a communal voice.

When Hayden contrasts the living memory of the people with unconvinc-
ingly static tributes like "statues" and "wreaths of bronze," he might be reflecting
on the difference between the original and later versions of his own poem. By
complementing his modernist poetics with a vernacular element, he avoids
the somewhat stilted declamation and derivative imagery of the first version
and merges his tribute into the collective memory he envisions as Douglass'
greatest legacy. This multi-level synthesis was central not only to Hayden's

mature poetics, but to the entire Afro-modernist project. Some of its many manifestations can be found in the sonnets discussed in this chapter: Hughes retained a considerable measure of vernacular words and structures; Brooks developed a dense modernist idiom occasionally informed by the vernacular; Hayden remained wary of vernacular language but drew on the vernacular for its rhythm and the communal spirit it evoked. Beyond these outstanding examples, the synthetic vernacular ramified through much Afro-modernist poetry, drama, and prose of the time, including such classics as *Invisible Man* (1952) and *A Raisin in the Sun* (1959). In effect, it made all of Afro-modernist literature into a synthetic realm where formerly segregated cultural voices were brought into a necessarily artificial and fabricated yet idealistic consensus. Both as a formal and as an epistemological principle, its legacy can be traced all the way to the twenty-first century, where many African American poets cite Hughes, Brooks, or Hayden as precursors (Nelson and Dove 169).

The vernacular and the sonnet were crucial factors in the resurgence of Afro-modernism, and both were transformed in the process. The sonnet was not so much a white as a synthetic form for Afro-modernist poets. It signaled that African American themes and concerns merited the same attention as those of European canonic poetry, but also that black expressive strategies could rival, alter, and enrich one of the most durable forms of the European tradition. The vernacular, on the other hand, was disentangled from minstrelsy, dialect verse, and parochial conceptions of black cultural authenticity. As one element among many of an experimental modernist poetics it became widely acceptable to the black intellectual avant-garde. If the "indisputable modern moment in Afro-American discourse" arrived, as Houston Baker argues in *Modernism and the Harlem Renaissance,* with Sterling Brown's inclusion of the blues into his "masterful" poetry (92–93), it was Hughes's synthesis of the blues with the sonnet that brought the vernacular together with literary high modernism. His "Un-Sonnet Sequence in Blues" opened a way into the literary mainstream for the post-war generation and anticipated the productive ambivalences that would pervade the Afro-modernist project of the 1940s and beyond.

Chapter 5

POETICS OF THE ENCLAVE
The Sonnet in the Age of Black Nationalism

In the mid-1960s the social and aesthetic values of the post-war generation came under attack from a group of writers who rejected its universalist and integrationist premises. The Black Arts movement, as it was soon called, charged that "when Western man speaks of universality, he is referring to an Anglo-Saxon universality," and criticized integrationist conceptions of poetry such as Robert Hayden's. The controversy around Hayden's self-description as "a poet who happens to be Negro" contributed to the movement's sense of mission, which indicates not only its political focus but also its oppositional approach.[1] The Black Arts movement tended to define its political and aesthetic program against white culture and everything associated with it, including the sonnet, whose status in African American poetry changed drastically as a result. The form that had been at the center of poetic innovation in the preceding decades found itself pushed to the margins and had to subsist in enclaves within the cultural sphere that the movement conceptualized as the black nation. In these marginal spaces, the sonnet reshaped itself in response to pressures from the Black Arts orthodoxy, and in its very subsistence questioned the ideological boundaries of the black nation.

These fraught relationships are among many other tensions within the Black Arts movement identified in recent scholarship. While early critics tended to celebrate or dismiss the movement outright, more recent studies such as James Smethurst's *The Black Arts Movement* (2005) and Howard Rambsy's *The Black Arts Enterprise and the Production of African American Poetry* (2011) stress the interplay of enabling and confining influences it exerted on black writing of the 1960s and 1970s.[2] The fate of the sonnet is an instructive example of the ambivalences at work in the Black Arts movement, including its complicated stance on formally innovative writing. The 'black aesthetic' it sought to establish included some kinds of formal experimentation but pointedly excluded others. Don L. Lee/Haki Madhubuti, one of the main theorists of the black aesthetic, named polyrhythm, intensity, irony, sarcasm, direction, concrete subject matter, and musicality as desirable strategies (*Dynamite Voices* 35). Stephen Henderson's *Understanding the New Black Poetry* (1973), the first scholarly study of the new aesthetic, works with an overlapping set of criteria: jazz rhythmic effects; virtuoso free-rhyming; hyperbolic and metaphysical imagery; understatement; compressed and cryptic images; worrying the line (33–42). As later scholars pointed out, the black aesthetic privileged oral over written poetry and rejected experimentation inspired by postmodernism and other predominantly white traditions.[3] These principles led many writers and theorists of the movement to dismiss the sonnet outright. At the same time, the very disconnect between the sonnet and the black aesthetic motivated a number of African American poets to revise the form. This chapter examines how their revisions troubled the boundaries of both the sonnet and the black nation.

BLACK SPACE: LITERARY FORM AND THE
BOUNDARIES OF CULTURAL NATIONALISM

As Smethurst notes in *The Black Arts Movement*, black nationalism was probably the most widely shared political principle in the Black Arts and Black Power movements (15). The idea of a black nation had influenced debates around African American culture for more than a century, from the expatriation societies of the antebellum period to Marcus Garvey's "Back to Africa" project and from the cultural nationalism of the early New Negro movement to the communist Black Belt thesis (see Chapters 2–3). Over the years the black nation had been imagined in a number of different, sometimes contradictory ways: as a goal or a reality, as a sovereign state or a cultural realm, as a global Pan-African project or a local anticolonial one, as a call on African Americans to return to Africa or to organize politically within the United States. One of the most influential figures in the Black Arts movement, Amiri Baraka, admits in his autobiography that he had no clear idea of black nationalism when he first adopted the concept (312). The scholar-activist James Turner, writing for *Black World* in 1971, identified as many as six strands of black nationalism operating within the Black Arts and Black Power movements: religious, cultural, Marxist-revolutionary, economic, political, and Pan-African. There were many crossovers between these strands both programmatically and in terms of the persons involved, but in the literary scene it was the cultural strand of black nationalism that exerted the strongest influence.[4]

National cultures often define themselves by exclusion, as historians have shown, and the cultural nationalism of the Black Arts movement found its common denominator not so much in a shared African heritage as in its opposition to the white-dominated mainstream culture of the United States. "All of the various influences" on the movement, Baraka notes in his autobiography, "focused on white people as enemies" (313). While its theorists made a point of developing a positive agenda, the focus remained on the struggle against white-dominated social structures. "Black art . . . must respond positively to the reality of revolution," Karenga proclaimed in his manifesto "Black Art." "It becomes very important then, that art . . . not bog itself down in the meaningless madness of the Western world wasted" (477–78). Similarly, Askia Touré's "Black Magic" opens with the assertion that the movement needs to "redefine the role of the Black poet," only to specify this redefinition as a "cancelling out" of "the western literary 'negro' poet" (9). Much of this oppositional energy was directed against the concept of "individuality," which Black Arts leaders branded a white strategy of stultifying collective black empowerment.[5]

Unlike their New Negro predecessors, these leaders propagated a distinctly territorial conception of black cultural nationalism. With the slogan "black is a country" they revived the communist idea that black people form an oppressed nation within the United States. They tended to locate this black country not only in the South but also in the inner cities, which in Baraka's words would become "liberated territory" once black officials had been elected and "foreign" elements expelled.[6] The obvious problem of defining the geographical boundaries of his territory made it the more important to proclaim cultural, discursive, and behavioral boundaries that could determine membership in the black nation. As Philipp Brian Harper, Michael Dawson, and others have pointed out, the vocabulary of nationalism—belonging, exclusion, community, boundaries, unity—served to project a homogeneous black people and to police ideological commitment.[7] Black culture, in this view, delineated and evolved within a bounded discursive space.

The black aesthetic was an important means of legitimizing the exclusive, oppositional conception of the black nation. Literary references pervaded black radical discourse throughout the period, and Wahneema Lubiano has convincingly argued that literary criticism stood in for the institutional and ideological structures the black nation lacked. Literary criticism played "the state's role in delimiting and representing acceptable . . . forms and images," Lubiano notes, "including the means by which the black nationalist versions of

the black American past, present, and future can be authorized and dissemi-
nated." The vocabulary of bounded space and its ideological functions congeal
in the concept of "black space," which regularly appears in debates around
the black aesthetic. In a metaphorical superimposition it designates both the
space filled by black writing on a white page and, analogously, the space to be
occupied by self-governed black communities in a white-dominated America.[8]

The cultural boundaries of the black nation were troubled by the subsis-
tence of white forms and traditions within these boundaries. The sonnet, with
its European ancestry and its recognizable structure, appears with striking
frequency in Black Arts debates and invariably serves to denounce older,
non-nationalist poetry. In his preface to Gwendolyn Brooks's autobiography,
Madhubuti argues that Brooks's early use of the sonnet diminished "the force
of her poetic song"; he singles out her poem "the sonnet-ballad" as an example
(14; 17). Brooks followed suit in *A Capsule Course in Black Poetry Writing*
(1975), telling prospective poets that "we must chase out Western measures,
rules, models," especially "all lovely little villanelles and sonnets" (5–7). The
novelist Ishmael Reed, whose aesthetics intersected with those of the Black Arts
movement, went so far as to call black poets who wrote in traditional forms
"slaves" who "excelled at 'Sonnets,' 'Odes,' and 'Couplets,' the feeble pluckings
of musky Gentlemen" (406).

Not all writers of the period went along with this exclusive cultural national-
ism. Considerable portions of the black middle class remained suspicious of
the movement and, if they were interested in poetry at all, read the modernists
of the previous generation or the conventional mediocrities churned out by
undeterred vanity publishers. The Black Arts movement itself was a heteroge-
neous group, recent scholars have pointed out, that comprised Latino poets like
Victor Hernández Cruz and joined forces with Asian American writers on the
West Coast. Nevertheless, it developed a tightly bounded set of "acceptable . . .
forms and images" that avant-garde writers needed to engage if they wanted
to be included in its meetings, magazines, and anthologies.[9] The exclusion of
the sonnet from these boundaries amounted to an unprecedented caesura in
its African American history. For the first time in a century it dropped from
view among the black avant-garde. While the number of politically aware
and aesthetically innovative poets grew considerably in the 1960s, very few of
these poets wrote sonnets, and none made the sonnet central to their oeuvre
the way Claude McKay, Countee Cullen, and Gwendolyn Brooks had. The
few sonnets that did find an audience within the Black Arts movement, on
the other hand, were among the most popular poems of the period. Margaret

Walker's "Malcolm X" was one of them; Hayden's "Frederick Douglass," despite its author's controversial stance, became another.

The sonnet did not vanish from the black nation but remained a troubling force within and along its boundaries. Subsisting in enclaves, it negotiated the intraracial distinctions of belonging and exclusion that Harper has shown to be a primary if unacknowledged concern of the movement ("Nationalism" 225–26). In doing so it defied many of the poetological objections raised by black cultural nationalists and proved remarkably adaptable to the black aesthetic. The effort to salvage the sonnet for a Black Arts agenda was spearheaded by James A. Emanuel, a tangential figure known for his scholarly and editorial work more than for his poetry. In a 1975 *Black World* article titled "Renaissance Sonneteers: Their Contributions to the Seventies," Emanuel argued that the "revolutionary spirit of the Seventies" was indebted to the political protest of the Harlem Renaissance and that the sonnets of the period, of which he quoted a generous selection, proved the suitability of the form for "racial pride, racial history, and racial guidance" (40; 33). Emanuel ultimately failed to generate large-scale interest in the sonnet, maybe because his own efforts in the form stayed well within conventional boundaries. Yet he was not alone in championing the Harlem Renaissance sonnet as an inspiration for black radicalism. A similar idea seems to inform Henderson's influential *Understanding the New Black Poetry,* where McKay appears as a venerated precursor and the sonnet is mentioned with remarkable frequency.

Other poets who attempted to reconcile the sonnet with the black aesthetic were more innovative than Emanuel in adapting the form to the new cultural environment. They developed three main adaptation strategies, all of which responded to the pressures of black nationalism. The first strategy can be described as formal camouflage: the attempt to make the sonnet indistinguishable from Black Arts poetry through changes in its traditional formal structure and through blackness markers like music, the spoken word, and vernacular expressions. The second strategy involves camouflage as well but operates on the thematic level. It attempts to sneak the sonnet into black nationalist discourse by choosing topics whose racial and political relevance outweigh the association of the form with whiteness. Tributes to black leaders were the main occasion for such thematic camouflage. Inversely, the third strategy draws specifically from the outside status signaled by the sonnet to mark off an enclave from the communal project of the black nation—a space in which to express the intimacy and individuality for which the nation had no official use. This strategy resulted in a somewhat paradoxical revival of the love sonnet, which had long been abandoned by the poetic avant-garde. On the other hand, the first two strategies continued to destabilize and vernacularize the classic sonnet form. They accelerated the process that had begun in Langston Hughes's "unsonnets" and Gwendolyn Brooks's modernist experiments (see Chapter 4) and further blurred the boundaries between the sonnet and vernacular free verse.

FORMAL CAMOUFLAGE: BLACKENING THE SONNET

Borderline cases that meet some of the conventional criteria for sonnets but seem consciously to refuse identification with the genre can be found throughout the Black Arts period. The authors of these poems add or subtract lines, dismantle traditional stanza patterns by means of typographical or syntactic changes, allude to classic themes, or add immaculate concluding couplets to otherwise amorphous free-verse poems. It is difficult to draw the line, for example, on a scale ranging from fourteen-line poems that make no reference whatever to the sonnet tradition, to poems whose syntactic patterns resemble those of the sonnet (Larry Tyner's "On Climbing" divides into units of four, three, five, and two lines), to poems that emphasize such patterns typographically (Baraka's early "The Turncoat" looks like a sonnet whose fifth line has switched stanzas), to poems whose typography, syntax, and argument follow a Petrarchan or Shakespearean pattern even though they use neither a rhyme scheme nor a regular meter. In some cases it is not even clear whether a departure from traditional aesthetics indicates a subversive agenda or merely ineptitude. Arnold J. Kelley's "Guide to Living and Working" (1974), for instance, can be read as a sonnet deformed into a kind of chant-like rap poetry, but his other work is so clumsily written that his unwieldy verse seems the result of inability rather than innovation.

While this brief survey already indicates the difficulty of distinguishing the "white" form of the sonnet from the "black" poetry propagated by cultural nationalists, the boundary between the two was challenged most decisively by avant-garde poets who turned the very permeability of the sonnet into a source of creative inspiration. Perhaps the most talented of these poets was Conrad Kent Rivers, who went furthest in adapting the sonnet to racial themes in the tradition of the Harlem Renaissance sonneteers. Rivers might have exerted considerable influence had it not been for his premature death in 1968. An unruly presence in the incipient stages of the movement, he freely admitted that he was "not at peace with myself or my world" (quoted in Ramey 215). His poetry reflects both his mental conflicts and the wide range of sources from which he built his racial identity. Western poetry was one of these sources, and Rivers approached it in the re-formative spirit of the Harlem Renaissance poets (see Chapter 2). "All the standards for which the western world has lived so long," he declared, "are in the process of break-down and revision" (quoted in Ramey 215). The few sonnets he published bear the traces of this revisionary poetics.

"Underground (black cat)" evokes Hughes's jazz poems of the 1920s and signifies on racial stereotypes in cleverly phrased tropes. When the speaker reminisces about "basement parlors / where jazz freaks a blonde / drunk on black jazzmen" (*Still Voice* 7), he initially suggests a pejorative perception of the players as "jazz freaks," only to transfer that perception to the blonde (and hence presumably white) woman as the line continues. In the opening lines of "Albany," an introspective poem in free verse with a Shakespearean stanza pattern, Rivers echoes the ambivalence of McKay's sonnets:

> If this unknown city will set me free
>   and admit that I too am a man,
> tired of begging and walking in darkness
>   let it be. (*These Black Bodies* 4, lines 1–4)

While Rivers successfully updates the form and sensibility of the sonnet for a contemporary discussion of racial identity, his diffident approach failed to resonate with the new radicalism that had emerged by the time of his death. Both the sonnet and the compromises of Harlem Renaissance protest were now widely regarded as instances of subservience to whites, which forced poets interested in either to intensify strategies of camouflage if they wanted to remain within the cultural and discursive space of the black nation.

This challenge is behind many formal experiments of the period and explains why these experiments rarely resulted in the sort of self-sufficient playfulness that characterizes white postmodernism (cf. Nielsen, *Black Chant* 107; 123). Rather than attending to the breakdown of signification, black poets of the 1960s and 1970s pursued a positive political goal—the definition and celebration of blackness—and embraced such essentialist concepts as nationality and authenticity. In the sonnet, metapoetic allusions like the play on the number 14 in Quincy Troupe's "Weather Report in Lincoln Nebraska" (1972) remained the exception. Poets experimenting with the form usually camouflaged it with the blackness markers propagated by Madhubuti, Henderson, and other theorists of the black aesthetic. Applied to a European form like the sonnet, such devices resulted in both defamiliarization and deformation.

This displacement of the cultural norm took the strategy of signifying into the postmodern age. If the subversive protest poets of the Harlem Renaissance used the regular sonnet to signify on white cultural presuppositions, the experimental poets of the Black Arts movement signified on the very forms of thought and expression in which such presuppositions were conceived. A few pages into his experimental collection *Another Kind of Rain* (1970), for example, Gerald Barrax presents a generically titled "Poem" that begins:

> That black bitch of a muse had refused
> To touch me with her fire when I had to sing
> In the dead silence of sterile white space
> And she's gone, selling it now, because I couldn't pay her price. (14, lines 1–4)

The drastic imagery signifies on the traditional, "white" concept of poetic inspiration in several ways. It exposes the repressed sexual overtones of being "kissed by the muse," ironically notes the implications of sterility or even impotence for the poet waiting for the muse, and moves on to a semantic shift that exposes both the material prerequisites of artistic production and their absence in black daily life. Barrax draws on such techniques as sarcasm, hyperbolic imagery, playing the dozens, and vernacular orality to replace a classic theme of the European poetic tradition with an assertion of black poetic self-expression in an economic and ideological environment that often prevented such self-expression.

This strategy is reflected in the overall structure of the poem. While there is no rhyme scheme, both the punctuation and the tripartite argument evoke the three quatrains of the Shakespearean sonnet. A line break after line 12 seems to announce a concluding couplet, but Barrax ironically undercuts these expectations by extending his concluding statement to three lines. Without the muse, he says,

> I find myself wrapped in self
> Embrace
> And wild to hear my soul's applause.

This could easily have been a couplet, so that the artificial separation of "self-embrace" into two lines suggests a willful, capricious deformation of the traditional structure. In these lines the speaker becomes both a caricature of the self-centered poet of the Romantic-aestheticist tradition and, in his desire for the "black bitch of a muse," a spokesman for a collective vernacular aesthetic that alone can save him from such solipsistic impotence. This double-voiced message allows Barrax to signify on white cultural norms from a position of strength rather than weakness. He can ridicule the sterility of the white voice through, and in contrast with, the vernacular vitality of the black voice, which emerges as the more successful cultural standard from the comparison. His ability to make the sonnet form into a vehicle for this message is another indicator of cultural strength and creative potency. The extension of the concluding lines is interestingly ambivalent in this context, however, since the double-voiced structure of the poem suggests two very different readings: as yet another disruption of the white norms from a position of black strength, and as the inability of the sterile white(y) poet to harness his outpourings into the compact fourteen-line pattern. While the former reading dismisses the sonnet in accordance with Black Arts politics, the latter amounts to a revalorization of the form in line with McKay's forceful, controlled protest sonnets.

THEMATIC CAMOUFLAGE: THE BLACK NATIONALIST PRAISE SONNET

Its collectivist politics notwithstanding, the Black Arts movement channeled much of its political energy through a few outstanding figures. Among the most noted of these figures were Malcolm X and John Coltrane, the former embodying political radicalism, the latter cultural authenticity. Malcolm's assassination ignited the movement and inspired so many poetic tributes that the Broadside Press published an anthology dedicated entirely to his memory. In the most extensive analysis to date of this phenomenon, Howard Rambsy calls tribute poems a "signature mode" of the Black Arts era and notes their "strong presence" in both anthologies and popular magazines.[10] For poets interested in traditional forms, this combination of popularity and cultural authority offered an opportunity to sneak sonnets into black national discourse. This sort of thematic camouflage also provided an entryway for the older generation. Poets like Gwendolyn Brooks and Margaret Walker found in praise poetry a familiar mode in which to navigate the technical and ideological challenges of the black aesthetic. While Brooks discarded the sonnet altogether as part of her conversion to that aesthetic, Walker attempted to reconcile the two, and her sonnet to Malcolm X became her strongest link to the black nation.

The revival of the praise sonnet, which had been in decline since its heyday around the turn of the twentieth century, was an unlikely byproduct of black cultural nationalism, and the younger poets took a markedly different approach from their precursors. They were interested in propagating positive "images" of blackness (a favorite expression of the time) as a path to cultural and aesthetic autonomy. Previous praise sonnets also offered positive images of outstanding black figures, of course, but as we have seen they usually commended these figures to a white-dominated mainstream culture by highlighting their conformity to traditional models of heroism (see Chapter 1). The conciliatory stance necessitated by this strategy contrasts sharply with the confrontational vocabulary of the Black Arts poets, who praised their heroes as "warriors" against the established order rather than exemplars within that order (Reese 38). On the other hand, there are continuities with the older model that highlight both the complexities of the praise situation and the relative conservatism of sonneteers within the Black Arts movement. The tension between individual and collective concerns, for example, reappears in the new wave of praise sonnets and is exacerbated by the collectivist demands of the black nation. In the same vein, the self-positioning inherent to poetic tributes was inevitably fraught with political demands and individualist innuendoes.

These tensions are palpable in Walker's "For Malcolm X," which first appeared in the aforementioned anthology of posthumous tributes and became the best-known praise sonnet of the period. Like many posthumous tributes of the time, Walker's sonnet tries to reflect the entire range of responses to Malcolm in the black community. It expresses sadness and anger, veneration and resistance, anxiety and a faint glimmer of hope. In order to integrate all of these conflicting moods, Walker relies on a Whitmanian elegiac tone and on the structuring devices offered by the sonnet form. The octave is framed by the lofty poetic imagery of "All you violated ones with gentle hearts / . . . / Gather round this coffin and mourn your dying swan" (*Prophets* 18, lines 1, 8), but contained within this frame are the more drastic images of "devils" and "hollowed pits for eyes" as well as the political interpellation of the oppressed black masses, "[h]ating white devils and black bourgeoisie" (lines 4–6). While the octave addresses the masses gathering around the coffin, the sestet reverses this pattern and addresses the dead Malcolm from the perspective of a collective "we" gazing into the coffin. The volta thus becomes another structural device for encompassing different responses to Malcolm's death. The octave could also be read as a speech by the dead leader himself, with the sestet recording the reaction of his people in the call-and-response pattern of the African American tradition. Walker successfully evokes a range of emotions by juxtaposing these individual and collective voices. Her handling of stylistic devices, on the other hand, reveals the problems inherent in such condensation. Juxtapositions like "white devils and black bourgeoisie" are stylistically incongruous, and the disparate imagery of the sestet runs into contradictions and mixed metaphors (a Muslim Christ figure who is bleeding and performing an operation the same time) instead of evoking the range and magnitude of Malcolm's example.

In choosing a reliable form like the sonnet, Walker might be trying to rep-licate Malcolm's influence and reach a wide audience, thus positioning herself in direct succession to the leader she celebrates. This reading is sustained by the address patterns of her poem, which make her a spokesperson for both the leader (in the octave) and the masses responding to him (in the sestet). Walker consciously positions herself in the Black Arts movement through the poem's categorical rejection of both whites and assimilationist blacks, a move that parallels the well-publicized conversions of such leading figures as Baraka and Madhubuti a few years earlier. In the preface to her collected poems, *This Is My Century* (1989), Walker notes that her "friends, the black male scholars and critics, speak disparagingly of my sonnets" (xvii), a comment that indicates both her desire for acceptance by these figures and the practical consequences of formal choices in a Black Arts environment. Nevertheless the rich heritage of the praise sonnet seems to have exerted some influence on the movement. An unusual number of Malcolm tributes are fourteen-liners, a length free-verse poets usually avoided because of its association with the sonnet tradition. Even experimental free-verse tributes like Ted Joans' "My Ace of Spades" (1969) and Ethelbert Miller's "Malcolm X, February 1965" can thus be read as approximat-ing the sonnet form and echoing the tradition of the black praise sonnet.[11]

The tension between individual and collective considerations also pervades the second type of praise sonnet revived during the period: tributes from one poet to another. Like the 'vertical' tributes to leader figures, these 'horizontal' tributes combined conventional features of the praise sonnet with strategies favored by the experimental poets at the core of the Black Arts movement. One widely available model for such experiments was Gwendolyn Brooks's broad-side *Family Pictures* (1970), which appeared well after her sonnet-writing days and features tributes to colleagues like Madhubuti and Keorapetse Kgositsile. Madhubuti reciprocated with an entire series of poems to Brooks over the years. As we have seen in Chapter 1, horizontal tributes foreground the author's self-positioning and relationship to the addressee, often at the expense of politi-cal content and collective appeal. This was less consequential for distinguished poets like Brooks and Madhubuti, who were also cultural leaders, than it was for marginal figures who incurred the additional risk of writing in a form discouraged in the black nation. As a result, few of these tributes are marked as sonnets in any obvious way. None employ pentametric lines or a rhyme scheme, and poems like Quincy Troupe's "A Sense of Coolness" (1972), Alvin Aubert's "Dayton Dateline" (1975), and Sarah Carolyn Reese's "Alhamisi" (presumably from the mid-1970s) make no formal references beyond the length of fourteen lines.[12] They evoke the tradition of the praise sonnet by naming the addressee in the title or subtitle but ultimately leave it to the reader to make (or ignore) the connection. All of them can profitably be read in that tradition, however, which suggests it had an impact on the composition process.

Tributes to black people were an obvious means of evoking the collective ethos at the core of black cultural nationalism. Depending on the addressee, such tributes signaled commitment to the political struggle and/or the black aesthetic, and even if some formal choices failed to reflect that agenda, the popularity of tribute poems among readers, writers, and critics was reason enough to regard them as community-building activism (cf. Rambsy 14–15; 32). These credentials seem to have provided thematic camouflage that allowed poets to allude to the sonnet form without risking their position inside the ideological boundaries of the black nation. As we have seen, however, the praise sonnet can create a sense of intimacy between speaker and addressee, and it has a long tradition of foregrounding the speaker's personal views and feelings. This tension between communal pressure and self-assertion makes itself felt in most praise sonnets of the Black Arts period. It generates an ambivalence that can both destabilize the poem and enrich its layers of meaning.

Troupe's "A Sense of Coolness," a fourteen-line poem dedicated to Stanley Crouch, is the exception to this rule. Instead of negotiating the demands of the collective, it ignores them altogether and creates an imaginative space to which only the speaker and the addressee have access: "the odor of ancestors and water / reeds bending the softness / of the blends of evening" (lines 4–6). Troupe seems to be taking a timeout from political concerns to establish a purely personal and aesthetic connection with Crouch, who had been vocal in his rejection of would-be writers confusing "craft" with the "name-calling fad masked as 'Revolutionary Black Nationalism'" ("Toward" 28). Troupe honors his friend and colleague by adopting his high-cultural aesthetic preferences, which results in a style reminiscent of Charles Olson rather than black street poetry. Troupe's allusion to the praise sonnet can be read as one of these high-cultural formal markers, and it points to the third strategy African American sonneteers developed in response to black nationalism: the use of the sonnet as an enclave in the midst of the collective struggle against racism.

Enclaves of Individuality

The set of aesthetic revalorizations summarized by the slogan "black is beautiful" gave the expression of love a cultural and political significance it had not possessed in the previous history of African American literature. Almost all major poets of the period wrote love poetry, and some published entire volumes of it. Prominent examples include Dudley Randall's *Love You* (1970), Sonia Sanchez's *Love Poems* (1973), Linda Brown Bragg's *A Love Song to Black Men* (1974), LeRoy Clarke's *Taste of Endless Fruit* (1974), and Frank John/ Nkemka Asika's *Love in Black Soul* (1977). The titles of these collections indicate that the Black Arts movement extended the concept of love beyond the personal sphere. Both masculinity and female beauty were redefined in collective terms. If black was beautiful, this was because it counteracted oppressive white standards of social, cultural, and political worth. Leading thinkers of the movement held that such beauty could, and should, be appreciated by all black people, and indeed that it emanated from a collective aesthetic tradition.[13] The love poetry inspired by these ideas typically praises the black woman or man for embodying this tradition and inspiring racial pride.

These developments generated various ambivalences within the black nation—ambivalences that went unnoticed in scholarship because the role of love and intimacy in the Black Arts movement has only recently come under scrutiny. Two groundbreaking publications, Kevin Quashie's *The Sovereignty of Quiet* (2012) and Keith Leonard's "Love in the Black Arts Movement" (2013), begin to examine these ambivalences. Quashie points out, among other things, that the argument for black equality presupposes but at the same time represses shared human traits such as disinterested love and vulnerability (76–79; 101–2). Leonard stresses the political functions of love in the black nation, especially in contributing to the "affective identification" and "emotional unity" presupposed by the imagined community of nationalism (619). While core figures of the movement did publish love poetry that enacted this sort of collective subjectivity, the love sonnets of the period took a different stance. In line with the long tradition of the genre, they sustained a more conventional notion of love as an intimate romantic exchange outside the collective sphere. Bounded off from the black nation both by its topic and by its form, the love sonnet echoed the nationalist argument for black desirability but explored the interior dimensions and emotional complexities of individual love relationships. By carving out an enclave in which these problems could be negotiated, it became a marginal but vitalizing presence in the black nation.

These dynamics are most clearly illustrated by formally regular sonnets published in a Black Arts environment. Linda Brown Bragg's "Winter Sonnet," for example, appeared in her abovementioned collection *A Love Song to Black Men,* published by the Broadside Press. It establishes an intimate space for romantic love both through its distinctive form and through the setting evoked in the opening lines: "We walked and blinked at sunlight on the snow, / The silence broken only by our tread" (27, lines 1–2). The motifs of snow and silence in the first two lines remove the poem from the bustle of daily life and from the urban sphere in which Black Arts poetry usually situated itself. The chivalrous gesture of the next two lines introduces the theme of conventional romantic love, and the rest of the poem is devoted to developing these motifs. A more complex expression of intimate love can be found in June Jordan's "Sunflower Sonnets," written in 1975, whose title image similarly evokes pristine nature as an enclave while at the same time gesturing toward Hayden's use of the sunflower as a symbol for the endurance of the black lower classes. Well-connected with both the Black Arts movement and mainstream publishing, Jordan anticipated the poets of the 1980s and 1990s in that she worked to situate the black aesthetic in a wider societal and generational context.[14] This agenda manifests in her "Sunflower Sonnets," which establish an enclave for intimate love while at the same time defining that enclave in terms reminiscent of Edna St. Vincent Millay. The whimsical, ambivalent voice she adopts from Millay allows her to trace the minute complexities of a romantic relationship without sacrificing it either to individual disillusionment or to the claims of the collective.

Jordan also adopts the formal pattern of Millay's sonnets, a Shakespearean rhyme scheme that accommodates modern speech patterns through enjambments and caesuras. While the first "Sunflower Sonnet" is rather imitative in this respect, the second achieves a more original, contemporary sound through its colloquialisms and syncopations:

> . . . Which is to say
> I guess the costs of long term tend to pile
> up, block and complicate, erase away
> the accidental, temporary, near
> thing/pulsebeat promises one makes
> because the chance, the easy new, is there
> in front of you. . . . (lines 6–12)

These lines present a more comprehensive version of the black national subject, one that admits and negotiates its own emotional vulnerability along the lines of Quashie's argument (76–77). The threat of disruption is at work on several levels in the poem. The lovers' relationship is threatened by "the chance, the easy new" that might draw them away from each other; the poem's expression of intimacy is threatened by the political exigencies of its black nationalist environment; and the stability of the sonnet form is threatened by the "pulsebeat" of the black aesthetic. This latter aspect prefigures the poetics of the sonnet Rita Dove would formulate in her preface to *Mother Love* (1995): the notion that the traditional sonnet is an "intact world," a protection from both change and vulnerability, that will collapse as soon as its presuppositions are questioned or its formal boundaries punctured (xiii). By interlinking all of these aspects, Jordan makes her "Sunflower Sonnets" into an enclave, a shelter from disruption in which love, intimacy, and vulnerability can subsist.

Not all love sonnets of the period fortify their boundaries that assiduously. Poets like Lance Jeffers and Joe H. Mitchell construct their enclaves in a more open manner, both formally and semantically. Their example suggests that intimacy could be communicated not just within but beyond the enclave, and could thus be disseminated into the black nation as a whole. The most accomplished sonnets in this vein are those of the prolific Mitchell, a now forgotten figure who founded his own press, Natural Resources Unlimited, and brought out eight volumes of his poetry in rapid succession in 1973 and 1974. One of his titles, *Lovin' You* (1974), announces his characteristic approach: he synthesizes the traditional love poem with modern, often vernacular elements. His technique is informed by both the street vernacular and the associative style of William Carlos Williams and Charles Olson. Where the latter influence predominates, the stanzas of Mitchell's sonnets, which he always sets apart typographically, turn into vignettes of their own that offer different perspectives on the subject of the poem.

Mitchell's metapoetic reflection on the sonnet form comes to the fore in "paper-back" from another of his vernacularly titled collections, *O Woman* (1974). The speaker of the poem comments ironically on his efforts to "whisper / at least 3 to 8 minutes / of sweet nothings" to his partner after the sexual act. Neither of the lovers is interested in such whispering, it turns out, but both have read an "art-of-loving paperback" that prescribes the activity (lines 6–8, 14). The poem signifies not only on mercantile advice books but also on the sonnet tradition. On a surface level, that tradition represents the true "art of loving" and serves as a counterpart to the rule-book routines of the speaker's relationship. The speaker's rendering of these routines, however, is itself marked as a sonnet by the Shakespearean layout. Moreover, that sonnet is named for the very rule-book that creates them, which deflates the romantic ideals associated with the form and in effect parallels it with the mundane quantifications of a cheap advice book.

Even a love sonnet can merely reiterate "3 to 8 minutes / of sweet nothings," the poem suggests, and it reinforces this suggestion through a conspicuously self-referential play on numbers: "3 to 8" comes in between lines 3 and 8; the "12 minutes" the woman has to wait for her cigarette appear in line 12. The hyphenated title also encourages a metapoetic reading, especially by evoking the classic Shakespearean tropes of materiality and signification. While Mitchell uses the sonnet form to comment ironically on his own poem, he also uses his poem, and maybe his autobiographical experience, to signify on the sonnet form. In the same vein, he evokes the conventional boundaries that prevent direct communication between lovers but ultimately overcomes them by establishing a common ground beyond the "art-of-loving paperback." He masters these conventions, and the formal conventions of the sonnet, in a gesture of uninhibited self-expression and interpersonal communication. Mastery of form was no longer of interest for the political vanguard in the Black Arts period, but Mitchell modernizes the strategy in a way that allows him to negotiate intimate concerns in a self-assertive manner that projects a politically progressive stance as well.

The notion of the love sonnet as an enclave within the black nation suggests two general observations regarding the sonnet in the Black Arts period. First, it indicates that the sonnet became one of the preserves of individuality in an environment dominated politically and poetologically by the collective. The sonnet was a formal option for poets who believed, as James Cunningham wrote in a rejoinder to Karenga's "Black Art" manifesto, that "art with its diversity of points of view always manages to reveal people to be far more complex and various than we are otherwise willing to admit" (487). It was poets like Jordan, Jeffers, and Mitchell who created enclaves for private concerns and individual expression. At the same time, their experiments indicate the wide range of strategies for which the sonnet was appropriated at the time. While the love sonnet subsisted in a personal sphere at odds with the orthodoxy of black cultural nationalism, the praise sonnet served for political declarations and position-takings in the center of the black nation—declarations echoing those of the radical avant-garde that rejected the sonnet in principle. What most of these strategies had in common was a tendency to defamiliarize the sonnet, either in order to imprint a recognizable personal signature as in Rivers and Mitchell, or to incorporate black aesthetic elements as a way of making the sonnet acceptable to the new avant-garde.

This latter impulse suggests a second concluding observation: The African American sonnet underwent a fundamental ideological shift in the Black Arts period. Techniques like mimicry, defamiliarization, and signifying had previously served to articulate a black political agenda against the racism or indifference of a white-dominated mainstream. For the sonneteers of the Black Arts period they served the opposite purpose. They allowed these poets to defend their use of the sonnet form, and by extension their freedom to engage the white mainstream, against the indifference of (or rejection by) the black avant-garde. The racial ambivalence of the African American sonnet, which had previously posed a threat to white racial prejudice, now intruded onto the discursive space of the black nation and destabilized the boundaries by which that nation was defined. The genre that had long been "almost . . . but not white," in Homi Bhabha's phrase, was now almost but not black, which left it in a doubly marginalized position (*Location* 128). The handful of capable poets who continued to use the form on a consistent basis did so on their own device, often disconnected from larger developments. It was not until the mid-1980s that the sonnet reemerged as an option for avant-garde poets, but when it did, its marginal status in the Black Arts movement made it a favorite among a new generation that was challenging the precepts and boundaries of the black nation.

Chapter 6

THE SPACES OF BLACK EXPERIMENTAL POETRY

When Rita Dove was awarded the Pulitzer Prize for poetry in 1987, many took this to confirm the end of the black aesthetic. Dove had distanced herself from the Black Arts movement early on, portrayed black life from an individual rather than a collective point of view, and acknowledged the European cultural heritage as a formative influence. She was taken to represent a new generation of African American poets, a generation that has since been labeled cosmopolitan, postmodern, post-black, and many other things.[1] Some scholars have questioned not only these labels but the notion that the black aesthetic was replaced or superseded by the new generation. On the contrary, these scholars argue, the black aesthetic continues to encourage formally experimental writing, "shape editorial decisions" and inform "conceptions of the canon and the larger tradition."[2] The previous chapter has shown that the Black Arts movement did inspire formally innovative writing by African Americans—but within clearly defined boundaries. It privileged the oral over the graphic and the collective over the individual, insisted on referentiality and accessibility, rejected putatively white influences, and championed black ones such as jazz and blues music.

Following the seminal work of Aldon Nielsen, scholars have shown that these preferences excluded substantial portions of African American poetry from anthologies and literary histories, for example poetry that prioritizes written language, fosters ambiguity, is elusive rather than accessible, subverts conventionalized meanings, or adapts strategies from white-associated movements such as poststructuralism.[3] African American poets working in these modes have been among the foremost critics of the black aesthetic and its boundaries. Harryette Mullen influentially claimed that the notion of an "authentic black voice" rooted in the oral tradition silences other voices and "results in the impoverishment of the tradition." Rather than delimiting black expression,

Mullen argues, poetry should challenge its boundaries and expand its range. It should be "explorative and interrogative, an open-ended investigation into the possibilities of language, the aesthetic and expressive, intellectual and *transformative* possibilities of language." In the same vein Nathaniel Mackey praises contemporary experimental poetry for its "pursuit of greater complexity and sophistication in technical and formal matters, . . . a more complex accommodation between technique and epistemological concerns, between ways of telling and ways of knowing." This kind of poetry, Mackey and Mullen suggest, probes into the covert presuppositions and conventions of African American life rather than establishing clear guidelines or boundaries. It has struggled for visibility because it troubles the pervasive assumption that black writing is not experimental and experimental writing is not black.[4]

Scholars have taken important steps in recovering black experimental poetry, but arguably have allowed another blind spot to develop in the process. Many studies of such poetry privilege its temporal dimension over the spatial. Nielsen's *Integral Music: Languages of African American Innovation* (2004), for example, situates experimental poetry in the "future anterior" because it is driven by the tension between blackness and modernity (xv–xvi). The future anterior reappears in Anthony Reed's insightful *Freedom Time: The Poetics and Politics of Black Experimental Writing* (2014), which stresses the liberatory potential of temporal writing and reading. By deferring conventional meanings and revising dominant histories, Reed argues, experimental writing destabilizes existing social and perceptual orders and projects the very utopian, liberated future for which the Black Arts movement was yearning. Even spatial formations like concrete poems and sonnets have a temporal dimension, Reed suggests, in that they draw attention to the shape and sound of words, which disrupts old meanings and generates new ones. Philipp Brian Harper's *Abstractionist Aesthetics* (2015) similarly privileges temporality as the site of innovation and resistance. Harper aims to revalorize art that subverts the epistemological foundations of race rather than criticizing racism in positive terms. Music and narrative are the most effective venues of such art, he argues, because their temporal progression creates an illusion of direct experience whose disruption can then draw attention to the historicity and constructedness of all experience.[5]

This focus on temporality is not accidental. To a considerable extent it is borne out by the poetry itself. Harryette Mullen emphasizes the transformative quality of poetic language in her definition of experimental writing, and the multilayered wordplay in her poetry continually triggers such transformations. Nathaniel Mackey draws on the disruptive effects of music, seriality, and other temporalizing devices throughout his oeuvre. A closer look at the role of the sonnet in contemporary African American poetry, however, questions the tendency in scholarship to equate temporality with formal innovation and radical politics or vice versa.

The explosion of interest in the sonnet from the 1980s onward is among the strongest indicators of the receding influence of the black aesthetic, which as we have seen excluded the sonnet from the realm of black poetry. The sheer number of sonnets published since the 1990s is unprecedented in the history of African American poetry, as is their prominence and diversity. They range from banal everyday scenes to ambitious negotiations of African American history and culture, from self-centered meditations in the confessional tradition to radical displacements of structure and meaning, from heartfelt eulogies to irreverent revisions of poetic precursors. The sonnet has a prominent place in the work of leading poets of the time, including Gerald Barrax, Wanda Coleman, Yusef Komunyakaa, Marilyn Nelson, Afaa Michael Weaver, and Al Young. Rita Dove's *Mother Love* (1995), an entire collection of experimental sonnets, confirmed the revival of the form and ensured its continuing popularity with a younger generation, including one of her successors as Poet Laureate, Natasha Trethewey.[6]

Perhaps the most striking aspect of this revival is the sudden popularity of the sonnet sequence. When Dove received the Pulitzer, only a handful of sonnet sequences had been published by African American poets. The following decade saw the appearance of no less than eleven sequences, including two book-length ones.[7] One reason behind the sudden interest in the sonnet sequence, this chapter argues, was its suitability for negotiating and revising the legacy of black cultural nationalism. The new generation of poets used the familiar structure of the sonnet to foreground the materiality of language and subvert conventional forms and meanings. Many of these poets work with serial and procedural techniques. As defined by the scholar Joseph Conte, serial poetry is characterized by "the discontinuous and often aleatory manner in which one thing follows another" (3), while procedural poems use a set of predetermined, often arbitrary constraints as a generative principle. The sonnet sequence enhances the deconstructive effect of such techniques by introducing a temporal dimension. Through repetition and transformation, it multiplies potential meanings and further undermines conventional forms and expectations. This spatiotemporal dynamic made the sonnet sequence a particularly productive site of experimental writing—writing that subverted the cultural and aesthetic boundaries of the Black Arts movement.

This chapter traces the spatiotemporal dynamics in the sonnet sequences of Ed Roberson, Wanda Coleman, Rita Dove, and two poets of the early twenty-first century, G. E. Patterson and Wanda Phipps. Roberson began to experiment with the sonnet on the margins of the Black Arts movement and worked almost exclusively in the form from the mid-1980s to the early 2000s. Coleman published an open-ended series of "American Sonnets" in the early 1990s that made the most prolific African American sonneteer in quantitative terms. Dove turned to the sonnet in the mid-1990s and has continued working in the form. Patterson and Phipps take this tradition into the twenty-first century to explore identities that, like their sonnet sequences, are both fractured and interconnected. All of these poets challenge existing accounts of black experimental poetry in that they explore transformative and disruptive effects that are neither limited to nor dependent on temporal poetics. Their work shows that such effects can also be attained by troubling the spatial arrangement of rhymes, lines, and sections in a predetermined form like the sonnet. It is no accident that the most succinct theorizations of the sonnet in an African American context, Fred Moten's "in the break" and Dove's "intact world," emerged from discussions of experimental poetry and draw on spatial metaphors to conceptualize the formally, politically, and epistemologically disruptive effect of experimental work in the form (see introduction). Both Moten and Dove locate the political import of formal experimentation in its transgression of boundaries, as we have seen, and make the boundaries of the sonnet stand in for those of conventional ideas, meanings, and worldviews. The sonnet sequences discussed in the following exacerbate this dynamic by combining spatial and temporal transgression.

Ed Roberson's Spaces of Indeterminacy

When the young, little-known poet Ed Roberson published the poem "18,000 feet" in his collection *When Thy King Is a Boy* (1970), readers saw fourteen lines in standard typesetting, jaggedly but consistently diminishing in length. The poem is a fragmentary interior monologue inspired by the speaker's observation of a high-altitude scenery; it ends with a new sense of ease at having left the complexities of social life behind. One of the last lines, "how much a prison freedom is" (*When Thy King* 11, line 12), evokes the disappointments of a century of African American life after the official end of slavery. Given that "18,000 feet" appears next to a poem titled "sonnet" in the collection, the line might also signify on Wordsworth's "Nuns fret not at their Convent's narrow room," which celebrates the sonnet form as an escape from "the weight of too much liberty" (*Poems* 133, line 13). By implication, "18,000 feet" is itself a variation on the sonnet form.

Shortly before Roberson's collection was published, however, the poem had appeared in a volume of the *New Directions* series and in the extended edition of Langston Hughes and Arna Bontemps' anthology *The Poetry of the Negro*. Readers of these publications saw a very different poem: a fourteen-liner still, but one whose layout resists identification as a sonnet. Its organization is vertical rather than horizontal, and indentations divide it into sections of two, five, six, and one lines. Some of the lines feature expanded spaces between words or phrases, which has a decelerating effect similar to the later version. The word order remains unchanged with the exception of line 12, which here reads "how much a freedom prison is." This might be an editorial blunder that Roberson corrected in his own volume, but the change might also indicate a conscious attempt on the author's part to point readers to his experiments with traditional conceptions of the sonnet.

Since he did not achieve wider recognition until the 1990s, Roberson is usually grouped with Mackey, Mullen, Coleman, and other experimental poets who emerged after the Black Arts movement. When "18,000 feet" is read as a modification of the sonnet form, however, it recalls the sonnet-variants of the Black Arts period whose authors were marginalized because their work did not satisfy the formal and thematic expectations of the movement (see Chapter 5). Roberson's work and reception are thus representative of the changing fates of the African American sonnet in the late twentieth century. The volumes that secured his reputation, *Lucid Interval as Integral Music* (1984), *Voices Cast Out to Talk Us In* (1995), and *Atmosphere Conditions* (2000), largely consist of experimental sonnet sequences. While these sequences have a strong temporal dimension, the titular motifs of the interval and the atmosphere indicate Roberson's interest in spatial modes. Many of his sequences follow "18,000 feet" in negotiating the experience and perception of spaces such as mountains, cities, and the sky. They redouble this spatial dimension on the page, where the arrangement of words, lines, sections, and poems creates gaps and connections, contrasts and parallels, that open up a variety of possible meanings.

In interviews, Roberson recalled that he was attracted to the sonnet because its boundedness draws attention to individual words and enhances the interplay between its constitutive parts.[8] His experiments in the form considerably widened the formal range of the African American sonnet by opening it up to influences from postmodernist and language poetry. At the same time, they demonstrated that the rather hermetic language resulting from these influences could effectively negotiate racial concerns. Roberson's poems are not openly political statements, nor do they directly revise racial histories. They create a semantically autonomous realm that implicates language conventions, including racially connoted words, in the indeterminacy of the signifier and thus destabilizes conventional stereotypes and innuendoes. Roberson has claimed that African American poetry is often read as "some sort of a sociological marker or token of black writing" (Horton, "Structure" 764), and his poetics of indeterminacy avoids such limiting ascriptions without denying the African American experience underlying his poems. His experiments seem to aim less at foregrounding the ideological implications of language than at deforming linguistic conventions, so as to create a shared space of liberated signification in which an individual-yet-racial experience can be communicated.

This shared space emerges on the thematic level as well. Many of Roberson's sonnets are set in a natural environment that transcends (but does not deny) the limitations of the cultural realm and of such racially charged settings as the levee or the cotton field. Roberson's nature is a sphere of personal experience in which cultural signifiers dissolve and transform, offering poet and reader opportunities for reinterpreting these signifiers. In the title poem of *Atmosphere Conditions* (2000), for example, this transformative sphere is the sky:

> That weather when you can't tell whether
> what you see is yours, nature's or some curve
> a public careering through throws on the wall (7, lines 1–3)

The sky offers the observing poet not escape from culture but a new perspective on its patterns of signification. The poet's impression that certain atmospheric phenomena look like graffiti ("New York subway art," line 5) becomes a leitmotif of the poem and establishes its racial subtext. Where some Black Arts representatives dismissed nature poetry as disconnected and escapist—a black poet "need not talk about the aesthetics of a tree," Don L. Lee asserted in *Dynamite Voices* (1971), because "there are no trees in Harlem or on the westside of Chicago" (49)—Roberson explores its potential for the deconstruction of racial signifiers and thus makes it into a space of unrestrained communication. In doing so he anticipated the recent discovery of nature in African American poetry, signaled by the anthology *Black Nature* (2009) and several scholarly studies, just as he anticipated the resurgence of the sonnet.[9] The title poem of *Atmosphere Conditions*, like several others in the collection, draws on the sonnet form to reflect the poet's transformative vision. Just as the sky reflects cultural patterns and interweaves them in new variations, the poem interweaves tercets and couplets in ways that recall the stanza patterns of the sonnet without ever adding up to a complete, conventional specimen.

While his transformative spheres are often spatial, Roberson's first book-length collection of sonnets indicates that they can be temporal as well. *Lucid Interval as Integral Music* consists of three sections, "The Form," "This Week's Concerts," and "Interval and Final Day's Concerts." In calling his sonnets "concerts," Roberson stresses their temporal unfolding and implicates them in his poetics of indeterminacy. Like concert music, they draw on a shared set of signs without referents, signs that do not have meaning in any narrow sense but create an aesthetic effect through the complexity of their interaction. Music typifies the indeterminate, ever-evolving process of signification Roberson envisions for his shared communicative space, a kinship he puts to work on various levels of *Lucid Interval.*

On a motivic level, he plays with the double meanings of musical terms to negotiate racial and political themes in a fresh, flexible language. The very first poem of "This Week's Concerts" establishes a new perspective on lynching, a well-worn theme of African American poetry, by rendering it in acoustic terms. The speaker of the poem is a collective "we" that takes on the shapes of a lynch mob but also of workers burning a corpse in a crematorium or death camp. This collective entity emphasizes the musical connotations of the process: "taking the body down / we thought was a solo for fuel"; and "shoving it in for warmth" they create "naked jarring blast" (11, lines 5–7, 11). The concert theme established by the volume and section titles emphasizes the musicality of the language on both the semantic and the acoustic levels. The lynching creeps into the poem through its sounds, which captures the reader on a different level than most lynching poems and subtly evokes the horror of the act. Another example for this strategy is Roberson's evocation of police violence in poem 22: "The black cats / had given blue feet to police siren such / that I thought the scream a jazz jade bowl and a step" (32–33, lines 11–13).

Beside such motivic uses, Roberson's deconstruction of musical terms also serves to manifest his poetological agenda. The titular concept of the interval is of particular importance in this respect. It pervades the volume from the macro-level (the temporal interval between the two sections of the concert) through the layout of the poems (Roberson characteristically works with spaces of unequal lengths between words) to the micro-structure of signification. Like its counterpart the "bridge" (poems 20, 22), the interval has a temporal and a spatial component. The temporal intervals between utterance and understanding give rise to the indeterminacy at the heart of Roberson's poetics. The spatial intervals between white and black engender both the oppression he depicts and the shared communicative space in which the conditions of such oppression can be exposed and counteracted.

The interval thus disrupts the intact world of Roberson's sonnets, both in a formal and a semantic sense. The critic Kathleen Crown registers this semantic disruption when she reads Roberson's intervals as "the breaks in historical consciousness produced by traumatic events such as the Middle Passage," breaks "that symptomatically reenact the original trauma and, at the same time, bear witness to a culture's ability to survive, adapt, and innovate." Brent Hayes Edwards points out that such breaks "are not only a concern of the content of the book, but also the principle of its form": "the graphic break between the parts of the poem" suggests both silence and adaptation.[10] Yet another function of these intervals, in both time and space, is their evocation of seriality. They blur the boundaries of individual sonnets but also of the sonnet sequence as a whole, so that the open-endedness of interpretation is enhanced by a sense of open-endedness on the page. The serial arrangement of Roberson's collections evokes but deconstructs the narrative temporality of classic sonnet sequences.

Roberson provides only the vaguest semantic frames for his sequences: any kind of stable narrative framework would encroach on the indeterminacy of his poems by imposing causal coherence and limiting the number of possible meanings and connotations. He uses the sequence to multiply meanings instead by putting the individual sonnets and their constitutive parts into relation. He expands the sphere of indeterminacy onto the entire sequence and, implicitly, onto the discourses and preconceptions the sequence negotiates. Instead of closing gaps in signification, plot, and layout, Roberson's sequencing draws attention to them. Words stand out of context, sentences remain incomplete or trick the reader into premature conclusions, and the typographical arrangement of the poems creates open spaces that leave it unclear how the different parts relate to each other. These devices require the reader to construct his own connections, and ultimately his own narrative. They are "generative," as Moten says of the gaps and cuts in jazz montages, and render "inoperative any simple opposition of totality to singularity" (89).

Moten's interpretation of the gap or break as a generative indeterminate space captures the creative energy the sonnet sequence produces in its very disruption. Roberson arranges his sonnets in ways that enhance not only the indeterminacy within the sonnets but that open up the boundaries of these sonnets, thus questioning the very definition of the form. The sequence "This Week's Concerts" from *Lucid Interval,* for example, begins rather innocuously with a single sonnet, numbered with a Roman numeral, but upon turning the page the reader discovers a second sequence underneath the first one: sonnet II is followed by a sonnet 2 (Arabic numeral) on the lower half of the page. There is no sonnet 1, nor is there a sonnet 3: underneath sonnet III is an unnumbered sonnet that has no discernible semantic connections with any of the others. It can be read as a poem of its own, or as a counterpart to sonnet III, or as a sequel to either sonnet 2 (continuing horizontally) or sonnet III (continuing vertically). The confusion persists through the entire sequence: the bottom half of the page often carries an Arabic-numbered complement but sometimes an unnumbered one, or it is left empty. Some of the Arabic-numbered sonnets take up phrases or motifs from their Roman-numbered counterparts, others reference an earlier Arabic-numbered one. In a few instances the Roman-numbered sonnet is printed squarely in the middle of the page, disrupting the horizontal division.

The challenge, and the ultimate impossibility, of ascertaining the boundaries of individual sonnets is enhanced by the uneven line counts and layouts of these sonnets. The Roman-numbered sonnets are typographically divided into three quatrains and a single concluding line, which foregrounds their incompleteness and suggests that the bottom-half sonnets might furnish completion—especially since some of the latter have 15 lines. This arrangement has been read as a postmodernist deferral of meaning, an unearthing of suppressed memories, and, by Roberson himself, as a call-and-response pattern.[11] Importantly in our context, it engenders what Derrida would call a supplementary dynamic between the sonnets, suggesting completion and superfluity at the same time. While these readings stress the temporal dimension of Roberson's work in the sonnet, the dynamics they describe gain their force through his spatial experimentation. His fragmentation of the sonnet sequence creates the indeterminate spaces in which conventions of meaning, including racial stereotypes, can be suspended and revised.

Wanda Coleman, Rita Dove, and the Interstices of Myth and Nation

The disruptive potential of the in-between was widely recognized in literary and cultural theory of the late twentieth century, most influentially perhaps by the postcolonial theorist Homi Bhabha. Like Roberson's poetics, Bhabha's reflections on the "interstice" play on the overlap of the material and the semiotic. In the essays collected in *The Location of Culture* (1994), Bhabha suggests that the world of globalized capitalism is best understood by examining "the interstitial, disjunctive spaces and signs" that engender its characteristic indeterminacy (311). Spaces and signs are mutually constitutive in this view, or rather, they are mutually deconstructive. Space seems to stabilize meaning and vice versa, but on closer inspection the gaps and fissures—the interstices—loom so large that conventional interpretations of either spaces or signs collapse. Bhabha is an important theorist of such spatio-semiotic disruption, as his comments on the "Third Space of enunciations" attest (56). His conceptualization of the interstice, however, presupposes that disruptive energies are generated in time rather than space—an assumption we have found in contemporary scholars of black experimental poetry as well.

Bhabha introduces this assumption in his critique of Fredric Jameson, whom he faults for constricting the "radical discontinuity" of global capitalism by focusing on its spatial representations. This focus introduces notions of "distance" and "separation," Bhabha claims, while ignoring "the interstitial passages and processes of cultural difference that are inscribed in the 'in-between,' in the temporal break-up" (310; 314). The example of Roberson has shown that spatial formations too have their interstices. The tension between the material and semiotic layers of the sonnet sequence, for example, can unfold disruptive energies in both time and space. While Roberson's explorations of semantic indeterminacy have an obliquely political significance, other poets turned the sonnet sequence into a more directly referential tool for exploring the interstices of racialized thought and behavior. Wanda Coleman's "American Sonnets," which she published in discontinuous installments from 1993, break the sonnet sequence apart to explore the mental and social underworlds of contemporary America. Rita Dove's *Mother Love* (1995) widens the scope toward other continents and histories as it fractures the intact worlds of myth and nation.

Coleman was a poet of lower-class Los Angeles, and her best work draws from popular culture and everyday impressions rather than academic debates. Her sonnets show little concern for boundaries of form, layout, theme, and tradition. Scattered across four of her poetry collections, the American Sonnets break the fourteen lines up into seemingly arbitrary units ranging from fairly conventional patterns to disruptive rearrangements. American Sonnet 1, for example, replaces two of its lines with a mathematical equation, while other sonnets cut some of the lines down to one or two words, evoking the sharp pace and interactive quality of call and response. Some lines are interrupted by virgules, as if to signal a line break, while others omit even the spaces between words.

The uses to which Coleman puts these and other disruptive effects are illustrated by one of the first American Sonnets she published, number 5. The sonnet opens with a string of playful, internally rhymed words that might or might not indicate a leitmotif ("rusted busted and dusted"). The second line further postpones semantic completion, which in most of the sonnets never actually occurs, by refusing to clarify the subject or object of the verbs in the first line:

the spurious chain of plebian events
(aintjahmamaauntjemimaondapancakebox?) (lines 2-3)

While the second line adopts an authoritative, formal stance, the third switches registers and introduces a black vernacular voice that draws attention to racial stereotypes in everyday life. The following section, the longest in the poem, returns to an authoritative stance to suggest that the statistics that define African Americans in public debate—"largest number of homicides," "largest number of deaths by cancer," "largest / number of institutionalized men," and so on—lack the profound causality they imply. In effect, such statistics are a "spurious" interpretation of the "chain of plebian events" chronicled in the sequence. The concluding lines provide an inside perspective on the conditions in a black lower-class environment. They point out the imprisoning quality of this lifestyle, in which most African Americans are involuntary participants, "preoccupied with perfecting plans of escape" (line 11). The sonnet then switches back to the vernacular voice, which repeats this finding in a playful variation.

The second line of the sonnet is not only pivotal to its argument but can be read as a self-reflexive description of the entire sequence. "American Sonnets" describes the "plebian events" in the urban lower class and remains highly skeptical toward the pseudo-causal notion of a "chain of events." It severs both the semantic connections within individual sonnets and the connectedness of the sonnet sequence: a few isolated instances aside, the sequence has no narrative or motivic links. Its bombastic title further emphasizes the spuriousness of teleological grand narratives in that it evokes a representativeness that the poems cannot—and do not want to—sustain. Instead of patching over societal rifts and injustices with a national narrative, Coleman's American Sonnets question and undermine received notions of both America and the sonnet. Like her white contemporary Gerald Stern, who also published a sequence of *American Sonnets* (2003), Coleman turns the generic title into an individualizing gesture. In contrast to Stern's rather self-centered meditations, however, the best of Coleman's sonnets—the early ones—do more than inscribe the poet's perspective into the American narrative.[12] They reach out to encompass the poet's environment, whether it is made up by her acquaintances, her city, or the entire country. In calling attention to the numerous, often overlooked narratives this environment offers, her sonnets redefine what it means to be American. They expose the mainstream narrative of America as another of those intact worlds of the Western tradition that hide an underworld of inequality and injustice, violence and suffering.

The earliest American Sonnet that Coleman chose to include in one of her collections, sonnet 3, introduces myth as both topic and material of the sequence:

> fair splay/pay—the stuff myths are made of
> (cum grano salis) (lines 1–2)

These opening lines suggest that the sequence will draw on myth as the raw material of its collages, while at the same time questioning the making, the construction process, of the myths that sustain American society. The second line evokes the classical tradition, the myths of Rome, many of which were colonial appropriations of their Greek counterparts. It also announces the irreverent approach Coleman will take in her revised appropriation of American culture. The classicist reference signals the double disruption Coleman practices in that it recalls the double meaning of "myth" in ancient Greece. Aristotle used "mythos" to refer to "the arrangement of the incidents" in literary texts, as Mackey points out in the preface to his collection *Splay Anthem,* which opens up intriguing implications for self-reflexive experimental writing (xiii). Sonnet sequences such as Coleman's explore these implications by foregrounding the process of arrangement, thus disrupting the very notion of a linear narrative implied in Aristotle's definition—and in a title such as "American Sonnets." At the same time, Coleman's opening lines evoke the literary tradition that emerged from the mythic stories of gods and heroes. This literary tradition is the core of the intact world of Western poetry, for which it provides an epistemology, a template of foundational stories, and a rich source of images, symbols, and metaphors—as can be seen in the sonnet tradition from Sidney and Shakespeare to Yeats, Heaney, Walcott, and Dove. Coleman's American Sonnets continue this lineage but with a crucial, revisionist difference. By rearranging the spatial building blocks of the sonnet, they draw attention to the constructedness of the etiological stories underlying and defining American culture.

In her foreword to *Mother Love,* Dove describes each individual sonnet as a world in itself. She then follows Coleman, however, in negotiating the intact worlds of myth and nation in the more extensive form of the sonnet sequence, which provides more opportunities than a single sonnet for disengaging the links and interrupting the progression required by such narratives. The sequence may weave together grand narratives of national identity, but once its coherence is broken up these narratives unravel and the arbitrary, porous quality of national and cultural boundaries is exposed. Dove works toward this effect by disrupting both the temporal and the spatial order of these such narratives. As Mackey notes in his comments on myth, experimental writing can counteract "presumptions of an objective ordering of history" by rearranging the incidents so that they blur, redouble, or vanish in the play of signifiers (xiii). Dove draws on ancient Greek and Roman myths throughout her poetic oeuvre and often modifies them in the manner Mackey envisions. The revisionist impulse behind these modifications has been widely noted in scholarship.[13] Myths work toward a coherent epistemology, or in Dove's terms, toward an intact world whose boundaries can be punctured by poetic variation. By revising these foundational narratives of Western culture, Dove asserts the specificity and relevance of the black experience within a shared but heterogeneous cultural sphere.

Like Claude McKay before her, Rita Dove finds such a sphere in the richly layered historical contact zone of the Mediterranean. A book-length rewriting of the Demeter and Persephone myth, *Mother Love* draws on the Mediterranean setting and the cultural afterlives of that myth to chronicle a modern mother-daughter relationship. While numerous scholars have examined Dove's revisionist variations of mythical intertexts, few have noted that in *Mother Love* she draws on the parallels between myth and sonnet to redouble the revisionist dynamic.[14] The boundaries of the sonnet come to represent the cultural and epistemological boundaries of Western foundational myths, while the temporal linearity of the sonnet sequence evokes the straightforward etiology of these myths. *Mother Love* reworks its mythical intertexts in variations on the sonnet that trouble both the spatial boundaries and the temporal progression implied by the form. A reading of "Her Island," the concluding section of the volume, will show how Dove negotiates the boundaries of racism, colonialism, and economic imperialism from ancient Sicily to the globalized world of the present.

The autobiographical sequence "Her Island" depicts Dove as a tourist in search of classical sites on Sicily, an island that has a long history of intercultural encounters. Sicily is where the sonnet form originated, at the court of Frederick II, from contacts between ancient and medieval, between German, Italian, and Arabian culture. Many of the sites her travelers visit, moreover, are associated with Greek colonization, which made its way West through Southern Italy and brought new cultural impulses but also physical violence and economic exploitation (Finley, Smith, and Duggan 1–20). These ambivalent backgrounds shape the sequence on several levels. Dove personalizes the myth by paralleling herself with Persephone and her daughter with Demeter, drawing on the collective template for an autobiographical negotiation of contemporary individuality. At the same time, she links the emotional ravages of the mother-child relationship—forced separation, growing apart—with the political implications of mother-child figurations in a colonial situation (the Greek 'metropolis' translates as "mother city" or "mother country"). This multi-layered negotiation effectively disrupts the discursive and spatial claims of colonializing countries even while acknowledging the creative potential of the intercultural encounters colonialism has brought about.

The myth is introduced obliquely in the very first line of "Her Island," where the seemingly innocuous scene-setting ("Around us: blazed stones, closed ground") alludes to Persephone's abduction to the underworld, which allegedly took place in Sicily. The allusion unfolds gradually and proleptically as images of the underworld accrue throughout the sequence. It culminates in the last line of the last sonnet, a variation on the first in which the ground suddenly becomes the agent of abduction: "around us: blazed stones, the ground closed" (77.14).[15] In a striking example of spatiotemporal variation, Dove uses the corona device—the last line of each sonnet is also the first line of the next—but not in the strict form tradition demands. It is precisely her departure from exact repetition that allows a glimpse into the psychological and cultural abysses beneath Sicily's scorched earth. Her sequence is almost a crown but not quite, and the interstices of the traditional European structure reveal the underworlds on which the structure rests, and which it seeks to conceal.

One such interstitial revelation occurs when Dove's travelers have arrived, in a series of concentric circles that mirror the cyclical structure of the corona sequence, at Lake Pergusa, the "perfect oval" (74.10) at the center of the island where popular mythography locates the abduction of Persephone.

> Our maps have not failed us: this is it,
> the only body of water for twenty miles,
> water black and still as the breath
> it harbored; and around this perfect ellipse
> they've built . . . a racetrack. (75.2–6)

Dove organizes the entire poem to center on the word "racetrack," whose revelatory force she emphasizes with the three dots (a perfect ellipsis to match the perfect ellipse of the lake) and with a typographical space that sets these lines off from the rest of the poem. The underworld imagery is strong here, black being the dominant color in the visual image the poem evokes, and the focus on the word "racetrack" links the blackness of the underworld with that of race and racism. Dove makes no further reference to this thematic layer it in the rest of the sonnet, nor in the next, where she imagines herself as one of the racers in "this / godawful roar, this vale of sound":

> Your head's a furnace: you don't feel it.
> [. . .]
> A vital rule: if two vehicles ahead of you
> crash, drive straight toward the fire
> and they will have veered away before you get
> there. Bell lap, don't look to see who's
> gaining. Aim for the tape, aim *through* it.
> Then rip the helmet off and poke your head
> through sunlight, into flowers. (76.5–14)

In the narrow, heated, reeking cockpit of the race car she ceases to feel anything but the "godawful roar" of this "furnace." In this imaginary trance she metamorphoses from a racer into a racing Orpheus, not allowed to look back at those behind her, and then into Persephone plunging back up onto the field from which she has been sucked down while picking flowers. The references to Greek myth are more or less obvious to the well-trained Western reader. A well-trained reader of black poetry might find that the furnace of the race evokes a journey through the underworld often evoked as a foundational myth of African American cultural identity: the Middle Passage.

In an earlier scene the travelers meet an old Italian who guides them from the tourist-ridden ruins of Agrigento to the forgotten remnants of a temple of Vulcan. The man, whom Dove presents as a Charon figure, takes them on a long walk "down ever-dwindling streets" through the waste land of the "city dump," until they believe they are "about to turn into / the latest victims of a tourist scam" (72.3–8). The phrasing suggests yet another metamorphosis, an ominous one, during this descent into the underworld. While the rest of the collection is written from Demeter's perspective, Dove here imagines herself as a Persephone, abducted by the mysterious old Italian who is familiar with the territory. Ripped out of the ordinary tourist experience, she realizes that she is a foreigner on this ancient ground and that her position toward the core of Western civilization, whose remnants have drawn her to the island, remains peripheral for all her interest and education. In paralleling this problem with the Persephone myth, however, Dove points to yet another ambivalence: historically speaking, Hades is a foreigner as well, since he only came to Sicily when the Greeks colonized the island. The hybrid cultural heritage of the island troubles dichotomies such as native/foreigner, victim/perpetrator, or colonizer/colonized and reflects Dove's ambivalence on Western civilization and its foundational myths.

When Dove introduces the idea of the sonnet as an intact world in her foreword, she calls the Demeter and Persephone myth "a tale of a violated world" that is best told in disrupted sonnets (xiii). The foreword itself anticipates this disruption by evoking several canonic Western writers as precursor figures and by taking its title, "An Intact World," from the German phrase *heile Welt*. Such crossings of linguistic and cultural boundaries occur throughout the volume and especially in "Her Island." The autobiographical speaker of this poem is traveling together with her German husband, on whose nationality she reflects with both affection and irony. Observing Sicilians eager to pass their "rented / Chrysler" on the highway, she exclaims, "Ha! Can't they guess a German / plies the wheel?" (73.4–6). They cannot, of course, since the car is American and the country Italy; the putative German national character vanishes with its signifiers. They speak German with the old man who guides them to the temple as neither his English nor her Spanish suffice. The language conveys a vague threat: her husband speaks it better than she does and is thus drawn into a privileged relationship with the guide—"man to man" (71.8)—that potentially excludes her. More poignantly, when she recognizes the word "Krieg" (war) in the old man's explanations she comes to realize that his German was "gathered word by word / half a century ago," when Italy was collaborating with the Nazis in World War II (71.5–7). His is a very different German from hers, which for a moment forces her to gaze into another historical underworld.

Dove's definition of the "common language" they speak with the old Italian brings the historical implications of the sonnet form into focus. She first simply calls that common language "German" but at the beginning of the next poem— again playing on the corona structure—adds that it is really "German, / laced with tenth-grade Spanish and / residual Latin" (70.1–3). This hybrid language crosses a number of spatial and temporal boundaries. If the high-school Spanish evokes the increasing cultural diversity of the United States and its ambivalent attitude toward its Southern national border, the "residual Latin" suggests that the linguistic and cultural lineage of Dove's poetry reaches as far back as ancient Rome. It also indicates that the Greek colonies were later colonized in their turn by the Romans, who like the Europeans in Africa and America succeeded in imposing their language but failed to erase the colonized culture. The word "residual" evokes these backgrounds, being of Latin origin itself, and its original meaning, "left behind," links it with the Orpheus theme. Latinate words appear throughout the sequence, but like the sonnets of Petrarch—one of the most renowned Latin scholars of his age—"Her Island" ultimately relies on the poet's mother tongue as the most sensitive, though inevitably hybridized, medium for autobiographical and psychological expression.

THE AFRICAN AMERICAN SONNET
INTO THE TWENTY-FIRST CENTURY

While her negotiation of borders and border-crossings has a stronger referential dimension than those of other experimental poets, Dove retains an interest in the power of language to erect and undermine discursive boundaries. This aspect takes center stage in the sequences of the next generation of poets, who reconnect with Roberson in exploring the interstices of language itself. Wanda Phipps and G. E. Patterson draw on the formal constraints of the sonnet sequence to evoke a spatiotemporal dynamic that reflects the identities they are negotiating: identities that are both fragmented and whole, both individual and universal. The genre they activate for this purpose is the love sonnet, which had already served as an enclave for negotiations of individuality at the time of the Black Arts movement (see Chapter 5). Patterson's *To and From* (2008), a collection that consists entirely of sonnets, foregrounds the repetitiveness but also the persistent inspirational force of poetic language by filling the space around the sonnets with quotations from canonic precursor figures. This amounts to a new strategy for troubling the sonnet space. The very material of which the sonnets are composed, their language, exceeds their boundaries—both materially, on the page, and semantically, as the words within the sonnet enter into transformative referential relations with the words around it. At the same time, the language of Patterson's precursors is transformed by the meanings and connotations it acquires in the new context of his sequence. *To and From* thus combines spatial and temporal strategies of destabilization to create a space in which identities can be negotiated beyond the restrictions of conventional meanings and stereotypes. The unusual arrangement of words and phrases on the page engenders numerous repetitions with a difference, and the sequentiality of the sonnets amplifies this transgressive play with signification.

Wanda Phipps' *Your Last Illusion or Break Up Sonnets* (2000) also foregrounds the materiality and ambiguity of language but draws on procedural techniques to achieve this effect. Procedural poems as defined by Conte use a set of predetermined, often arbitrary constraints as a generative principle. These constraints are usually defined in spatial terms, for example by the number of words or lines; in some cases, such as concrete poetry, the boundaries of the layout set the generative constraint. The sonnet seems to fit Conte's definition:

it is constituted by the predetermined boundaries of the fourteen lines, the division into sections, and the rhyme scheme. In Conte's view these boundaries are not generative, however, because most sonnets foreground a thematic message rather than formal principles. Unlike procedural poetry, Conte claims, the sonnet is concerned with closure not rupture, which shows in its preference for variation over exact repetition (39–43). While these observations are largely accurate, they are challenged by the experimental strategies of contemporary sonnet sequences. The formal and semantic open-endedness of Coleman's "American Sonnets" continually defers expectations of closure, for example, and the formal constraints of the sonnet arguably play a generative role in Roberson's poetics of indeterminacy.

Phipps' *Your Last Illusion* is the most consistently procedural of these sequences. Its subtitle plays on the double meaning of "breaking up" to announce the experimental twist of the sequence: its 19 sonnets trace the breaking up of a relationship by breaking up both the tradition of the love sonnet and, quite literally, the sonnets themselves, which are made up of repetitive, seemingly aleatory combinations of lines. The device of repetition is introduced in its various manifestations in the first sonnet of Phipps' sequence, where it evokes a sense of disorientation, of inability to process the conflicting thoughts and emotions incited by the end of the speaker's relationship. The sonnet begins with anaphoric expressions of surprise ("'what a planet!' / 'what a life!'") and follows the speaker's attempts to organize her thoughts in fits and starts. It ends in confused questions about the reasons and consequences of the breakup that suggest the speaker's desire to suspend the temporal chain of events:

> what will my mother say?
> who sleeps with who?
> I sleep with you
> "this is as good as it gets" (lines 11–14)

The different kinds of repetition used in the first sonnet reappear in the following ones, which also take up lines and phrases from the first—sometimes in identical repetition but more often in recombinations that offer new interpretations and perspectives on the speaker's situation ("who sleeps with you?," "this is as good as it is odd"). Phipps' approach is inspired, as the subtitle of her volume confirms, "by Ted Berrigan's Sonnets," and her sequence relies strongly on both the diary approach and the cut-up techniques Berrigan used in the 1960s. Berrigan's sonnets are among the first manifestations of procedural poetry in American literature (cf. Huntsperger 41–48), and like Phipps' "break up sonnets" they evoke the stable framework and the intimacy of the sonnet form in order to destroy the intact world suggested by this convention. For Berrigan, however, such destruction encompasses the speaking persona itself, whereas Phipps identifies closely with her lyrical I and makes its quest for wholeness a guiding thread of her sequence. And while Berrigan uses procedural techniques to emphasize the arbitrariness and ultimate meaninglessness of his experiences, Phipps depicts the chaos of the break-up as a temporary problem and turns her sequence into a quest for wholeness, for reassembling the fragments she has shored against her ruins.

The development toward wholeness as the lyrical I comes to terms with the breakup is first indicated on the formal level, when the disjunctive, repetitive lines of the first sonnets begin to congeal into larger semantic units. An expository passage at the beginning of sonnet 12 provides the first coherent explanation of the speaker's situation, and thus a belated narrative frame that imposes some degree of coherence on the earlier sonnets. This development culminates in the two concluding sonnets, where the sequence shifts its emphasis from the procedural to the narrative principle. Coherent semantic units now dominate the poems. Isolated, fragmentary lines still occur but become explainable as the speaker's stream of consciousness, induced by the thoughts and situations clarified in the narrative sections. While these concluding sonnets present the culmination of the story on a semantic level, however, they lose some of their aesthetic appeal. In contrast with the challenging urgency evoked by procedural techniques in the earlier sonnets, they seem more facile, sometimes even banal in a way, the sequence becomes just another break-up story. It is the procedural elements that give the sequence its distinct appeal and that ultimately save it from banality. In a few instances the chaos of the earlier sonnets resurfaces even in the concluding lines, disrupting the coherence of the narrative and suggesting that the gaps and fissures created by the break-up (of both the relationship and the sonnet form) will not simply go away. The intact world of stable identities and social relationships no longer exists.

What makes *Your Last Illusion* representative of the contemporary African American sonnet is the generative function of its spatial boundaries. As in Roberson's work, the sonnet sequence is not merely—and not even primarily—a narrative device. Neither the content of Phipps' story nor the way she tells it require a sequence of that length, but the sequence, and also the single sonnets in it, provides a predetermined formal framework in which the repetitions and variations that furnish its generative principle can play out. It is these repetitions and variations that give the sequence its formal and epistemological complexity as they complement the linear development of the story with a different temporality—one that works both retroactively (providing context, and thus meaning, for earlier uses of the same line) and simultaneously (aligning all sonnets in which that line occurs). This effect, too, is reminiscent of Berrigan's sonnets, which his wife, the poet Alice Notley, described as incorporating "the past into the present becoming the future, and so each sonnet seems to have invisible arrows pointing out from it backwards, forwards, and sideways too" (3).

On the semantic level, *Your Last Illusion* avoids close association with African American culture. The speaker lives not in Harlem but in Flatbush, a migrant quarter, where her apartment resonates with the "rumbles" of subway trains but also "hovers above / Bistrot La Marseillaise" (3.4–6). While the underworlds of her traumas—personal and, perhaps, cultural—rumble through her life every now and then, her primary experience seems to be that of the cosmopolitan, bourgeois avant-garde. She hovers in bistrots and East Village restaurants, sips "too much wine on the Upper West Side" (19.1), and frequents the Gargoyle Mechanique, a 1990s avant-garde performance space. Like Roberson's sequences, *Your Last Illusion* draws on spatiotemporal experimental technique to destabilize essentialist conceptions of the black experience and negotiate the individual views, identities, and allegiances of contemporary African American poets. The African American sonnet thus continues to partake of various cultural backgrounds and trouble the formal and discursive boundaries of black writing. Over a century and a half, generations of poets have found in the sonnet what Nathaniel Mackey identifies as a goal of much innovative writing by African Americans: an opportunity "to expand the poetic space to practice in" as part of "that larger black quest for social space."[16]

Notes

Introduction

1. Since many nineteenth-century poems were published by anonymous or unidentifiable magazine contributors, it is impossible to determine whether "The Montenegrin" was the first regular sonnet written by an African American. It can be said to have inaugurated the African American sonnet tradition in that it is the first sonnet in a volume by an African American listed in the Library of Congress catalog. A survey of the major newspapers and magazines still accessible from the period has not yielded any earlier specimens whose authors could be identified as African American. For earlier sonnets that appeared in African American newspapers see DeSimone and Louis, *Voices Beyond Bondage* 92, 140, 156.—This study focuses on sonnets by black poets from the United States but includes poets from the anglophone Caribbean who influenced the development of the genre in the United States. It omits writers whose ethnic background could not be ascertained. Individual poems will be cited by line number; sonnet sequences, unless otherwise noted, by poem and line number.

2. Eighteenth- and nineteenth-century poets, including Phillis Wheatley and George Moses Horton, occasionally published fourteen-line poems in heroic couplets. These poems were not regarded as sonnets at the time and are therefore not treated as such in this study. See Horton, *Poetical Works* xiii–xix; Wheatley, *Poems* 53. On definitions of the sonnet see Burt and Mikics, introduction; Fuller, *The Sonnet*; Müller, "Theorien des Sonetts"; Spiller, *Development of the Sonnet* 3–4. On the American sonnet tradition see Bromwich, introduction; Link, *Das moderne amerikanische Sonett*; Neubauer, *Zwischen Tradition und Innovation*.

3. Donne, *Songs and Sonnets* 239. See Müller, "Theorien des Sonetts" 102–7, on Romanticism; Ahearn, "Frost's Sonnets" 35–36, on the continuity of the spatial conception in Frost; see also Oppenheimer, *Birth of the Modern Mind* 23, 190. For a discussion of space in Wordsworth's sonnet see Hollander, *Melodious Guile* 86–90; Phelan, *Nineteenth-Century Sonnet* 12–14; for space in the Romantic sonnet more generally see Burwick, "'Narrow Rooms' or 'Wide Expanse'" 49–64. While John Kerrigan regards Wordsworth's conception of the sonnet as domestic and architectural ("Wordsworth and the Sonnet"), rural and agricultural imagery is frequent in both his sonnets and his theoretical comments on the form. In a letter to Alexander Dyce, for example, he writes, "Instead of looking at this composition as a piece of architecture, making a whole out of three parts, I have been much in the habit of preferring the image of an orbicular body,—a sphere or a dew-drop" (1833; quoted in Havens, *Influence of Milton* 533).

4. Hess, "Wordsworth's Aesthetic State" 10; Cronin, "Wordsworth's *Poems* of 1807" 33–34; Ross, "Romancing the Nation-State" 62. On the Romantics' and particularly Wordsworth's

nationalism, see Bate, "Inventing"; Behrendt, "Wordsworth and Nation"; Kaiser, *Romanticism, Aesthetics, and Nationalism* 20–21; Woodring, *Politics in English Romantic Poetry* 115–28. Wordsworth's conclusion that the boundaries of the sonnet offer respite from "too much liberty" participates in an ongoing discussion of the meaning and value of liberty. As scholars of the Romantic period have pointed out, the term had acquired positive connotations in the late eighteenth century, when it was associated with nature and natural rights, only to come under suspicion when the liberty proclaimed by the French Revolution turned into terror and dictatorship (Hess, "Wordsworth's Aesthetic State" 9–10; Beer, "Nature and Liberty" 201–4). Writing in 1802 (Wordsworth, *Poems* 133), Wordsworth presents the sonnet as a solution to this problem: by imposing time-tested boundaries on human endeavor it affords freedom without excess. On the popularity of Wordsworth's emphasis on balance and self-control among a Victorian public see Phelan, *Nineteenth-Century Sonnet* 4–17; Wiley, *Romantic Geography* 121–22. On Wordsworth as a Burkean see Chandler, "Wordsworth and Burke"; Ross, "Romancing the Nation-State" 58–64.

5. Gates, *Signifying Monkey* 64–88; cf. Feith, "Henry Louis Gates" 59–78. Gates draws on poststructuralist theory in conceptualizing the term and spells it "Signifyin(g)" to distinguish it from the linguistic concept of the same name and to emphasize its oral quality after the manner of Derrida's "différance" (*Signifying Monkey* 46). Scholars today tend to retain the original spelling. With reference to Gates's elaboration on the term, Deborah McDowell has suggested that the notion of signifying as a necessarily confrontational activity is contradicted by the example of female writers, whose signifying on each other is usually complementary rather than confrontational ("Changing Same" 281–302).

6. Jarvis, "What Is Historical Poetics?"; Prins, "What Is Historical Poetics?"; Wilson, *Specters of Democracy* 7; see also A. Reed, *Freedom Time* 8. This strand of historical poetics has affinities with the Russian theorists who originally used the term, especially Alexander Veselovsky (see Kliger and Maslov, *Persistent Forms*), but differs from these theorists in its insistence on historicizing the cultural work of poetic form rather than identifying transhistorical components. For a similar approach see DuPlessis, "Social Texts and Poetic Texts." For samples of historical poetics scholarship on the nineteenth century see Adams, Calahan, and Hansen, *Historical Poetics*; McGill, *Traffic in Poems*.

7. Other nuanced discussions include Fisher, *Habitations of the Veil*; Nathans, *Slavery and Sentiment*; Smethurst, *African American Roots* 24–39. Recent publications that use mask or veil metaphors without problematizing them include Bérubé, "Masks, Margins" 65–66; Zafar, *We Wear the Mask* 3–4, 9–10; Black, "Literary Subterfuge"; Wyman, "Beyond the Veil"; Sexton, "Lifting the Veil."

8. Edwards, *Practice of Diaspora*; Gruesser, *Confluences*; see also Knadler, *Remapping Citizenship and the Nation*; Nwankwo, *Black Cosmopolitanism*; Ramazani, *A Transnational Poetics* 45–47.

9. Bregman, *Golden Way* for Hebrew; Friedrich, "Unheralded Revolution" 199 n. 1 for Bengal; Steffen, *Crossing Color* 128 for Latin America.

Chapter 1

1. Frazier, *Black Bourgeoisie* 148–49; Bruce, *Black American Writing* 19–32; see also McHenry, *Forgotten Readers* 225–27; Sherman, *Invisible Poets* xx–xxi, xxvi–xxix. Frazier's

seminal study *The Black Bourgeoisie* (1955) covers the mid-twentieth century but includes several asides on the "old black bourgeoisie" of the postbellum period from which this description draws (146–49). On the genteel tradition generally see V. Brooks, *America's Coming-of-Age* 8–16, 58–59; Kindilien, *American Poetry in the Eighteen Nineties* 1–22; McClay, "Two Versions of the Genteel Tradition"; Sedgwick, "American Genteel Tradition"; Tomsich, *A Genteel Endeavor.*

2. Gayle, *Way of the New World* 11; Wagner, *Black Poets of the United States* 85–82, 128; and more moderately Redmond, *Drumvoices* 86–91. Even Sherman, who recovers a broad range of genteel poetry in *Invisible Poets,* associates gentility with a weak, apolitical approach (xxvi–xxvii).

3. Leonard, *Fettered Genius* 4. On Dunbar see Smethurst, *African American Roots* 24–39, 81–95; on Whitman see I. Wilson, "Introduction" 11; on the classics see Cook and Tatum, *African American Writers and Classical Tradition* 93–124; Hairston, *Ebony Column* 11–12 and passim; Walters, *African American Literature and the Classicist Tradition* 6–8. Moses, "Lost World" offers a benevolent view of the genteel tradition but does not address literature in any detail. Bruce, *Black American Writing From the Nadir,* and Bennett, "Rewriting Dunbar," are among the few scholars to do justice to the pervasiveness of genteel conventions, but they too stress the confining effect of these conventions more than their enabling one.

4. Redding, *To Make a Poet Black* 89; Wagner, *Black Poets* 128. Claude McKay rejected Braithwaite as an accommodationist (Szefel, "Beauty and William Braithwaite" 579). On Braithwaite's influence see Abbott, "Magazine Verse and Modernism"; Szefel, "Encouraging Verse"; Smethurst, *African American Roots* 151–53; K. Williams, "An Invisible Partnership."

5. J. W. Johnson, *Fifty Years* 22. On Johnson's attitudes to race see Carroll, "Black Racial Spirit"; Levy, *James Weldon Johnson.* For an extended discussion of "Mother Night" against the background of the genteel tradition see Müller, "James Weldon Johnson."

6. For contemporary assessments see Hunt, "An Essay on the Cultivation" 17–18; Minto, *Characteristics of English Poets;* Pattison, *Sonnets of John Milton;* Sanderlin, "Influence of Milton" 249; Sharp, "Sonnet." The latter's comment on Shakespeare is representative: "It is because this great master over the passions and follies and heroisms of man has at least once dropped the veil of impersonality that we are so fascinated by the sonnets" (lix). On the Romantics' influence on the nineteenth-century sonnet see Phelan, *Nineteenth-Century Sonnet* 37–45. For a modern view on Shakespeare's authenticity see Ferry, *"Inward" Language* 4. It is worth noting that until recently most critics of early African American poetry adopted the authenticity standard, such as Loggins, *Negro Author* 349.

7. S. Wilson, *Melting-Pot Modernism* 99–102. On expectations of authenticity in slave narratives and dialect verse see Bland, *Voices of the Fugitives;* Keeling, "Paul Dunbar and the Mask of Dialect"; and more generally Jarrett, *Deans and Truants* 29–51; Zafar, *We Wear the Mask* 67–88. There is occasional evidence of a subjective voice in the poetry of George Moses Horton and the actress Adah Isaacs Menken, but these examples show the ways in which even personal poetry was tangibly public in its themes and rhetoric. See Barrett, *To Fight Aloud Is Very Brave* 225–50; Sherman, *Invisible Poets* 11–19, 37, 183–91.

8. Quashie 6–8; E. Alexander, *Black Interior;* Pardlo, "To Whom It May Concern." Ivy G. Wilson suggests (but does not develop) a similar conception of interiority as both spatial and psychological in "Writing on the Wall" 57. On strategies of self-inscription see also Baker, "Theoretical Returns" 422–24; Leonard, *Fettered Genius;* Zafar, *We Wear the Mask.*

9. Barrett, "Abraham Lincoln and Poetry" 33. On the political functions of Civil War tributes see Barrett, "American Poetry Fights the Civil War" 324. Poetic tributes are mentioned in passing or not at all in such standard literary histories of the Civil War as Aaron, *Unwritten War;* Barrett, *To Fight Aloud;* and Fahs, *Imagined Civil War.* An exception is Griffin, *Ashes of the Mind,* which includes detailed analyses of praise poetry by Lowell, Melville, and Dunbar.

10. Elliott, "Story of Our Magazine" 47; cf. Dworkin, *Daughter of the Revolution;* Johnson and Johnson, "Away From Accommodation" 325–27; Schneider, "*Colored American*" 159–60. For history books, see W. Brown, *Negro in the American Rebellion;* W. Brown, *Rising Son;* Cromwell, *Negro in American History;* Simmons, *Men of Mark;* G. Williams, *A History of the Negro Race.* The praise sonnets mentioned are Bibb, *Poems* 100; Dunbar, *Complete Poems* 191, 339, 341, 360; Cotter, Sr., *Collected Poems* 62; Middleton, *Dreams of an Idle Hour* 22; C. Ray, *Poems* 74–88; for praise poetry of the time see also Rowe, *Our Heroes.*

11. Goodman, *Republic of Words* 59–68. Hedrick, *Harriet Beecher Stowe* 394; F. Wilson, *Crusader in Crinoline* 609–19. Barbara Hochman points out, however, that Northern readers in the 1890s tended to subsume the race politics of the novel under a narrative of national and racial unity (255–57). See Winship, "Greatest Book of its Kind" for the new editions; Robbins, *Cambridge Introduction to Harriet Beecher Stowe* 103 on the Southern response. For a more conventional sonnet to Stowe by an African American poet see Holly, *Freedom's Offering* 36.

12. Longfellow, *Poetical Works* 342–47. On the speaker-addressee relationship in the Petrarchan sonnet see Bermann, *Sonnet Over Time* 23–31; Dubrow, *Echoes of Desire* 32–35, 39–48.

13. Aaron, *Unwritten War* 160–61; Smethurst, *African American Roots of Modernism* 69–70, 88–89. By contrast, Griffin stresses the political dimension of the poem, which he locates in the tension between the boundedness of the sonnet form and the unbounded, existential questions the poem raises (*Ashes of the Mind* 188–97). On the wide publication of the poem see Smethurst, *African American Roots of Modernism* 88; on African Americans' views of Shaw see Flint, "Black Response to Colonel Shaw" 210–12.

14. Originally planned as a sequence of twelve sonnets, Corrothers published his sonnet to Dunbar first in the *Voice of the Negro* (1906) and later, as a double sonnet, in *Book of American Negro Poetry* (1922); see Corrothers, *In Spite of the Handicap* 227; "A Tribute to Paul Laurence Dunbar." On Dunbar's influence in general see Bruce, *Black American Writing* 57, 98–101. Other praise sonnets from the decade following his death can be found in Brawley, *Desire of the Moth for the Star* 7, 12; Fortune, *Dreams of Life* 25; Middleton, *Dreams of an Idle Hour* 22; Paisley, *Voice of Mizraim* 28; Ray, *Poems* 86–88.

15. Quoted from Fortune, *Dreams of Life* 60. A slightly different, earlier version of the sonnet was published in newspapers including the *Baxter Springs News* in the early 1890s (*Chronicling America*).

CHAPTER 2

1. S. Brown, "A Poet and His Prose" 256; Arna Bontemps quoted in Maxwell, "Introduction" xxi; J. W. Johnson, *Book of American Negro Poetry* 168; Douglass, *Terrible Honesty* 324–25; McWhirther, *Red Summer* 85. See also McLeod, "Claude McKay" 66; McKible and Churchill, "In Conversation" 427–8; Tillery, *Claude McKay* 37. Beach suggests 1922 as the beginning of the Harlem Renaissance and points specifically to the publication of McKay's *Harlem Shadows,*

the volume in which "If We Must Die" was collected (*Cambridge Introduction* 114–17). On the poem's wide impact see Bronz, *Roots of Negro Racial Consciousness* 74; Kent, *Blackness and the Adventure of Western Culture* 25, 37, 42; McKay, *A Long Way From Home* 31–32.

2. Huggins, *Harlem Renaissance* 54, 303; Foley, *Spectres of 1919* 1–5; cf. Gates and Jarrett, introduction 6–14. Among the few scholars who do justice to the influence of genteel conventions are Moses, "Lost World"; Nowlin, "Race Literature"; Cook and Tatum, *African American Writers and Classical Tradition* 107–24.

3. McKay, *Complete Poems* 177–78. For scholarly debate and interpretation of the poem see Condit, "An Urge Toward Wholeness" 361; Hieglar, "Claude McKay's 'If We Must Die'"; Jenkins, *Language of Caribbean Poetry* 38–41; Keller, "A Chafing Savage" 450; Lederer, "Didactic and the Literary" 219–22; Lee, "On Claude McKay's"; Tillery, *Claude McKay* 33–36.

4. Of the many examples already cited, "If We Must Die" and Clifford's "Three Sonnets" (*Widening Light* 31–32) can be seen as paradigms; noteworthy specimens not mentioned so far include Hill's "Freedom" (*Wings of Oppression* 15) and McKay's "The Little Peoples" and "Birds of Prey" (*Complete Poems* 136; 174–75) all of which are voiced by a collective "we."

5. On McKay's Fabianism see James, *A Fierce Hatred* 57; Maxwell, "Introduction" xiv; on the Fabian program see Pease, *History of the Fabian Society* 32; on the term "collectivism" see Semmel, *Imperialism and Social Reform* 133 and in a specifically African American context A. Reed, *W.E.B. Du Bois and American Political Thought* 18–26.

6. Standard readings of Brown as a dialect poet include Rowell, "Sterling A. Brown"; Sanders, "Sterling A. Brown," which makes the Afro-modernist "poetic vocabulary" Brown derives from the black vernacular a touchstone of his modernism (394); Lamothe, *Inventing the New Negro*, which pits his "modern" vernacular against the "conservative," "bourgeois" standards of the older generation (91–114). Tidwell and Tracy's *After Winter: The Life and Art of Sterling A. Brown*, an edited collection that includes several of the essays cited here, does not feature discussions of Brown's sonnets except for a reprint of an article about two newly discovered specimens. Smethurst, *New Red Negro*, recuperates the formal poetry into a folk reading by ascribing it "a sense of orality in which a narrative voice actually speaking is strongly present in every poem" (77). For dismissals of Brown's formal poetry see Anderson, "Sterling Brown's Southern Strategy" 1025. Sources that discuss the formal poetry on an equal footing include Manson, "Sterling Brown"; and, more convincingly, Sanders, *Afro-Modernist Aesthetics* 81–88.

7. For example Baker, *Afro-American Poetics*; Pinckney, "Sweet Singer of Tuckahoe"; Shucard, *Countee Cullen*. A notable exception is James Emanuel, who commended Cullen's poetry for criticizing the entire "range of discriminations against Black people." Significantly, Emanuel singled out the sonnets "Yet Do I Marvel" and "From the Dark Tower" as main examples for this race-conscious approach and went so far as to claim them as precursor texts to Richard Wright's *Native Son* ("Renaissance Sonneteers" 43–35). For portrayals of Cullen as weakly imitative see Blyden, *Waiting Years* 45; Redding, *To Make a Poet Black* 108. The "poet and not Negro poet" comment is quoted in Sperry, "Countee P. Cullen"; "Negro Wins Prize in Poetry Contest" E1. See also Molesworth, *And Bid Him Sing* 103–10; Shucard, *Countee Cullen* 16–31; Smith, "Poetry of Countee Cullen" 218; Turner, *In a Minor Chord* 61–72. Jonathan Shandell has pointed out another newspaper article, in which Cullen said he wanted to be *known* as a poet, not a Negro poet—a significant difference in phrasing that further undermines criticisms such as Hughes's in "The Negro Artist and the Racial Mountain" (Shandell, "How Black Do You Want It" 155).

8. Henry, "Countee Cullen" 311; McCall, "Countee Cullen" 68. On Cullen's broad audience see Canaday, "Major Themes" 103–4; Smethurst, "Lyric Stars" 118; see also Baker, *Modernism and the Harlem Renaissance* 86. For disempowering readings of the poem see Smith, "Poetry of Countee Cullen" 217; see also Fetrow, "Cullen's 'Yet Do I Marvel'" 103.

9. On the poem's contextualization in *Southern Road* see also Manson, "Sterling Brown" 24; Sanders, "Sterling A. Brown" 393–97; Smethurst, *New Red Negro* 78.

CHAPTER 3

1. De Jongh, *Vicious Modernism* 48–70; A. Douglass, *Terrible Honesty*; R. Miller, "Café de la Paix"; see also Berlin, *Making of African America* 152–200; Whitlow, *Black American Literature* 71–72; Putnam, "Provincializing Harlem"; Philipson, "Harlem Renaissance as Postcolonial Phenomenon"; Glasrud and Wintz, *Harlem Renaissance*; Baldwin, Minkah, and Kelley, *Escape From New York*.

2. See for example Aaron, *Writers on the Left*; Bogardus and Hobson, *Literature at the Barricades*; Denning, *Cultural Front*; Gabbin, *Sterling A. Brown*; Young, *Black Writers of the Thirties* 166–202. Exceptions from this tendency include Maxwell, "Introduction"; Smethurst, *New Red Negro*.

3. On communism and nationalism see Mevius, "Reappraising Communism and Nationalism"; Dawahare 73–91; C. Robinson, *Black Marxism* 218–25. On communist internationalism see Dawahare xii–xiv; Makalani, *In the Cause of Freedom*. Scholars such as Dawahare and Barbara Foley (*Spectres of 1919*) have pointed out that communist (and more broadly leftist) ideas enjoyed considerable popularity in the Harlem Renaissance of the 1920s as well. James Edward Smethurst, by contrast, argues for a distinct shift in African American political thought and cultural production around 1930 (*New Red Negro* 3).

4. Kelley, *Race Rebels* 108. For a critical view of communist Pan-Africanism see Schuyler, "Rise of the Black Internationale." On African Americans' relationship to Moscow and the Comintern see Foley, *Radical Representations* 170–212; Horne, *Black Liberation/Red Scare* 67–72, 202–204; Maxwell, *New Negro, Old Left*; and also K. Baldwin, *Beyond the Color Line*; Kelley, *Race Rebels* 105–21; Smethurst, *New Red Negro* 8.

5. Cullen, *Black Christ* 36; J. Miller, *Remembering Scottsboro* 52–55; Hill, *Men, Mobs, and Law* 209–11, 228–36.

6. Gates, *Loose Canons* 26–28; Foley, *Radical Representations* 182–85; Ford quoted in Smethurst, *New Red Negro* 44. On African American folk writing see Retman, *Real Folks*. On the communist debate of the relationship between social and folk art see Dawahare, *Nationalism* 86–89. On the Black Belt thesis see Draper, *American Communism and Soviet Russia* 320–50; Klehr, *Heyday of American Communism* 324–48; Foley, *Radical Representations* 170–87; Horne, *Black Liberation/Red Scare* 69. On its consequences for African American identity see Smethurst, *New Red Negro* 24; Horne, *Black Liberation/Red Scare* 69; Horne, "Red and the Black" 204. On communist sonnets by white writers see Filreis, *Modernism From Right to Left* 253–54.

7. Woodson, *Anthems, Sonnets, and Chants* 69–141, esp. 82; cf. Retman, *Real Folks* 5. While Woodson claims his corpus is "representative" (90; 93), it consists of only 33 sonnets and excludes important volumes like Cullen's *The Medea* and Baxter's *Sonnets to the Ethiopians*.

Woodson overstates and distorts his valorization of individualism in the 1930s sonnet because he is unfamiliar with the history of the form. In presenting the mere expression of black subjectivity as a new way of subverting racist constraints and prejudices (70–73), he effectively ascribes to the writers of the 1930s a strategy that had been developed half a century earlier, as we have seen in Chapter 1 of the present study. Moreover, Woodson's strategy of discussing the sonnets as part of a collective "pantext" (11) imposes a construed notion of organic unity and development on the individual poems in his corpus, which were written by a range of authors from very different backgrounds and subject positions.—On leftist discussion of the "high" literary tradition see Calverton, *New Ground of Criticism* 58; Foley, *Radical Representations* 129–69; Smethurst, *New Red Negro* 56.

8. For accounts that posit continuity with the slave narrative see Coles, *Black Writers Abroad* 10–11; Smith, "African American Travel Literature"; on African American travel writing in the Harlem Renaissance see Griffin and Fish, introduction.

9. Clark, introduction 3; Holland and Huggan, *Tourists with Typewriters* 47–65; cf. Korte, *English Travel Writing*. Examples for such binary reinscription can be found, for example, in Behdad, *Belated Travelers*; Pratt, *Imperial Eyes*; Grewal, *Home and Harem*; Spurr, *Rhetoric of Empire*; P. Smethurst, introduction 1–18.

10. Totten, *African American Travel Narratives*; Pettinger, *Always Elsewhere*; Griffin and Fish, *A Stranger in the Village*. On the special situation of African American travelers see Holland and Huggan, *Tourists with Typewriters* 14–19; Shaw-Thornburg, "Problems of Genre" 47–51.

11. Butler, *Make Way for Happiness* 13–25; cf. Holland and Huggan, *Tourists with Typewriters* 27–47; Thompson, *Travel Writing* 137–62.

12. Quoted in Maxwell, "Introduction" xi; cf. Conroy, "Vagabond Motif" 15–23; Edwards, *Practice of Diaspora* 190–210; Makalani, *In the Cause of Freedom* 45–102; Maxwell, "Introduction" xvii.

13. Breitinger, "In Search of an Audience" 178; Stoff, "Claude McKay and the Cult of Primitivism" 263. For attempts to recuperate McKay into an America-centered leftist or black nationalist agenda see Jarrett, *Representing the Race* 101–2; Griffin, "Last Word" 158; see also Perry, *Silence to the Drums* 28. The Cities sonnets are quoted from McKay, *Complete Poems* 223–40, where they were eventually published in 2004. Only a few of these sonnets are datable and remaining manuscripts are equivocal about the intended arrangement, so that the Cities sonnets cannot reliably be analyzed in their sequentiality. The division into African and European sonnets is undercut by the order of composition and by the close resemblance of the Spanish sonnets to the African ones. Walonen, "Land of Racial Confluence" 79, 85–86 discusses individual sonnets from the sequence; Müller, "Postcolonial Pursuits in African American Studies" is the only comprehensive analysis of the sequence so far. On the publication history of the Cities sonnets see McKay, *Complete Poems* 352–53.

14. LeSeur notes that both *A Long Way From Home*, which was written in the early 1930s, and McKay's letters from the period show his continuing discussion of the communist movement (229). On McKay and communism generally see K. Baldwin, *Beyond the Color Line* 25–82; Holcomb, *Code Name Sasha* 1–90; LeSeur, "Claude McKay's Marxism" 219–20, 230; Nickels, "Claude McKay and Dissident Internationalism"; Tillery, *Claude McKay* 62–75, 149.

15. On the political debates around the crisis see Dugan and Lafore, *Days of Emperor and Clown* 149–57; Harris, *United States and the Italo-Ethiopian Crisis* 53–61; Jones, *In Search of Brightest Africa* 211–17. On the waning interest among many African Americans, partly because of reports that the Abyssinian ruling class did not consider themselves to be Negroes,

see Gruesser, *Black on Black* 10; Scott, *Sons of Sheba's Race* 106–64; Toynbee, *Abyssinia and Italy* 239–48. On the literature inspired by these issues see Ottley, *New World A-Coming* 111; cf. Asante, *Pan-African Protest* 1–8; Scott, *Sons of Sheba's Race* 210. This literature is often discussed under the heading of Ethiopianism. Originally the name of a movement to establish Christian churches controlled by blacks across the African continent, Ethiopianism had become an umbrella term for a Biblically inspired Pan-Africanism by the early twentieth century (Moses, *Golden Age* 157–61; Drake, *Redeption of Africa*; Gruesser, *Black on Black* 6–14; Shepperson, "Ethiopianism and African Nationalism" 10–11). While "Ethiopia" was commonly taken to refer to the entire continent it was also in use as a synonym for Abyssinia, so that priests, orators, and other public speakers could easily reinterpret the passage when that nation came under threat from Italy (Esedebe, *Pan-Africanism* 121; Shepperson, "Pan-Africanism and 'Pan-Africanism'" 352).

16. Gruesser, *Black on Black* 94–95; Takayoshi, *American Writers* 49–50; Woodson, *Anthems, Sonnets, and Chants* 161; 147–54. Langston Hughes's "Air Raid Over Harlem" has incited some scholarly response but is often discussed outside of this historical context; see Gruesser, *Black on Black* 100–1; Smethurst, *New Red Negro* 112–14; Takayoshi, *American Writers* 50–51.

17. On the conceptual debates around Pan-Africanism in black scholarship see Edwards, "Uses of *Diaspora*" 46–56. On the Pan-African Congress see Esedebe, *Pan-Africanism* 52–57; Legum, *Pan-Africanism* 38–39. On Garvey's Pan-Africanism see Esedebe, *Pan-Africanism* 72–79; Fergus, "From Prophecy to Policy." On Pan-Africanism and black nationalism see Appiah, *In My Father's House* 3–46; Esedebe, *Pan-Africanism* 72–73, 80; Simeon-Jones, *Literary and Sociopolitical Writings* 22–24. On transatlantic Pan-Africanism see Drake, "Diaspora Studies and Pan-Aficanism" 355; Esedebe, *Pan-Africanism* 45–110; and with particular attention to its origins, Esedebe, *Pan-Africanism* 25; Prah, "Wish to Unite" 21; Taylor, *Black Nationalism in the United States* 117.

18. Gruesser, *Black on Black* 100–104; cf. Woodson, *Anthems, Sonnets, and Chants* 147–65, 171–89.

19. McKay quoted in Lee, "On Claude McKay's" 220; cf. Tillery, *Claude McKay* 34–36. Drake, "Diaspora Studies and Pan-Africanism" 397; Drake, "Meaning of 'Negritude'" 48; Legum, *Pan-Africanism* 15. On primitivism see Gruesser, *Black on Black* 16–17; Lemke, *Primitivist Modernism*; Perry, *Silence to the Drums* 9.

20. Gruesser, *Black on Black* 1, 94–95. On civilizationism see Moses, "Africa and Pan-Africanism" 127. Many earlier sonnets about Africa use similarly clichéd images in calling on the continent to rise and rejoin the progress of civilization; see for example L. Alexander, "Africa" 142; Clifford, *Widening Light* 60; McKay, *Complete Poems* 168–69. Outright primitivism was rare in the African American sonnet; for an exception, written by an undergraduate student, see C. Johnson, *Ebony and Topaz* 151.

CHAPTER 4

1. Rampersad, *Life of Langston Hughes* 215–22. On Brown as modernist see Gabbin, *Sterling A. Brown*; Glaser, "Folk Iambics"; Sanders, *Afro-Modernist Aesthetics;* on Hughes see A. Patterson, "Jazz, Realism, and the Modernist Lyric"; Scanlon, "Death Is a Drum."

On the New Modernist Studies see Mao and Walkowitz, "New Modernist Studies"; Altieri, "Afterword"; on the heterogeneity of African American modernism see Hutchinson, *Harlem Renaissance;* Sanders, *Afro-Modernist Aesthetics;* Smethurst, *African American Roots.*—An earlier, shorter version of this chapter was published as Müller, "The Vernacular Sonnet."

2. Bolden, *Afro-Blue* 13; Jackson, *Indignant Generation* 1–14. For general discussions of the African American vernacular see Lemke, *Vernacular Matters* 11–51; Scanlon, "Poets Laureate" 220–23. On modernism and the vernacular see Byerman, "Vernacular Modernism" 253–55.

3. Hughes, "Songs Called the Blues" 133; Tracy, *Langston Hughes and the Blues* 107.

4. Smethurst, *New Red Negro* 146–48. The studies are Chinitz, *Which Sin to Bear;* Sylvanise, *Langston Hughes;* Tracy, *Langston Hughes and the Blues.* For the contemporary reviews see Dace, *Langston Hughes* 279–95. On Hughes's return from social activism to blues poetry see Smethurst, *New Red Negro* 144–46; Tracy, *Langston Hughes and the Blues* 141–46. *Shakespeare in Harlem* will be quoted by page and line number from *The Poems: 1941–1950* 24–28.

5. Neal, "Any Day Now" 55; cf. Baker, *Blues, Ideology, and Afro-American Literature* 8 ("Only a *trained* voice can sing the blues."); Tracy, *Langston Hughes and the Blues* 99–100. On the introspective quality of the blues see Jemie, *Langston Hughes* 40. The parallel between the blues and the sonnet has also been drawn by Gladys Williams, who stresses the shared "sense of intimacy" and the emotions "poured into and overflowing" both forms. Her claim, however, that both the sonnet and the blues feature "a poet-singer speaking-singing directly to another" is at odds with the clear speaker-addressee and poet-beloved distinctions of the Renaissance sonnet ("Gwendolyn Brooks's Way With the Sonnet" 215).

6. Blount, "Preacherly Text" 583. For the critique of Hughes's use of slant rhyme see Emanuel, *Langston Hughes* 138; for commentary in support of it see Tracy, *Langston Hughes and the Blues* 209–10.

7. Brooks, Foreword 11–12; cf. Smethurst, *Black Arts Movement* 238. On Brooks' admiration for and exchange with Hughes see Kent, *A Life of Gwendolyn Brooks* 27, 40, 60, 112; on their shared concerns see Melhem, *Gwendolyn Brooks* 23; Shaw, *Gwendolyn Brooks* 62–64; G. Smith, "Gwendolyn Brooks's *A Street in Bronzeville*" 44. For a sample of African American literary criticism at the time see the 1950 "Symposium" on contemporary African American literature in the pages of *Phylon,* especially Chandler, "A Major Problem of Negro Authors"; Reddick, "No Kafka in the South"; Tillman, "Threshold of Maturity."

8. Kent, "Gwendolyn Brooks' Poetic Realism" 90; Leonard, *Fettered Genius* 119–21. Brooks's poetry will be quoted by page and line number from *The World of Gwendolyn Brooks.*

9. K. Williams, "World of Satin-Legs" 50–53. For earlier African American love sonnets see Cullen, *Black Christ* 46–49; *Medea* 247–49; Dunbar-Nelson, *Works* 81–82, 86; Mitchell, *This Waiting for Love* 51, 56–57. On the dialectical structure of Brooks's sonnets see Hubbard, "A Splintery Box" 53; on her lower-class settings see Davis, "Gwendolyn Brooks" 114–25; Kent, "Gwendolyn Brooks' Poetic Realism" 88–105; Smith, "Gwendolyn Brooks's *A Street in Bronzeville*" 46; on her demystification of love see Shaw, *Gwendolyn Brooks* 89.

10. On her individualism see Duncan, "And I Doubt All" 39; Leonard, *Fettered Genius* 118–123; Miller, "Define . . . the Whirlwind" 161–63.

11. G. Brooks, *World of Gwendolyn Brooks* 102. For close readings of this popular sonnet see K. Ford, "Sonnets of Satin-Legs Brooks" 358–59; Hubbard, "A Splintery Box" 52–54;

Neubauer, *Zwischen Tradition und Innovation* 240–41; G. Williams, "Gwendolyn Brooks's Way With the Sonnet" 233–37.

12. Hayden, *Collected Prose* 94, 118. On Hughes's criticism of the volume see Fetrow, *Robert Hayden* 48–51; P. Williams, *Robert Hayden* 15.

13. Hayden, *Ballad of Remembrance* 71. The second version of the poem had "to our children" at the end of line 3, for which Hayden substituted "to all" in this final version.

14. For example Moramarco and Sullivan, *Containing Multitudes* 37. For attempts to recuperate Hayden as an individualist see Leonard, *Fettered Genius* 156–59; 196; Pavlić, "Something Patterned, Wild, and Free" 534. On the progressive outlook of Hayden's poems see W. Williams, "Covenant" 740.

CHAPTER 5

1. Quoted in Llorens, "Writers Converge" 62; the previous quotes are from Killens, "The Black Writer " 381. On Hayden and the Black Arts movement see Llorens, "Writers Converge" 60–64; Smethurst, *Black Arts Movement* 76; Smith, "Quarreling in the Movement"; on Hayden as a politically conscious poet see Franke, *Pursue the Illusion* 218–34.

2. Mathes, *Imagine the Sound* 19, questions the notion of confining elements altogether but addresses the oral and musical aesthetics of the movement, which were central to its orthodoxy and thus safely removed from its exclusionary boundaries. Other studies of the movement that arrive at ambivalent assessments include Harper, "Nationalism and Social Division"; Shockley, "Black Arts Movement"; Shockley, *Renegade Poetics*; Van Deburg, *New Day in Babylon*; and the collections edited by Collins and Crawford, *New Thoughts on the Black Arts Movement*, and Glaude, *Is It Nation Time*. For celebratory criticism see Henderson, *Understanding the New Black Poetry*; Karenga, *Introduction to Black Studies*; Redmond, *Drumvoices*, Thomas, "Shadow World"; Woodard, *A Nation Within a Nation* 9–34; for dismissive commentary see Baker, *Blues, Ideology, and Afro-American Literature* 74–81; Baker, "On the Criticism"; Crouch, "Introduction"; Gates, *Figures in Black* 33–40; Gates, "Preface to Blackness."

3. Nielsen, *Black Chant* 21–22; Shockley, *Renegade Poetics* 1–2.

4. Chapman, introduction 37–38; Levine, "African American Literary Nationalism"; Street, *Culture War* 123–24. For typologies detailing some or all of the variants of black nationalism see Dawson, *Black Visions* 91; Levine, "African American Literary Nationalism" 119–21; Simeon-Jones, *Literary and Sociopolitical Writings* 9–31; Stout, "Theses on Black Nationalism" 242–43.

5. Neal, *Visions of a Liberated Future* 62; cf. Ferdinand, "Blkartsouth/get on up!"; Baraka, *Home* 137–41; Karenga, "Black Art" 480; Madhubuti, *From Plan to Planet* 95–97. On the oppositional approach of the Black Arts movement see Martin, "New Black Aesthetic Critics" 376; Rambsy, *Black Arts Enterprise* 144; Sherman, *Invisible Poets* xxxi. For research on the exclusionary self-definition of national cultures see Rubin, *A Shattered Nation* 133–34; Sharifi, *Imagining Iran* 165–66.

6. Baraka, *Home* 101–106; 363; 277–78; cf. Cruse, "Revolutionary Nationalism" 57–58. The only theoretical analysis of black nationalist territoriality so far is Dawson, *Black Visions* 97–100.—The communists had located the black nation in the South, and organizations like

the Republic of New Africa adopted this model to claim black self-government for the Southern states (Dawson, *Black Visions* 94; Umoja, "Searching for Place" 538). The Black Panther Party included the demand for a blacks-only referendum on an independent black nation in its party program and made its own position clear by quoting the United States' Declaration of Independence on self-government ("October 1966" 206).

7. Dawson, *Black Visions* 88–91; Harper, "Nationalism and Social Division" 237; see also Van Deburg, *New Day in Babylon* 53–55; Bernard, "A Familiar Strangeness" 263–6. On black nationalist territorialism see Neal, *Visions of a Liberated Future* 13–14; Baraka, *Home* 269–70; Dawson, *Black Visions* 99–100; Woodard, *A Nation Within A Nation* 5–6.

8. Crawford, "Poetics of Chant" 99; Lubiano, "Standing in for the State" 159–63; 160; see also Flowers, *African American Nationalist Literature of the 1960s*. Critics have pointed out the contradictions inherent in the black nationalist notion that literature was a means of creating a national culture that had supposedly existed all along (such as Shockley, "Black Arts Movement" 186). This contradiction was further complicated by a curious adoption of the genteel, integrationist argument for literature as a means of proving African Americans' full humanity. Don L. Lee mustered this argument in support of black nationalism when he argued that the black nation was a prerequisite for achieving cultural acceptance: "The literature of a nation like other arts forms, is not taken seriously by those who rule the world," he writes in *Dynamite Voices*, "until the creators themselves achieve some type of power or autonomy, e.g., the Jews in Israel and the WASP's in America" (78).

9. Lubiano, "Standing in for the State" 160; see also Rambsy, *Black Arts Enterprise* 132 and passim; on magazines cf. Johnson and Johnson, *Propaganda and Aesthetics* 161–200. On the heterogeneity of the Black Arts movement see Shockley, "Black Arts Movement" 188; Smethurst, *Black Arts Movement* 285–90. On the persistence of middle-class tastes among African Americans see Nielsen, *Black Chant* 40; Street, *Culture War* 104–5; 116–20.

10. Rambsy, *Black Arts Enterprise* 76; 32; see also 101–24; Henderson, *Understanding the New Black Poetry* 25. The anthology is Randall and Burroughs, *For Malcolm*. Other tributes published in the Black Arts movement include Gwendolyn Brooks's broadside *Family Pictures* (1970) and Arnold Adoff's aptly named anthology *Celebrations* (1977), which features tributes to Muhammad Ali, Langston Hughes, Martin Luther King, Patrice Lumumba, Rosa Parks, Paul Robeson, and Emmett Till.

11. Joans, *Black Pow-Wow* 96; E. Miller, *First Light* 97. Joans published "My Ace of Spades" as a fourteen-liner in his collection *Black Pow-Wow* (1969), but in the Malcolm X anthology of the same year it is shortened to thirteen lines, which obliterates the potential genre reference (Randall and Borroughs, *For Malcolm* 5).

12. Troupe, *Embryo* 22; Aubert, *Feeling Through*, n. pag.; Reese, *Songs of Freedom* 38. Reese's collection *Songs of Freedom* was published after much back and forth in 1983, but most of the poems were written during the Black Arts period.

13. On the "black is beautiful" slogan and its socio-historical background see Craig, *Ain't I a Beauty Queen* 23–44. The Malcolm X anthology exemplifies the pervasive notion that beauty and masculinity were closely linked at the time (Randall and Borroughs, *For Malcolm* xxi–xxvi, 3).

14. Baker, "Black Arts Era" 1849; Kinloch, *June Jordan* 75–78; MacPhail, "June Jordan and the New Black Intellectuals" 62–66. On Hayden see P. Williams, *Robert Hayden* 45. June Jordan's "Sunflower Sonnets" were published two years later in *Things That I Do In The Dark* 77.

CHAPTER 6

1. For cosmopolitan see Pereira, "The Poet in the World"; Pereira, *Rita Dove's Cosmopolitanism*. For postmodern see Dubey, *Signs and Cities*; Lott, "Response" 244–45; and with a broader perspective that includes marginalized writers of the Black Arts period, Nielsen, *Black Chant*. For post-black see Golden, "Introduction" 14–15; Taylor, "Post-Black, Old Black" 634; Touré, *Who's Afraid of Post-Blackness*; and critically, Kennedy, "Fallacy." A related term is "post-soul"; see Ashe, "Theorizing the Post-Soul Aesthetic" 609–11; Tate, *Flyboy in the Buttermilk* 198–210.

2. Shockley, *Renegade Poetics* 8; cf. Shockley, "Black Arts Movement" 186–89. For scholarship in support of the narrative see Moramarco and Sullivan, *Containing Multitudes* 314–18; Rowell, "Writing Self"; cf. Rowell, "Interview With Rita Dove" 716.

3. Nielsen, *Black Chant*; Nielsen, *Integral Music*; Moten, *In the Break*; Shockley, "Black Arts Movement"; Shockley, *Renegade Poetics*. Nielsen's theoretical premises and focus on recovery are shared by the contributors to the *MELUS* special issue *Black Modernism and Post-Modernism* (1991–1992).

4. Mullen, *Cracks* 79–80; Mullen quoted in Shockley, *Renegade Poetics* 10; Mackey, *Paracritical Hinge* 239–40. See also Harper, *Abstractionist Aesthetics* 12; Mullen, *Cracks* 9–12; Nielsen, *Black Chant* 9–13; A. Reed, *Freedom Time* 9.

5. Harper, *Abstractionist Aesthetics* 10–12; A. Reed, *Freedom Time* 28–32.

6. Komunyakaa, *Thieves of Paradise* 90–104; *Warhorses* 1–16; Nelson, *Homeplace* 11–20; *Fields of Praise* 99–102; *A Wreath for Emmett Till*; Trethewey, *Bellocq's Ophelia*; *Native Guard* 25–30; *Thrall* 9–12; Weaver, *My Father's Geography* 22–25; 47; 56; *Stations in a Dream* 28–65; Young, *Heaven* 111; 176–83; 265; 269; *Straight No Chaser* 1; *Coastal Nights and Inland Afternoons* 15–38; Phipps, *Your Last Illusion*; G. Patterson, *To and From*. For surveys of important contemporary African American sonneteers see Francini, "Sonnet vs. Sonnet"; Westover, "African American Sonnets." As evidence of the range of the contemporary African American sonnet see Early, *How the War* 97; Dove, *On the Bus* 56; Trethewey, *Domestic Work* 52 for everyday scenes; Trethewey, *Native Guard* 25–30 for history; Barrax, *Leaning Against the Sun* 13 for meditations; Coleman's "American Sonnets," discussed in the second section of this chapter, for displacements; McElroy, *Travelling Music* 74 for eulogies; Jordan, *Directed by Desire* 587–88 for revisions. See also Jordan's less successful revision of Yeats (*Directed by Desire* 448) and her important essay on Phillis Wheatley and the sonnet, cited in the introduction to this study (*On Call* 87–98).

7. The volumes are Dove, *Mother Love*; Chase-Riboud, *Portrait*; the sequences are Barrax, *Leaning Against the Sun* 44–46; Komunyakaa, *Neon Vernacular* 28–33; *Thieves of Paradise* 90–104; Weaver, *My Father's Geography* 22–25; 47; 56; Nelson, *Fields of Praise* 99–102; *Stations in a Dream* 28–65; and the first three installments of Coleman's "American Sonnets": sonnets 3–11 in *Hand Dance* (1993), sonnets 1–24 in *American Sonnets* (1994), sonnets 26–86 in *Bathwater Wine* (1998). Sonnets 25 and 87–100 were published in *Mercurochrome* (2001).

8. Crown, "Down Break Drum" 655; Keller and Wagstaff, "An Interview With Ed Roberson" 400; cf. Horton, "Structure" 767.

9. Dungy, *Black Nature*; Finseth, *Shades of Green*; Ruffin, *Black on Earth*; on Roberson specifically see Shockley, *Renegade Poetics* 145–68.

10. Crown, "Reading" 190; Edwards, "Black Serial Poetics" 631.

11. Edwards, "Black Serial Poetics" 631; Crown, "Reading" 212; Roberson quoted in Crown, "Down Break Drum" 675.

12. Sonnets 1 to 24, which appeared in 1993–1994, are noticeably superior to the follow-ups published between 1998 and 2001. The later sonnets lack the incisive, ironic voice of the earlier ones; they often slip into didacticism or prosy banalities and mostly limit their scope to the poet's life and personality. Coleman herself explained that the 1998 sonnets were auto-biographical and psychotherapeutic in their inception (Brown and Coleman, "What Saves Us" 645–46).

13. Walters, *African American Literature and the Classicist Tradition;* Cook and Tatum, *African American Writers and Classical Tradition.* On the evocation and disruption of order in Dove and other contemporary American poets see Scheiding, "Ideas of Order."

14. On the mythical intertexts see Righelato, *Understanding Rita Dove* 169–73; Steffen, *Crossing Color* 128–39; Walters, *African American Literature and the Classicist Tradition* 150–71. The only substantial discussion of Dove's use of the sonnet is Steffen, *Crossing Color* 128–39; another brief discussion is provided by Link, *Das moderne amerikanische Sonett* 126–28. On Dove's appropriation of European traditions see Pereira, *Rita Dove's Cosmopolitanism.*

15. Since the individual sonnets are not numbered, the sequence is cited by page and line number from Dove, *Mother Love* 67–77.—My reading of the last line of the sequence differs from readings offered by other critics. Pat Righelato claims that the "poetic imagination has mined the ground . . . and chooses to close now" (*Understanding Rita Dove* 169), as if there was an agent in the sentence other than the ground. Therese Steffen excludes the active ele-ment altogether when she suggests that the "ground" stands for "myth" and can be "closed" now that Dove has "unearthed" it and completed her "revision and reevaluation" (*Crossing Color* 138). The guiding thought of the final sonnet, however, is that "no story's ever finished," and quite aside from the lexical substitutability of "story" and "myth," neither the sequence nor the collection as a whole seem to suggest any kind of poetic closure.

16. Quoted in Edwards, "Black Serial Poetics" 628.

Works Cited

Aaron, Daniel. *The Unwritten War: American Writers and the Civil War*. Madison: University of Wisconsin Press, 1987.

Aaron, Daniel. *Writers on the Left: Episodes in American Literary Communism*. 1961. New York: Columbia University Press, 1992.

Abbott, Craig S. "Magazine Verse and Modernism: Braithwaite's Anthologies." *Journal of Modern Literature* 19.1 (1994): 151–59.

Adams, Joshua, Joel Calahan, and Michael Hansen, eds. *Historical Poetics*. Special issue of *Modern Language Quarterly* 77.1 (2016).

Adoff, Arnold, ed. *Celebrations: A New Anthology of Black American Poetry*. Chicago: Follett Publishing, 1977.

Ahearn, Barry. "Frost's Sonnets, In and Out of Bounds." *Modernism Revisited: Transgressing Boundaries and Strategies of Renewal in American Poetry*. Ed. Viorica Patea and Paul Scott Derrick. Amsterdam: Rodopi, 2007. 35–52.

Alexander, Elizabeth. *The Black Interior*. Saint Paul, MN: Graywolf Press, 2004.

Alexander, Lewis G. "Africa." *Opportunity* 2.17 (1924): 142.

Altieri, Charles. "Afterword: How the 'New Modernist Studies' Fails the Old Modernism." *Textual Practice* 26.4 (2012): 763–82.

Anderson, David. "Sterling Brown's Southern Strategy: Poetry as Cultural Evolution in *Southern Road*." *Callaloo* 21.4 (1998): 1023–37.

Appiah, Kwame Anthony. *In My Father's House: Africa in the Philosophy of Culture*. New York: Oxford University Press, 1992.

Asante, S. K. B. *Pan-African Protest: West Africa and the Italo-Ethiopian Crisis, 1934–1941*. London: Longman, 1977.

Ashe, Bertram D. "Theorizing the Post-Soul Aesthetic: An Introduction." *African American Review* 41.4 (2007): 609–23.

Aubert, Alvin. *Feeling Through*. Greenfield Center, NY: Greenfield Review Press, 1975.

Baker, Houston A., Jr. *Afro-American Poetics: Revisions of Harlem and the Black Aesthetic*. Madison, WI: University of Wisconsin Press, 1988.

Baker, Houston A., Jr. "The Black Arts Era, 1960–1975." *The Norton Anthology of African American Literature*. Ed. Henry Louis Gates and Nellie Y. McKay. 2nd ed. New York: Norton, 2004. 1831–50.

Baker, Houston A., Jr. *Blues, Ideology, and Afro-American Literature: A Vernacular Theory*. Chicago: University of Chicago Press, 1984.

Baker, Houston A., Jr. *A Many-Colored Coat of Dreams: The Poetry of Countee Cullen.* Detroit: Broadside Press, 1974.

Baker, Houston A., Jr. *Modernism and the Harlem Renaissance.* Chicago: University of Chicago Press, 1987.

Baker, Houston A., Jr. "On the Criticism of Black American Literature: One View of the Black Aesthetic." *Reading Black: Essays in the Criticism of African, Caribbean, and Black American Literature.* Ed. Houston A. Baker Jr. Ithaca: Cornell University Press, 1976. 48–58.

Baker, Houston A., Jr. "Theoretical Returns." 1991. *African American Literary Theory: A Reader.* Ed. Winston Napier. New York: New York University Press, 2000. 421–42.

Baldwin, Davarian L., Minkah Makalani, and Robin D. G. Kelley, eds. *Escape From New York: The New Negro Renaissance beyond Harlem.* Minneapolis: University of Minnesota Press, 2013.

Baldwin, James. *Notes of a Native Son.* 1955. Boston: Beacon Press, 2012.

Baldwin, Kate A. *Beyond the Color Line and the Iron Curtain: Reading Encounters Between Black and Red, 1922–1963.* Durham: Duke University Press, 2002.

Baraka, Amiri. *The Autobiography of LeRoi Jones.* Chicago: Lawrence Hill, 1984.

Baraka, Amiri. *Home: Social Essays.* New York: William Morrow, 1966.

Baraka, Amiri. "The Turncoat." *Soon, One Morning: New Writing By American Negroes 1940–1962.* Ed. Herbert Hill. New York: Knopf, 1969. 613.

Barrax, Gerald W. *Another Kind of Rain.* Pittsburgh: University of Pittsburgh Press, 1970.

Barrax, Gerald W. *Leaning Against the Sun.* Fayetteville: The University of Arkansas Press, 1992.

Barrett, Faith. "Abraham Lincoln and Poetry." *The Cambridge Companion to Abraham Lincoln.* Ed. Shirley Samuels. Cambridge: Cambridge University Press, 2012. 22–39.

Barrett, Faith. "American Poetry Fights the Civil War." *The Cambridge History of American Poetry.* Ed. Alfred Bendixen and Stephen Burt. Cambridge: Cambridge University Press, 2015. 306–27.

Barrett, Faith. *To Fight Aloud Is Very Brave: American Poetry and the Civil War.* Amherst: University of Massachusetts Press, 2012.

Bate, Jonathan. "Inventing Region and Nation: Wordsworth's Sonnets." *Swansea Review* 14 (1994): 2–22.

Baxter, J. Harvey L. *Sonnets to the Ethiopians.* Roanoke, VA: Magic City Press, 1936.

Beach, Christopher. *The Cambridge Introduction to Twentieth-Century American Poetry.* Cambridge: Cambridge University Press, 2003.

Beadle, Samuel A. "Sonnets to My Love." *Sketches From Life in Dixie.* By Beadle. Chicago: Scroll Publishing and Literary Syndicate, 1899. 15–24.

Beer, John. "Nature and Liberty: The Linking of Unstable Concepts." *Wordsworth Circle* 14.4 (1983): 201–13.

Behdad, Ali. *Belated Travelers: Orientalism in the Age of Colonial Dissolution.* Durham: Duke University Press, 1994.

Behrendt, Stephen C. "Wordsworth and Nation." *The Oxford Handbook of William Wordsworth.* Ed. Richard Gravil and Daniel Robinson. Oxford: Oxford University Press, 2015. 662–78.

Bellay, Joachim du. *Antiquitéz de Rome.* Trans. Edmund Spenser. Ed. Malcolm Smith. Binghamton, NY: Center for Medieval & Early Renaissance Studies, 1994.

Bennett, Paula Bernat. "Rewriting Dunbar: Realism, Black Women Poets, and the Genteel." *Post-Bellum, Pre-Harlem: African American Literature and Culture, 1877–1919.* Ed. Barbara McCaskill and Caroline Gebhard. New York: New York University Press, 2006. 146–61.

Berlin, Ira. *The Making of African America: The Four Great Migrations.* New York: Penguin, 2010.

Bermann, Sandra. *The Sonnet Over Time: A Study in the Sonnets of Petrarch, Shakespeare, and Baudelaire.* Chapel Hill: University of North Carolina Press, 1988.

Bernard, Emily. "A Familiar Strangeness: The Spectre of Whiteness in the Harlem Renaissance and the Black Arts Movement." *New Thoughts on the Black Arts Movement.* Ed. Lisa Gail Collins and Margo Natalie Crawford. New Brunswick: Rutgers University Press, 2006. 255–72.

Bérubé, Michael. "Masks, Margins, and African American Modernism: Melvin Tolson's *Harlem Gallery.*" *PMLA* 105.1 (1990): 57–69.

Bhabha, Homi K. *The Location of Culture.* London: Routledge, 1994.

Bhabha, Homi K. "Unsatisfied: Notes on Vernacular Cosmopolitanism." *Text and Nation: Cross-Disciplinary Essays on Cultural and National Identities.* Ed. Laura García-Moreno and Peter C. Pfeiffer. Columbia, SC: Camden House, 1996. 191–207.

Bibb, Eloise. *Poems.* 1895. *Collected Black Women's Poetry.* Vol. 4. Ed. Joan R. Sherman. New York: Oxford University Press, 1988.

Black Modernism and Post-Modernism. Special issue of *MELUS* 17.4 (1991–1992): 1–129.

Black, Daniel P. "Literary Subterfuge: Early African American Writing and the Trope of the Mask." *CLA Journal* 48.4 (2005): 387–403.

Bland, Sterling L., Jr. *Voices of the Fugitives: Runaway Slave Stories and Their Fictions of Self-Creation.* Westport: Greenwood Press, 2000.

Blount, Marcellus. "Caged Birds: Race and Gender in the Sonnet." *Engendering Men: The Question of Male Feminist Criticism.* Ed. Joseph Boone and Michael Cadden. New York: Routledge, 1990. 225–38.

Blount, Marcellus. "The Preacherly Text: African American Poetry and Vernacular Performance." *PMLA* 107.3 (1992): 582–93.

Blyden, Jackson. *The Waiting Years: Essays on American Negro Literature.* Baton Rouge: Louisiana State University Press, 1976.

Bogardus, Ralph F., and Fred Hobson, eds. *Literature at the Barricades: The American Writer in the 1930s.* University: University of Alabama Press, 1982.

Bolden, Tony. *Afro-Blue: Improvisations in African American Poetry and Culture.* Urbana: University of Illinois Press, 2004.

Borgstedt, Thomas. *Topik des Sonetts: Gattungstheorie und Gattungsgeschichte.* Berlin: de Gruyter, 2009.

Braddock, Jeremy. "The Poetics of Conjecture: Countee Cullen's Subversive Exemplarity." *Callaloo* 25.4 (2002): 1250–71.

Braden, Gordon. "Love and Fame: The Petrarchan Career." *Pragmatism's Freud: The Moral Disposition of Psychoanalysis.* Ed. Joseph H. Smith and William Kerrigan. Baltimore: Johns Hopkins University Press, 1986. 126–58.

Bragg, Linda Brown. *A Love Song to Black Men.* Detroit: Broadside Press, 1974.

Braithwaite, William Stanley. *The House of Falling Leaves: With Other Poems.* Boston: Luce, 1908.

Braithwaite, William Stanley. *Lyrics of Life and Love.* Boston: Turner, 1904.

Brawley, Benjamin. *The Desire of the Moth for the Star.* Atlanta: Franklin-Turner, 1906.

Brawley, Benjamin. "Elizabeth Barrett Browning and the Negro." *Journal of Negro History* 3.1 (1918): 22–28.

Bregman, Dvora. *The Golden Way: The Hebrew Sonnet During the Renaissance and the Baroque.* Tempe: Arizona Center for Medieval and Renaissance Studies, 2005.

Breitinger, Eckhard. "In Search of an Audience: In Search of the Self: Exile as a Condition for the Works of Claude McKay." *The Commonwealth Writer Overseas: Themes of Exile and Expatriation.* Ed. Alastair Niven. Brussels: Didier, 1976. 175–84.

Bromwich, David. Introduction. *American Sonnets: An Anthology.* Ed. David Bromwich. New York: Library of America, 2007. xvii–xxxviii.

Bronz, Stephen H. *Roots of Negro Racial Consciousness: The 1920's: Three Harlem Renaissance Authors.* New York: Libra, 1964.

Brooks, Gwendolyn, et al. *A Capsule Course in Black Poetry Writing.* Detroit: Broadside Press, 1975.

Brooks, Gwendolyn. *Family Pictures.* Detroit: Broadside Press, 1970.

Brooks, Gwendolyn. *The World of Gwendolyn Brooks.* New York: Harper & Row, 1971.

Brooks, Jonathan Henderson. *The Resurrection and Other Poems.* Dallas: Kaleidograph Press, 1948.

Brooks, Van Wyck. *America's Coming-of-Age.* 1915. Revised edition. Garden City, NY: Doubleday, 1958.

Brown, Charles Armitage. *Shakespeare's Autobiographical Poems.* London: Bohn, 1838.

Brown, Priscilla Ann, and Wanda Coleman. "What Saves Us: An Interview with Wanda Coleman." *Callaloo* 26.3 (2003): 635–61.

Brown, Sterling. *The Collected Poems of Sterling A. Brown.* Ed. Michael S. Harper. New York: Harper & Row, 1980.

Brown, William Wells. *The Negro in the American Rebellion, His Heroism and His Fidelity.* Boston: Lee & Shepard, 1867.

Brown, William Wells. *The Rising Son; or, the Antecedents and Advancements of the Colored Race.* New York: Negro Universities Press, 1874.

Browning, Robert. *The Complete Works.* Vol. 13. Ed. Ashby Bland Crowder et al. Athens, OH: Ohio University Press, 1995.

Bruce, Dickson D., Jr. *Black American Writing from the Nadir: The Evolution of a Literary Tradition 1877–1915.* Baton Rouge: Louisiana State University Press, 1989.

Bruce, Dickson D., Jr. *The Origins of African American Literature, 1680–1865.* Charlottesville: University Press of Virginia, 2001.

Brunner, Edward. "Inventing an Ancestor: The Scholar-Poet and the Sonnet." *New Formalisms and Literary Theory.* Ed. Verena Theile and Linda Tredennick. New York: Palgrave Macmillan, 2013. 71–95.

Burt, Stephen, and David Mikics. Introduction. *The Art of the Sonnet.* Ed. Stephen Burt and David Mikics. Cambridge: Belknap, 2010. 5–25.

Burwick, Frederick. "'Narrow Rooms' or 'Wide Expanse': The Construction of Space in the Romantic Sonnet." *Re-mapping Romanticism: Gender, Texts, Contexts.* Ed. Christoph Bode and Fritz-Wilhelm Neumann. Essen: Blaue Eule, 2001. 49–64.

Butler, Alpheus. *Make Way For Happiness.* Boston: Christopher, 1932.

Byerman, Keith. "Vernacular Modernism in the Novels of John Edgar Wideman and Leon Forrest." *The Cambridge Companion to the African American Novel.* Ed. Maryemma Graham. Cambridge: Cambridge University Press, 2004. 253–67.

Calverton, V. F. *The New Ground of Criticism.* Seattle: University of Washington Book Store, 1930.

Canaday, Nicholas, Jr. "Major Themes in the Poetry of Countee Cullen." *The Harlem Renaissance Remembered.* New York: Dodd, Mead, 1972. 103–25.

Carroll, Richard A. "Black Racial Spirit: An Analysis of James Weldon Johnson's Critical Perspective." *Phylon* 32.4 (1971): 344–64.

Chandler, G. Lewis. "A Major Problem of Negro Authors in Their March Toward Belles-Lettres." *Phylon* 11.4 (1950): 383–86.

Chandler, James K. "Wordsworth and Burke." *ELH* 47. 4 (1980): 741–71.

Chapman, Abraham. Introduction. *New Black Voices: An Anthology of Contemporary Afro-American Literature.* Ed. Chapman. New York: Mentor, 1972. 25–53.

Chinitz, David E. *Which Sin to Bear? Authenticity and Compromise in Langston Hughes.* Oxford: Oxford University Press, 2013.

Chrisman, Robert. "Robert Hayden: The Transition Years, 1946–1948." *Robert Hayden: Essays on the Poetry.* Ed. Laurence Goldstein and Robert Chrisman. Ann Arbor: University of Michigan Press, 2001. 129–54.

Christian, Marcus. *High Ground.* New Orleans: Southern Publishing, 1958.

Chronicling America: Historic American Newspapers. Lib. of Congress. 3 Aug. 2015 < http://chroniclingamerica.loc.gov>.

Clark, Steve. Introduction. *Travel Writing and Empire: Postcolonial Theory in Transit.* Ed. Steve Clark. London: Zed Books, 1999. 1–28.

Clarke, LeRoy. *Taste of Endless Fruit: Love Poems and Drawings.* Brooklyn, NY: Self-published, 1974.

Clifford, Carrie Williams. *The Widening Light.* Boston: Reid, 1922.

Coleman, Wanda. *American Sonnets.* Milwaukee: Woodland, 1994.

Coleman, Wanda. *Bathwater Wine.* Santa Rosa: Black Sparrow Press, 1998.

Coleman, Wanda. *Hand Dance.* Santa Rosa: Black Sparrow Press, 1993.

Coleman, Wanda. *Mercurochrome: New Poems.* Santa Rosa, CA: Black Sparrow Press, 2001.

Coles, Robert. *Black Writers Abroad: A Study of Black American Writers in Europe and Africa.* New York: Garland, 1999.

Collins, Lisa Gail, and Margo Natalie Crawford, eds. *New Thoughts on the Black Arts Movement.* New Brunswick: Rutgers University Press, 2006.

Condit, John Hillyer. "An Urge Toward Wholeness: Claude McKay and His Sonnets." *CLA Journal* 22 (1979): 350–64.

Conroy, Mary. "The Vagabond Motif in the Writings of Claude McKay." *Negro American Literature Forum* 5.1 (1971): 15–23.

Conte, Joseph M. *Unending Design: The Forms of Postmodern Poetry.* Ithaca, NY: Cornell University Press, 1991.

Cook, William W., and James Tatum. *African American Writers and Classical Tradition.* Chicago: University of Chicago Press, 2010.

Corrothers, James D. "A Tribute to Paul Laurence Dunbar." *Voice of the Negro* 3.3 (Mar 1906): 184.

Corrothers, James D. *In Spite of the Handicap: An Autobiography.* 1916. Freeport, NY: Books for Libraries Press, 1971.

Cotter, Joseph S., Jr. *Complete Poems.* Ed. James Robert Payne. Athens: University of Georgia Press, 1990.

Cotter, Joseph S., Sr. *Collected Poems.* 1938. Freeport, NY: Books for Libraries Press, 1971.

Craig, Maxine Leeds. *Ain't I a Beauty Queen? Black Women, Beauty, and the Politics of Race.* Oxford: Oxford University Press, 2002.

Crawford, Margo Natalie. "The Poetics of Chant and Inner/Outer Space: The Black Arts Movement." *The Cambridge Companion to American Poetry Since 1945.* Ed. Jennifer Ashton. Cambridge: Cambridge University Press, 2013. 94–108.

Cromwell, John W. *The Negro in American History: Men and Women Eminent in the Evolution of the American of African Descent.* Washington, DC: American Negro Academy, 1914.

Cronin, Richard. "Wordsworth's *Poems* of 1807 and the War Against Napoleon." *Review of English Studies* 48.189 (1997): 33–50.

Crouch, Stanley. "Introduction: The Incomplete Turn of Larry Neal." *Visions of a Liberated Future: Black Arts Movement Writings.* By Larry Neal. Ed. Michael Schwartz. New York: Thunder's Mouth Press, 1989. 3–6.

Crouch, Stanley. "Toward a Purer Black Poetry Esthetic." *Journal of Black Poetry* 1.10 (1968): 28–29.

Crown, Kathleen. "'Down Break Drum': An Interview With Ed Roberson." Part 1. *Callaloo* 33.3 (2010): 651–82.

Crown, Kathleen. "Reading the 'Lucid Interval': Race, Trauma, and Literacy in the Poetry of Ed Roberson." *Poetics Today* 21.1 (2000): 187–220.

Cruse, Harold. "Revolutionary Nationalism and the Afro-American." *Black Fire: An Anthology of Afro-American Writing.* Ed. LeRoi Jones and Larry Neal. New York: William Morrow, 1968. 39–63.

Cueva, Edmund Paul. "The Classics and Countee Cullen." *Interdisciplinary Humanities* 30.2 (2013): 24–36.

Cullen, Countee. *The Black Christ and Other Poems.* New York: Harper, 1929.

Cullen, Countee. *Color.* New York: Harper, 1925.

Cullen, Countee. *Copper Sun.* New York: Harper's, 1927.

Cullen, Countee. *The Medea and Some Other Poems.* New York: Harper, 1935.

Cunningham, James. "Hemlock for the Black Artist: Karenga Style." *New Black Voices: An Anthology of Contemporary Afro-American Literature.* Ed. Abraham Chapman. New York: New American Library, 1972. 483–89.

Dace, Tish, ed. *Langston Hughes: The Contemporary Reviews.* Cambridge: Cambridge University Press, 1997.

Dandridge, Raymond Garfield. *The Poet and Other Poems.* Cincinnati: Powell & White, 1920.

Davis, Arthur. "Gwendolyn Brooks: Poet of the Unheroic." *CLA Journal* 7 (1963): 114–25.

Dawahare, Anthony. *Nationalism, Marxism, and African American Literature Between the Wars: A New Pandora's Box.* Jackson: University Press of Mississippi, 2003.

Dawson, Michael C. *Black Visions: The Roots of Contemporary African-American Political Ideologies.* Chicago: University of Chicago Press, 2001.

De Jongh, James. *Vicious Modernism: Black Harlem and the Literary Imagination.* New York: Cambridge University Press, 1990.

Denning, Michael. *The Cultural Front: The Laboring of American Culture in the Twentieth Century.* London: Verso, 1997.

DeSimone, Erika, and Fidel Louis, eds. *Voices Beyond Bondage: An Anthology of Verse by African Americans of the 19th Century.* Montgomery: NewSouth Books, 2014.

Dodson, Owen. Rev. of *Shakespeare in Harlem*, by Langston Hughes. *Phylon* 3.3 (1942): 337–38.

Douglass, Ann. *Terrible Honesty: Mongrel Manhattan in the 1920s.* New York: Farrar, Straus and Giroux, 1995.

Dove, Rita. *Mother Love: Poems.* New York: Norton, 1995.

Dove, Rita. *On the Bus With Rosa Parks.* New York: Norton, 1999.

Drake, St. Clair. "Diaspora Studies and Pan-Africanism." *Global Dimensions of the African Diaspora.* Ed. Joseph E. Harris. Washington, DC: Howard University Press, 1982. 341–402.

Drake, St. Clair. "The Meaning of 'Negritude': The Negro's Stake in Africa." *Negro Digest* 13.8 (1964): 33–48.

Drake, St. Clair. *The Redemption of Africa and Black Religion.* Chicago: Third World Press, 1970.

Draper, Theodore. *American Communism and Soviet Russia: The Formative Period.* New York: Viking Press, 1960.

Du Bois, W. E. B. "Criteria of Negro Art." *Crisis* 32 (Oct. 1926): 290–97.

Du Bois, W. E. B. *The Souls of Black Folk.* 1903. Ed. Brent Hayes Edwards. Oxford: Oxford University Press, 2008.

Dubey, Madhu. *Signs and Cities: Black Literary Postmodernism.* Chicago: University of Chicago Press, 2003.

Dubrow, Heather. *Echoes of Desire: English Petrarchism and Its Counterdiscourses.* Ithaca: Cornell University Press, 1995.

Dugan, James, and Laurence Lafore. *Days of Emperor and Clown: The Italo-Ethiopian War 1935–1936.* Garden City, NY: Doubleday, 1973.

Dunbar, Paul Laurence. *The Complete Poems of Paul Laurence Dunbar.* 1913. New York: Dodd, Mead, 1950.

Dunbar-Nelson, Alice. *The Works of Alice Dunbar-Nelson.* Vol. 2. Ed. Gloria T. Hull. New York: Oxford University Press, 1988.

Duncan, Bryan. "'And I Doubt All': Allegiance and Ambivalence in Gwendolyn Brooks's 'Gay Chaps at the Bar.'" *Journal of Modern Literature* 34.1 (2010): 36–57.

Dungy, Camille, ed. *Black Nature: Four Centuries of African American Nature Poetry.* Athens: University of Georgia Press, 2009.

DuPlessis, Rachel B. "Social Texts and Poetic Texts: Poetry and Cultural Studies." *The Oxford Handbook of Modern and Contemporary American Poetry.* Ed. Cary Nelson: Oxford: Oxford University Press, 2012

Dworkin, Ira, ed. *Daughter of the Revolution: The Major Nonfiction Works of Pauline E. Hopkins.* New Brunswick, NJ: Rutgers University Press, 2007.

Early, Gerald. *How the War in the Streets Is Won: Poems on the Quest of Love and Faith.* St. Louis, MO: Time Being Books, 1995.

Eaton, Estelle. "Spring-Time Scenes For the Painter." *Out of My Dreams and Other Verses.* By Eaton. Boston: Christopher Publishing, 1959. 17.

Edwards, Brent Hayes. "Black Serial Poetics: An Introduction to Ed Roberson." *Callaloo* 33.3 (2010): 621–37.

Edwards, Brent Hayes. *The Practice of Diaspora: Literature, Translation, and the Rise of Black Internationalism.* Cambridge: Harvard University Press, 2003.

Edwards, Brent Hayes. "The Uses of *Diaspora.*" *Social Text* 19.1 (2001): 45–73.

Elliott, R. S. "The Story of Our Magazine." *Colored American Magazine* 3 (1901): 47.

Emanuel, James A. "For a Farmer." *The Broken Bowl: New and Uncollected Poems.* By Emanuel. Detroit: Lotus Press, 1983. 22.

Emanuel, James A. *Langston Hughes.* New York: Twayne, 1967.

Emanuel, James A. "Renaissance Sonneteers: Their Contributions to the Seventies." *Black World* 24.11 (1975): 32–45, 92–97.

Esedebe, P. Olisanwuche. *Pan-Africanism: The Idea and the Movement 1776–1963.* Washington, DC: Howard University Press, 1982.

Fahs, Alice. *The Imagined Civil War: Popular Literature of the North and South, 1861–1865.* Chapel Hill: University of North Carolina Press, 2001.

Fanon, Frantz. *Black Skin, White Masks.* 1952. Trans. Charles Lam Markmann. New York: Grove Press, 1967.

Feith, Michel. "Henry Louis Gates, Jr.'s *Signifying Monkey*: A Diasporic Critical Myth." *African Diasporas in the New and Old Worlds: Consciousness and Imagination.* Ed. Geneviève Fabre and Klaus Benesch. Amsterdam: Rodopi, 2004. 59–80.

Ferdinand, Val (Kalamu Ya Salaam). "Blkartsouth/get on up!" *New Black Voices: An Anthology of Contemporary Afro-American Literature.* Ed. Abraham Chapman. New York: New American Library, 1972. 467–73.

Fergus, Claudius. "From Prophecy to Policy: Marcus Garvey and the Evolution of Pan-African Citizenship." *The Global South* 4.2 (2010): 29–48.

Ferry, Anne. *The "Inward" Language: Sonnets of Wyatt, Sidney, Shakespeare, Donne.* Chicago: University of Chicago Press, 1983.

Fetrow, Fred M. "Cullen's 'Yet Do I Marvel.'" *Explicator* 56.2 (1998): 103–5.

Fetrow, Fred M. *Robert Hayden.* Boston: Twayne, 1984.

Filreis, Alan. *Modernism From Right to Left: Wallace Stevens, the Thirties and Literary Radicalism.* Cambridge: Cambridge University Press, 1994.

Finley, M. I., Denis Mack Smith, and Christopher Duggan. *A History of Sicily.* London: Chatto & Windus, 1986.

Finseth, Ian Frederick. Shades of Green: Visions of Nature in the Literature of American Slavery. Athens: University of Georgia Press, 2009.

Fisher, Rebecka. *Habitations of the Veil: Metaphor and the Poetics of Black Being in African American Literature.* Albany, NY: State University of New York Press, 2014.

Flint, Allen. "Black Response to Colonel Shaw." *Phylon* 45.3 (1984): 210–19.

Flowers, Sandra Hollin. *African American Nationalist Literature of the 1960s.* New York: Garland, 1996.

Foley, Barbara. *Radical Representations: Politics and Form in U.S. Proletarian Fiction, 1929–1941.* Durham: Duke University Press, 1993.

Foley, Barbara. *Spectres of 1919: Class and Nation in the Making of the New Negro.* Urbana: University of Illinois Press, 2003.

Ford, Karen Jackson. "The Sonnets of Satin-Legs Brooks." *Contemporary Literature* 48.3 (2007): 345–73.

Fortune, Timothy Thomas. *Dreams of Life: Miscellaneous Poems.* 1905. Miami: Mnemosyne, 1969.

Francini, Antonella. "Sonnet vs. Sonnet: The Fourteen Lines in African American Poetry." *RSA Journal* 14 (2003): 37–66.

Franke, Astrid. *Pursue the Illusion: Problems of Public Poetry in America.* Heidelberg: Winter, 2010.

Franklin, John Hope. Editor's Foreword. *T. Thomas Fortune: Militant Journalist.* By Emma Lou Thornbrough. Chicago: University of Chicago Press, 1972. vii–viii.

Frazier, E. Franklin. *Black Bourgeoisie.* New York: Free Press, 1957.

Friedrich, Paul. "The Unheralded Revolution in the Sonnet: Toward a Generative Model." 1988. *Linguistics in Context: Connecting Observation and Understanding.* Ed. Deborah Tannen. Norwood, NJ: Ablex, 1988. 199–219.

Fuller, John. *The Sonnet.* London: Methuen, 1972.

Gabbin, Joanne. *Sterling A. Brown: Building the Black Aesthetic Tradition.* Westport, CT: Greenwood Press, 1985.

Gaines, Kevin. *Uplifting the Race: Black Leadership, Politics, and Culture in the Twentieth Century.* Chapel Hill: University of North Carolina Press, 1996.

Gates, Henry Louis, and Gene Andrew Jarrett. Introduction. *The New Negro: Readings on Race, Representation, and African American Culture, 1892–1938.* Ed. Gates and Jarrett. Princeton: Princeton University Press, 2007. 1–20.

Gates, Henry Louis, Jr. *Figures in Black: Words, Signs, and the "Racial" Self.* New York: Oxford University Press, 1987.

Gates, Henry Louis, Jr. *Loose Canons: Notes on the Culture Wars.* New York: Oxford University Press, 1992.

Gates, Henry Louis, Jr. "Preface to Blackness: Text and Pretext." *Afro-American Literature: The Reconstruction of Instruction.* Ed. Dexter Fisher and Robert B. Stepto. New York: MLA, 1978.

Gates, Henry Louis. *The Signifying Monkey: A Theory of African-American Literary Criticism.* New York: Oxford University Press, 1988.

Gayle, Addison. *The Way of the New World: The Black Novel in America.* Garden City: Anchor Press, 1975.

Gill, Jonathan. *Harlem: The Four Hundred Year History from Dutch Village to Capital of Black America.* New York: Grove, 2011.

Glaser, Ben. "Folk Iambics: Prosody, Vestiges, and Sterling Brown's *Outline for the Study of the Poetry of American Negroes.*" *PMLA* 129.3 (2014): 417–34.

Glasrud, Bruce A., and Cary D. Wintz, eds. *The Harlem Renaissance in the American West: The New Negro's Western Experience.* New York: Routledge, 2012.

Glaude, Eddie S., Jr. *Is It Nation Time? Contemporary Essays on Black Power and Black Nationalism.* Chicago: University of Chicago Press, 2002.

Goethe, Johann Wolfgang von. *Faust: A Tragedy: The First Part.* Trans. Bayard Taylor. Leipzig: Brockhaus, 1872.

Golden, Thelma. "Introduction: Post . . ." *Freestyle.* Ed. Thelma Golden. New York: Studio Museum in Harlem, 2001. 14–15.

Goodman, Susan. *Republic of Words: The* Atlantic Monthly *and Its Writers, 1857–1925.* Hanover: University Press of New England, 2011.

Gray, Richard. *American Poetry of the Twentieth Century.* London: Longman, 1990.

Grewal, Inderpal. *Home and Harem: Nation, Gender, Empire and the Cultures of Travel.* Durham: Duke University Press, 1996.

Griffin, Barbara Jackson. "The Last Word: Claude McKay's Unpublished 'Cycle Manuscript.'" *MELUS* 21.1 (1996): 41–57.

Griffin, Farah J., and Cheryl J. Fish, eds. *A Stranger in the Village: Two Centuries of African-American Travel Writing.* Boston: Beacon Press, 1998.

Griffin, Farah J., and Cheryl J. Fish. Introduction. *A Stranger in the Village: Two Centuries of African-American Travel Writing.* Ed. Farah J. Griffin and Cheryl J. Fish. Boston: Beacon Press, 1998. xiii–xvii.

Griffin, Martin. *Ashes of the Mind: War and Memory in Northern Literature, 1865–1900*. 2008. Amherst: University of Massachusetts Press, 2009.

Gruesser, John Cullen. *Black on Black: Twentieth-Century African American Writing about Africa*. Lexington: University Press of Kentucky, 2000.

Gruesser, John Cullen. *Confluences: Postcolonialism, African American Literary Studies, and the Black Atlantic*. Athens: University of Georgia Press, 2005.

Gruesser, John Cullen. *White on Black: Contemporary Literature About Africa*. Urbana: University of Illinois Press, 1992.

Harper, Michael S. "Every Shut-Eye Aint Asleep / Every Good-bye Aint Gone: Robert Hayden (1913–1980)." *Robert Hayden: Essays on the Poetry*. Ed. Laurence Goldstein and Robert Chrisman. Ann Arbor: University of Michigan Press, 2001. 104–11.

Harper, Phillip Brian. *Abstractionist Aesthetics: Artistic Form and Social Critique in African American Culture*. New York: New York University Press, 2015.

Harper, Phillip Brian. "Nationalism and Social Division in Black Arts Poetry of the 1960s." *Identities*. Ed. Kwame Anthony Appiah and Henry Louis Gates, Jr. Chicago: University of Chicago Press, 1995. 220–41.

Harris, Brice, Jr. *The United States and the Italo-Ethiopian Crisis*. Stanford: Stanford University Press, 1964.

Hart, Matthew. *Nations of Nothing But Poetry: Modernism, Transnationalism, and Synthetic Vernacular Writing*. Oxford: Oxford University Press, 2010.

Havens, Raymond Dexter. *The Influence of Milton on English Poetry*. Cambridge: Harvard University Press, 1922.

Hayden, Robert. *A Ballad of Remembrance*. London: Paul Breman, 1962.

Hayden, Robert. *Collected Prose*. Ed. Frederick Glaysher. Ann Arbor: University of Michigan Press, 1984.

Hedrick, Joan. *Harriet Beecher Stowe: A Life*. New York: Oxford University Press, 1994.

Henderson, Stephen. *Understanding the New Black Poetry: Black Speech and Black Music as Poetic References*. New York: William Morrow, 1973.

Henry, Thomas Millard. "Countee Cullen." *Messenger* 6.10 (1924): 311.

Hess, Jonathan M. "Wordsworth's Aesthetic State: The Poetics of Liberty." *Studies in Romanticism* 33.1 (1994): 3–29.

Hieglar, Charles J. "Claude McKay's 'If We Must Die,' *Home to Harlem*, and the Hog Trope." *ANQ* 8.3 (1995): 22–26.

Hill, Leslie Pinckney. "Vision of a Lyncher." *The Crisis* 3.3 (1912): 122.

Hill, Leslie Pinckney. *The Wings of Oppression*. 1921. Freeport, NY: Books for Libraries Press, 1971.

Hill, Rebecca. *Men, Mobs, and Law: Anti-Lynching and Labor Defense in U.S. Radical History*. Durham: Duke University Press, 2008.

Hochman, Barbara. "Sentiment Without Tears: *Uncle Tom's Cabin* as History in the 1890s." *New Directions in American Reception Study*. Ed. Philip Goldstein and James L. Machor. Oxford: Oxford University Press, 2008. 255–76.

Holcomb, Gary Edward. *Claude McKay, Code Name Sasha: Queer Black Marxism and the Harlem Renaissance*. Gainesville: University Press of Florida, 2007.

Holland, Patrick, and Graham Huggan. *Tourists with Typewriters: Critical Reflections on Contemporary Travel Writing*. Ann Arbor: University of Michigan Press, 1998.

Hollander, John. *Melodious Guile: Fictive Pattern in Poetic Language*. New Haven, CT: Yale University Press, 1988.

Holly, Joseph C. *Freedom's Offering*. Rochester: McDonnell, 1853.

Horne, Gerald. *Black Liberation/Red Scare: Ben Davis and the Communist Party*. Newark: University of Delaware Press, 1994.

Horne, Gerald. "The Red and the Black: The Communist Party and African-Americans in Historical Perspective." *New Studies in the Politics and Culture of U.S. Communism*. Ed. Michael E. Brown et al. New York: Monthly Review Press, 1993. 199–237.

Horton, George Moses. *The Poetical Works of George M. Horton, The Colored Bard of North Carolina*. Hillsborough, NC: D. Heartt, 1845.

Horton, Randall. "'The Structure, Then the Music': An Interview With Ed Roberson." *Callaloo* 33.3 (2010): 762–69.

Howells, William Dean. *Criticism and Fiction*. New York: Harper, 1891.

Hubbard, Stacy. "'A Splintery Box': Race and Gender in the Sonnets of Gwendolyn Brooks." *Genre* 25.1 (1992): 47–64.

Huggins, Nathan. *Harlem Renaissance*. New York: Oxford University Press, 1971.

Hughes, Langston, and Arna Bontemps, ed. *The Poetry of the Negro 1746–1970*. Garden City, NY: Doubleday, 1970.

Hughes, Langston. *The Big Sea: An Autobiography*. New York: Hill and Wang, 1940.

Hughes, Langston. "Jazz as Communication." *The Langston Hughes Reader*. Ed. Langston Hughes. New York: Braziller, 1958. 492–94.

Hughes, Langston. "The Negro Artist and the Racial Mountain." 1926. *The Politics and Aesthetics of "New Negro" Literature*. Ed. Cary D. Wintz. New York: Garland, 1996. 166–68.

Hughes, Langston. *The Poems: 1921–1940. The Collected Works of Langston Hughes*. Vol. 1. Ed. Arnold Rampersad. Columbia: University of Missouri Press, 2001.

Hughes, Langston. *The Poems: 1941–1950. The Collected Works of Langston Hughes*. Vol. 2. Ed. Arnold Rampersad. Columbia: University of Missouri Press, 2001.

Hughes, Langston. "Songs Called the Blues." *Phylon* 2.2 (1941): 143–145.

Hunt, Leigh, and S. Adams Lee. *The Book of the Sonnet*. 2 vols. Boston: Roberts, 1867.

Hunt, Leigh. "An Essay on the Cultivation, History, and Varieties of the Species of Poem Called the Sonnet." *The Book of the Sonnet*. Vol. 1. Eds. Leigh Hunt and S. Adams Lee. Boston: Roberts, 1867. 3–91.

Huntsperger, David. *Procedural Form in Postmodern American Poetry: Berrigan, Antin, Silliman, and Hejinian*. New York: Palgrave Macmillan, 2010.

Hutchinson, George. *The Harlem Renaissance in Black and White*. Cambridge, MA: Belknap Press, 1995

Jackson, Lawrence P. *The Indignant Generation: A Narrative History of African American Writers and Critics, 1934–1960*. Princeton: Princeton University Press, 2011.

James, Winston. *A Fierce Hatred of Injustice: Claude McKay's Jamaica and His Poetry of Rebellion*. London: Verso, 2000.

Jarrett, Gene Andrew. *Deans and Truants: Race and Realism in African American Literature*. Philadelphia: University of Pennsylvania Press, 2007.

Jarrett, Gene Andrew. *Representing the Race: A New Political History of African American Literature*. New York: New York University Press, 2011.

Jarvis, Simon. "What Is Historical Poetics?" *Theory Aside*. Ed. Jason Potts and Daniel Stout. Durham: Duke University Press, 2014. 97–126.

Jeffers, Lance. *O Africa, Where I Baked My Bread*. Detroit: Lotus Press, 1977

Jefferson, Thomas. *Notes From the State of Virginia*. 1785. Ed. William Peden. Chapel Hill: University of North Carolina Press, 1998.

Jemie, Onwuchekwa. *Langston Hughes: An Introduction to the Poetry*. New York: Columbia University Press, 1976.

Jenkins, Lee M. *The Language of Caribbean Poetry: Boundaries of Expression*. Gainesville, FL: University Press of Florida, 2004.

Joans, Ted. *Black Pow-Wow: Jazz Poems*. New York: Hill and Wang, 1969.

Jobs, Sebastian. *Welcome Home, Boys! Military Victory Parades in New York City 1899–1946*. Frankfurt: Campus, 2012.

John, Frank (Nkemka Asika). *Love in Black Soul*. New York: Self-published, 1977.

Johnson, Abby, and Roland M. Johnson. "Away From Accomodation: Radical Editors and Protest Journalism, 1900–1910." *Journal of Negro History* 62.4 (1977): 325–38.

Johnson, Abby, and Roland M. Johnson. *Propaganda and Aesthetics: The Literary Politics of Afro-American Magazines in the Twentieth Century*. Amherst: University of Massachusetts Press, 1979.

Johnson, Charles S., ed. *Ebony and Topaz: A Collectanea*. 1927. Freeport, NY: Books for Libraries Press, 1971.

Johnson, Georgia Douglas. *Bronze: A Book of Verse*. 1922. Freeport, NY: Books for Libraries Press, 1971.

Johnson, Herbert Clark. *Poems from Flat Creek*. Francestown, NH: Marshall Jones, 1943.

Johnson, James Weldon, ed. *The Book of American Negro Poetry*. Revised edition. 1931. San Diego: Harcourt Brace, 1969. 3–8.

Johnson, James Weldon. "The Dilemma of the Negro Author." *American Mercury* 15.60 (1928): 477–81.

Johnson, James Weldon. *Fifty Years and Other Poems*. Boston: Cornhill, 1917.

Johnson, James Weldon. *God's Trombones: Seven Negro Sermons in Verse*. New York: Viking, 1927.

Johnson, James Weldon. "Preface to Original Edition." *The Book of American Negro Poetry*. Ed. James Weldon Johnson. Revised edition. 1931. San Diego: Harcourt Brace, 1969. 9–48.

Jones, Jeannette Eileen. *In Search of Brightest Africa: Reimagining the Dark Continent in American Culture, 1884–1936*. Athens: University of Georgia Press, 2010.

Jordan, June. *Directed by Desire: The Collected Poems of June Jordan*. Ed. Jan Heller Levi and Sara Miles. Port Townsend, WA: Copper Canyon Press, 2005.

Jordan, June. *On Call: Political Essays*. Boston: South End Press, 1985.

Jordan, June. *Things That I Do In The Dark*. New York: Random House, 1977.

Kaiser, David Aram. *Romanticism, Aesthetics, and Nationalism*. Cambridge: Cambridge University Press, 1999.

Karenga, Maulana Ron. "Black Art: Mute Matter Given Force and Function." *New Black Voices: An Anthology of Contemporary Afro-American Literature*. Ed. Abraham Chapman. New York: New American Library, 1972. 477–82.

Karenga, Maulana. *Introduction to Black Studies*. Los Angeles: University of Sankore Press, 1993.

Keats, John. *The Poems*. Ed. Jack Stillinger. Cambridge, MA: Belknap Press, 1978.

Keeling, John. "Paul Dunbar and the Mask of Dialect." *Southern Literary Journal* 25.2 (1993): 21–38.

Keller, James R. "'A Chafing Savage, Down the Decent Street': The Politics of Compromise in Claude McKay's Protest Sonnets." *African American Review* 28.3 (1994): 447–56.

Keller, Lynn, and Steel Wagstaff. "An Interview With Ed Roberson." *Contemporary Literature* 52.3 (2011): 397–429.

Kelley, Arnold J. "Guide to Living and Working." *From the Depths of My Soul: Poetry in Motion.* By Kelley. Hicksville, NY: Exposition Press, 1974. 23.

Kelley, Robin D. G. *Race Rebels: Culture, Politics, and the Black Working Class.* New York: Free Press, 1994.

Kennedy, Randall. "The Fallacy of Touré's Post-Blackness Theory." *The Root* 11 Aug. 2011.

Kent, George. *Blackness and the Adventure of Western Culture.* Chicago: Third World Press, 1972.

Kent, George. "Gwendolyn Brooks' Poetic Realism: A Developmental Survey." *Black Women Writers (1950–1980): A Critical Evaluation.* Ed. Mari Evans. New York: Doubleday, 1984. 88–105.

Kent, George. *A Life of Gwendolyn Brooks.* Lexington: University Press of Kentucky, 1990.

Kerrigan, John. "Wordsworth and the Sonnet: Building, Dwelling, Thinking." *Essays in Criticism* 35 (1985): 45–75.

Killens, John Oliver. "The Black Writer vis-à-vis His Country." *The Black Aesthetic.* Ed. Addison Gayle, Jr. Garden City: Doubleday, 1971. 379–96.

Kindilien, Carlin T. *American Poetry in the Eighteen Nineties.* Providence, RI: Brown University Press, 1956.

Kinloch, Valérie. *June Jordan: Her Life And Letters.* Westport, CT: Greenwood, 2006.

Klehr, Harvey. *The Heyday of American Communism: The Depression Decade.* New York: Basic Books, 1984.

Kliger, Ilya, and Boris Maslov, eds. *Persistent Forms: Explorations in Historical Poetics.* New York: Fordham University Press, 2016.

Knadler, Stephen. *Remapping Citizenship and the Nation in African-American Literature.* New York: Routledge, 2010.

Komunyakaa, Yusef. *Neon Vernacular: New and Selected Poems.* Hanover, NH: Wesleyan University Press, 1993.

Komunyakaa, Yusef. *Thieves of Paradise.* Hanover, NH: Wesleyan University Press, 1998.

Komunyakaa, Yusef. *Warhorses.* New York: Farrar, Straus and Giroux, 2008.

Korte, Barbara. *English Travel Writing from Pilgrimages to Postcolonial Explorations.* Trans. Catherine Matthias. Basingstoke: Macmillan, 2000.

Lamothe, Daphne. *Inventing the New Negro: Narrative, Culture, and Ethnography.* Philadelphia: University of Pennsylvania Press, 2008.

Lederer, Richard. "The Didactic and the Literary in Four Harlem Renaissance Sonnets." *English Journal* 62.2 (1973): 219–23.

Lee, Don L. *Dynamite Voices I: Black Poets of the 1960's.* Detroit: Broadside Press, 1971.

Lee, Don L. "Gwendolyn Brooks: Beyond the Wordmaker: The Making of an African Poet." Preface to *Report From Part One,* by Gwendolyn Brooks. Detroit: Broadside Press, 1972. 13–30.

Lee, Robert A. "On Claude McKay's 'If We Must Die.'" *CLA Journal* 18 (1974): 216–21.

Legum, Colin. *Pan-Africanism: A Short Political Guide.* Westport, CT: Greenwood Press, 1962.

Lemke, Sieglinde. *Primitivist Modernism: Black Culture and the Origins of Transatlantic Modernism.* New York: Oxford University Press, 1998.

Lemke, Sieglinde. *The Vernacular Matters of American Literature.* New York: Palgrave Macmillan, 2009.

Leonard, Keith D. "Love in the Black Arts Movement: The Other American Exceptionalism." *Callaloo* 36.3 (2013): 619–24.

Leonard, Keith D. *Fettered Genius: The African American Bardic Poet from Slavery to Civil Rights.* Charlottesville: University of Virginia Press, 2006.

LeSeur, Geta. "Claude McKay's Marxism." *The Harlem Renaissance: Revaluations.* Ed. Amritjit Singh, William S. Shiver, and Stanley Brodwin. New York: Garland, 1989.

Levine, Robert S. "African American Literary Nationalism." *A Companion to African American Literature.* Ed. Gene Andrew Jarrett. Oxford: Wiley-Blackwell, 2010. 119–32.

Levy, Eugene. *James Weldon Johnson: Black Leader, Black Voice.* Chicago: University of Chicago Press, 1973.

Lilly, Octave, Jr. "Saint Charles Avenue." *Opportunity* 16.9 (1938): 264.

Link, Franz. *Das moderne amerikanische Sonett.* Heidelberg: Winter, 1997.

Llorens, David. "Writers Converge at Fisk University." *Negro Digest* 15.8 (1966): 54–68.

Locke, Alain. "Our Little Renaissance." 1927. *The Politics and Aesthetics of "New Negro" Literature.* Ed. Cary D. Wintz. New York: Garland, 1996. 115–16.

Loggins, Vernon. *The Negro Author: His Development in America to 1900.* 1931. Port Washington, NY: Kennikat Press, 1964.

Long, Richard A. "Black Studies: International Dimensions." *New Black Voices: An Anthology of Contemporary Afro-American Literature.* Ed. Abraham Chapman. New York: Mentor, 1972. 420–25.

Longfellow, Henry Wadsworth. *The Poetical Works.* Vol. 6. Boston: Houghton Mifflin, 1886.

Lott, Eric. "Response to Trey Ellis's 'The New Black Aesthetic.'" *Callaloo* 38 (1989): 244–46.

Lubiano, Wahneema. "Standing In For the State: Black Nationalism and "Writing" the Black Subject." *Is It Nation Time? Contemporary Essays on Black Power and Black Nationalism.* Ed. Eddie S. Glaude Jr. Chicago: University of Chicago Press, 2002. 156–64.

Lynes, Katherine. "'Sprung from American Soil': The 'Nature' of Africa in the Poetry of Helene Johnson." *ISLE* 16.3 (2009): 525–49.

Mackey, Nathaniel. *Discrepant Engagement: Dissonance, Cross-Culturality, and Experimental Writing.* Cambridge: Cambridge University Press, 1993.

Mackey, Nathaniel. *Paracritical Hinge: Essays, Talks, Notes, Interviews.* Madison: University of Wisconsin Press, 2005.

Mackey, Nathaniel. *Splay Anthem.* New York: New Directions, 2006.

MacPhail, Scott. "June Jordan and the New Black Intellectuals." *African American Review* 33.1 (1999): 57–71.

Madhubuti, Haki. *From Plan to Planet: Life Studies: The Need for Afrikan Minds and Institutions.* Detroit: Broadside Press, 1973.

Madhubuti, Haki. *Liberation Narratives: New and Collected Poems 1966–2009.* Chicago: Third World Press, 2009.

Makalani, Minkah. *In the Cause of Freedom: Radical Black Internationalism from Harlem to London, 1917–1939.* Chapel Hill: University of North Carolina Press, 2011.

Manson, Michael Tomasek. "Sterling Brown and the 'Vestiges' of the Blues: The Role of Race in English Verse Structure." *MELUS* 21.1 (1996): 21–40.

Mao, Douglas, and Rebecca L. Walkowitz. "The New Modernist Studies." *PMLA* 123.3 (2008): 737–48.

Martin, Reginald. "The New Black Aesthetic Critics and Their Exclusion from American 'Mainstream' Criticism." *College English* 50.4 (1988): 373–82.

Mathes, Carter. *Imagine the Sound: Experimental African American Literature After Civil Rights.* Minneapolis: University of Minnesota Press, 2015.

Maxwell, William J. "Introduction: Claude McKay—Lyric Poetry in the Age of Cataclysm." *Complete Poems.* By Claude McKay. Ed. William J. Maxwell. Urbana: University of Illinois Press, 2004. xi–xliv.

Maxwell, William J. *New Negro, Old Left: African-American Writing and Communism Between the Wars.* New York: Columbia University Press, 1999.

McCall, James Edward. "Countee Cullen." *Messenger* 10.3 (1928): 68.

McClay, Wilfred M. "Two Versions of the Genteel Tradition: Santayana and Brooks." *New England Quarterly* 55.3 (1982): 368–91.

McClellan, George Marion. "My Madonna." *Poems.* By McClellan. Nashville, TN: AME Publishing House, 1895. 28.

McDowell, Deborah. "'The Changing Same': Generational Connections and Black Women Novelists." *New Literary History* 18.2 (1987): 281–302.

McElroy, Colleen. *Travelling Music.* Ashland, OR: Story Line Press, 1998.

McGill, Meredith, ed. *The Traffic in Poems: Nineteenth-Century Poetry and Transatlantic Exchange.* New Brunswick: Rutgers University Press, 2008.

McHenry, Elizabeth. *Forgotten Readers: Recovering the Lost History of African American Literary Societies.* Durham: Duke University Press, 2002.

McKay, Claude. *A Long Way From Home.* 1937. New York: Arno Press, 1969.

McKay, Claude. *Complete Poems.* Ed. William J. Maxwell. Urbana: University of Illinois Press, 2004.

McKible, Adam, and Suzanne Churchill. "In Conversation: The Harlem Renaissance and the New Modernist Studies." *Modernism/Modernity* 20.3 (2013): 427–31.

McLeod, A. L. "Claude McKay, Alain Locke, and the Harlem Renaissance." *Literary Half-Yearly* 27.2 (1986): 65–75.

McWhirter, Cameron. *Red Summer: The Summer of 1919 and the Awakening of Black America.* New York: Henry Holt, 2011.

Melhem, D. H. *Gwendolyn Brooks: Poetry and the Heroic Voice.* Lexington: University Press of Kentucky, 1987.

Melucci, Alberto. "Getting Involved: Identity and Mobilization in Social Movements." *International Social Movement Research* 1 (1988): 329–48.

Menard, John Willis. *Lays in Summer Lands.* 1879. Ed. Larry Eugene Rivers, Richard Mathews, and Canter Brown Jr. Tampa: University of Tampa Press, 2002.

Mevius, Martin. "Reappraising Communism and Nationalism." *The Communist Quest for National Legitimacy in Europe, 1918–1989.* Ed. Martin Mevius. London: Routledge, 2011. 1–24.

Middleton, Henry Davis. *Dreams of an Idle Hour.* Chicago: Advocate, 1908.

Miller, E. Ethelbert. *First Light: New and Selected Poems.* Baltimore: Black Classic Press, 1994.

Miller, James A. *Remembering Scottsboro: The Legacy of an Infamous Trial*. Princeton: Princeton University Press, 2009.

Miller, R. Baxter. "'Define . . . the Whirlwind': Gwendolyn Brooks's Epic Sign for a Generation." *Black American Poets Between Worlds, 1940–1960*. Ed. Miller. Knoxville: University of Tennessee Press, 1986. 160–74.

Miller, R. Baxter. "Café de la Paix: Mapping the Harlem Renaissance." *South Atlantic Review* 65.2 (2000): 73–94.

Milnes, Josephine. "The Poetry of Praise." *Kenyon Review* 23.1 (1961): 104–25.

Minto, William. *Characteristics of English Poets: From Chaucer to Shirley*. Edinburgh: Blackwell, 1885.

Mitchell, Joe H. *Lovin' You*. Markham, IL: NRU, 1974.

Mitchell, Joe H. *O Woman*. Markam, IL: NRU, 1974.

Mitchell, Verner D. *This Waiting For Love: Helene Johnson, Poet of the Harlem Renaissance*. Amherst: University of Massachusetts Press, 2000.

Molesworth, Charles. *And Bid Him Sing: A Biography of Countée Cullen*. Chicago: University of Chicago Press, 2012.

Moramarco, Fred, and William Sullivan. *Containing Multitudes: Poetry in the United States Since 1950*. New York: Twayne, 1998.

Moses, Wilson Jeremiah. "Africa and Pan-Africanism in the Thought of Du Bois." *The Cambridge Companion to W.E.B. Du Bois*. Cambridge: Cambridge University Press, 2008. 117–30.

Moses, Wilson Jeremiah. *The Golden Age of Black Nationalism: 1850–1925*. Hamden, CT: Archon Books, 1978.

Moses, Wilson Jeremiah. "The Lost World of the New Negro, 1895–1919." *Black American Literature Forum* 21.1–2 (1987): 61–84.

Moten, Fred. *In the Break: The Aesthetics of the Black Radical Tradition*. Minneapolis: University of Minnesota Press, 2003.

Mullen, Harryette. *The Cracks Between What We Are and What We Are Supposed to Be: Essays and Interviews*. Introd. Hank Lazer. Tuscaaloosa: University of Alabama Press, 2012.

Müller, Timo. "James Weldon Johnson and the Genteel Tradition." *Arizona Quarterly* 69.2 (2013): 85–102.

Müller, Timo. "Postcolonial Pursuits in African American Studies: The Later Poems of Claude McKay." *Postcolonial Studies Across the Disciplines*. Ed. Jana Gohrisch and Ellen Grünkemeier. Amsterdam: Rodopi, 2013. 131–49.

Müller, Timo. "Theorien des Sonetts." *Theorien der Literatur: Grundlagen und Perspektiven*. Vol. 6. Ed. Günter Butzer and Hubert Zapf. Tübingen: Francke, 2013. 101–20.

Müller, Timo. "The Vernacular Sonnet and the Resurgence of Afro-Modernism in the 1940s." *American Literature* 87.2 (2015): 253–73.

Nathans, Heather. *Slavery and Sentiment on the American Stage, 1787–1861: Lifting the Veil of Black*. Cambridge: Cambridge University Press, 2009.

Neal, Larry. "Any Day Now: Black Art and Black Liberation." *Ebony* Aug. 1969: 54–62.

Neal, Larry. *Visions of a Liberated Future: Black Arts Movement Writings*. Ed. Michael Schwarz. New York: Thunder's Mouth, 1989.

"Negro Wins Prize in Poetry Contest." *New York Times* 2 Dec. 1923: E1.

Nelson, Marilyn. *The Fields of Praise: New and Selected Poems*. Baton Rouge: Louisiana State University Press, 1997.

Nelson, Marilyn Waniek. *The Homeplace*. Baton Rouge: Louisiana State University Press, 1990.

Nelson, Marilyn, and Rita Dove. "A Black Rainbow: Modern Afro-American Poetry." *Poetry after Modernism*. Ed. Robert McDowell. Brownsville, OR: Story Line Press, 1998. 142–98.

Neubauer, Paul. *Zwischen Tradition und Innovation: Das Sonett in der amerikanischen Dichtung des zwanzigsten Jahrhunderts*. Heidelberg: Winter, 2001.

Nickels, Joel. "Claude McKay and Dissident Internationalism." *Cultural Critique* 87 (2014): 1–37.

Nielsen, Aldon Lynn. *Black Chant: Languages of African-American Postmodernism*. Cambridge: Cambridge University Press, 1997.

Nielsen, Aldon Lynn. *Integral Music: Languages of African American Innovation*. Tuscaloosa: University of Alabama Press, 2004.

Notley, Alice. Introduction. *The Sonnets*, by Ted Berrigan. New York: Penguin, 2000. v–xv.

Nowlin, Michael. "Race Literature, Modernism, Normal Literature: James Weldon Johnson's Groundwork for an African American Literary Renaissance, 1912–20." *Modernism/Modernity* 20.3 (2013): 503–18.

Nwankwo, Ifeoma Kiddoe. *Black Cosmopolitanism: Racial Consciousness and Transnational Identity in the Nineteenth-Century Americas*. Philadelphia: University of Pennsylvania Press, 2005.

"October 1966 Black Panther Party Platform and Program." *SOS—Calling All Black People: A Black Arts Movement Reader*. Ed. John H. Bracey, Jr., Sonia Sanchez, and James Smethurst. Amherst: University of Massachusetts Press, 2014. 205–6.

Odum, Howard W., and Guy B. Johnson. *Negro Workaday Songs*. 1962. New York: Negro Universities Press, 1977.

Opp, Karl-Dieter. *Theories of Political Protest and Social Movements: A Multidisciplinary Introduction, Critique, and Synthesis*. London: Routledge, 2009.

Oppenheimer, Paul. *The Birth of the Modern Mind: Self, Consciousness, and the Invention of the Sonnet*. Oxford: Oxford University Press, 1989.

Ottley, Roi. *New World A-Coming: Inside Black America*. 1943. New York: Anro Press, 1968.

Paisley, John Walter. *The Voice of Mizraim*. New York: Neale, 1907.

Pardlo, Gregory. "'To Whom It May Concern': Toward Theorizing Poems of the Interior." *Callaloo* 36.3 (2013): 577–81.

Patterson, Anita. "Jazz, Realism, and the Modernist Lyric: The Poetry of Langston Hughes." *Modern Language Quarterly* 61.4 (2000): 651–82.

Patterson, G. E. *To and From*. Boise, ID: Boise State University Press, 2008.

Patterson, G. E. *Tug*. Saint Paul, MN: Graywolf Press, 1999.

Pattison, Mark, ed. *The Sonnets of John Milton*. 1892. London: Kegan Paul, 1908.

Payne, James Robert. "Joseph Seamon Cotter, Jr.: Toward a Reconsideration." *Joseph Seamon Cotter, Jr.: Complete Poems*. Ed. James Robert Payne. Athens: University of Georgia Press, 1990. 1–22.

Pease, Edward R. *The History of the Fabian Society*. 1918. London: Frank Cass, 1963.

Pereira, Malin. *Rita Dove's Cosmopolitanism*. Urbana: University of Illinois Press, 2003.

Perry, Margaret. *Silence to the Drums: A Survey of the Literature of the Harlem Renaissance*. Westport, CT: Greenwood Press, 1976.

Pettinger, Alasdair. *Always Elsewhere: Travels of the Black Atlantic*. London: Cassell, 1998.

Phelan, Joseph. *The Nineteenth-Century Sonnet*. Basingstoke: Palgrave Macmillan, 2005.

Philipson, Robert. "The Harlem Renaissance as Postcolonial Phenomenon." *African American Review* 40.1 (2006): 145–60.

Phipps, Wanda. *Your Last Illusion or Break Up Sonnets: Inspired by Ted Berrigan's Sonnets*. N.p.: Situations, 2000.

Pinckney, Darryl. "The Sweet Singer of Tuckahoe." *New York Review of Books* 5 Mar. 1992. Web.

Posmentier, Sonya. "The Provision Ground in New York: Claude McKay and the Form of Memory." *American Literature* 84.2 (2012): 273–300.

Prah, Kwesi Kwaa. "The Wish to Unite: The Historical and Political Context of the Pan-African Movement." *The Making of the Africa-Nation: Pan-Africanism and the African Renaissance*. London: Adonis & Abbey, 2003. 13–39.

Pratt, Mary Louise. *Imperial Eyes: Travel Writing and Transculturation*. 1992. 2nd ed. New York : Routledge, 2008.

Prins, Yopie. "What Is Historical Poetics?" *Historical Poetics*. Special issue of *Modern Language Quarterly* 77.1 (2016): 13–40.

Putnam, Laura. "Provincializing Harlem: The 'Negro Metropolis' as Northern Frontier of a Connected Caribbean." *Modernism/Modernity* 20.3 (2013): 469–84.

Quashie, Kevin. *The Sovereignty of Quiet: Beyond Resistance in Black Culture*. New Brunswick, NJ: Rutgers University Press, 2012.

Ramazani, Jahan. *A Transnational Poetics*. Chicago: University of Chicago Press, 2009.

Rambsy, Howard. *The Black Arts Enterprise and the Production of African American Poetry*. Ann Arbor: University of Michigan Press, 2011.

Ramey, Lauri, ed. *The Heritage Series of Black Poetry, 1962–1975: A Research Compendium*. Aldershot: Ashgate, 2008.

Rampersad, Arnold. *The Life of Langston Hughes*. Vol. 1. New York: Oxford University Press, 1986.

Randall, Dudley, and Margaret G. Borroughs, eds. *For Malcolm: Poems on the Life and the Death of Malcolm X*. Detroit: Broadside Press, 1969.

Ray, Charlotte E., and Henrietta Cordelia Ray. *Sketch of the Life of Charles B. Ray*. New York: Little, 1887.

Ray, Henrietta Cordelia. *Poems*. New York: Grafton Press, 1910.

Ray, Henrietta Cordelia. *Sonnets*. New York: Little, 1893.

Reddick, L. D. "No Kafka in the South." *Phylon* 11.4 (1950): 380–83.

Redding, J. Saunders. *To Make a Poet Black*. 1939. Ithaca, NY: Cornell University Press, 1988.

Redmond, Eugene B. *Drumvoices: The Mission of Afro-American Poetry: A Critical History*. Garden City, NY: Anchor Press, 1976.

Reed, Adolph L., Jr. *W.E.B. Du Bois and American Political Thought: Fabianism and the Color Line*. New York: Oxford University Press, 1997.

Reed, Anthony. *Freedom Time: The Poetics and Politics of Black Experimental Writing*. Baltimore: Johns Hopkins University Press, 2014.

Reed, Henry. *Lectures on the British Poets*. London: Shaw, 1859.

Reed, Ishmael. "Can a Metronome Know the Thunder or Summon a God?" *The Black Aesthetic*. Ed. Addison Gayle, Jr. Garden City: Anchor Books, 1972. 381–82.

Reese, Sarah Carolyn. *Songs of Freedom*. Detroit: Lotus Press, 1983.

Retman, Sonnet. *Real Folks: Race and Genre in the Great Depression*. Durham: Duke University Press, 2011.

Righelato, Pat. *Understanding Rita Dove*. Columbia, SC: University of South Carolina Press, 2006.

Rivers, Conrad Kent. *The Still Voice of Harlem*. Heritage Series 5. London: Breman, 1972.

Rivers, Conrad Kent. *These Black Bodies and This Sunburnt Face.* Cleveland, OH: Free Lance Press, 1962.

Robbins, Sarah. *The Cambridge Introduction to Harriet Beecher Stowe.* Cambridge: Cambridge University Press, 2007.

Roberson, Ed. "18,000 Feet." *New Directions* 22 (1970): 112.

Roberson, Ed. *Atmosphere Conditions.* Los Angeles: Sun & Moon Press, 2000.

Roberson, Ed. *Voices Cast Out to Talk Us In.* Iowa City: University of Iowa Press, 1995.

Roberson, Ed. *When Thy King Is a Boy.* Pittsburgh: University of Pittsburgh Press, 1970.

Roberts, Brian Russell. *Artistic Ambassadors: Literary and International Representation of the New Negro Era.* Charlottesville: University of Virginia Press, 2013.

Robinson, Cedric J. *Black Marxism.* 1983. Chapel Hill: University of North Carolina Press, 2000.

Robinson, Daniel. "To Scorn or to 'Scorn Not the Sonnet.'" *A Companion to Romantic Poetry.* Ed. Charles Mahoney. Chichester: Wiley-Blackwell, 2011. 62–77.

Robinson, Edwin Arlington. *Collected Poems.* New York: Macmillan, 1946.

Ronda, Margaret. "'Work and Wait Unwearying': Dunbar's Georgics." *PMLA* 127.4 (2012): 863–78.

Ross, Marlon B. "Romancing the Nation-State: The Poetics of Romantic Nationalism." *Macropolitics of Nineteenth-Century Literature: Nationalism, Exoticism, Imperialism.* Ed. Jonathan Arac und Harriet Ritvo. Durham: Duke University Press, 1995. 56–85.

Rowe, George Clinton. *Our Heroes: Patriotic Poems on Men, Women and Sayings of The Negro Race.* Charleston, SC: Walker, Evans, and Cogswell, 1890.

Rowell, Charles H. "Sterling A. Brown and the Afro-American Folk Tradition." *Studies in the Literary Imagination* 7.2 (1974): 131–52.

Rowell, Charles Henry. "Interview With Rita Dove: Part 2." *Callaloo* 31.3 (2008): 715–26.

Rowell, Charles Henry. "Writing Self, Writing Community: An Introduction." *Angles of Ascent: A Norton Anthology of Contemporary African American Poetry.* Ed. Charles Henry Rowell. New York: Norton, 2013. xxix–liii.

Rubin, Anne Sarah. *A Shattered Nation: The Rise and Fall of the Confederacy, 1861–1868.* Chapel Hill: University of North Carolina Press, 2005.

Ruffin, Kimberly N. *Black on Earth: African American Ecoliterary Traditions.* Athens: University of Georgia Press, 2010.

Sanderlin, George. "The Influence of Milton and Wordsworth on the Early Victorian Sonnet." *ELH* 5.3 (1938): 225–51.

Sanders, Mark A. *Afro-Modernist Aesthetics and the Poetry of Sterling A. Brown.* Athens: University of Georgia Press, 1999.

Sanders, Mark A. "Sterling A. Brown and the Afro-Modern Moment." *African American Review* 31.3 (1997): 393–97.

Santayana, George. "The Genteel Tradition in American Philosophy." *The Works of George Santayana.* Vol. 7. New York: Scribner's, 1937. 127–50.

Scanlon, Larry. "'Death Is a Drum': Rhythm, Modernity, and the Negro Poet Laureate." *Music and the Racial Imagination.* Ed. Ronald Radano, Philip V. Bohlman, and Houston A. Baker. Chicago, IL: University of Chicago Press, 2000. 510–53.

Scanlon, Larry. "Poets Laureate and the Language of Slaves: Petrarch, Chaucer, and Langston Hughes." *The Vulgar Tongue: Medieval and Postmedieval Vernacularity.* Ed. Fiona Somerset and Nicholas Watson. University Park, PA: University of Pennsylvania Press, 2003. 220–56.

Scheiding, Oliver. "Ideas of Order in Contemporary American Poetry." *Ideas of Order in Con-temporary American Poetry.* Ed. Oliver Scheiding and Diana von Finck. Würzburg: Königshausen & Neumann, 2007. 3–21.

Schneider, Mark R. *"The Colored American* and *Alexander's*: Boston's Pro-Civil Rights Bookerites." *Journal of Negro History* 80.4 (1995): 157–69.

Schuyler, George S. "The Rise of the Black Internationale." 1938. *The New Negro: Readings on Race, Representation, and African American Culture, 1892–1938.* Ed. Henry Louis Gates and Gene Andrew Jarrett. Princeton: Princeton University Press, 2007. 149–53.

Scott, William R. *The Sons of Sheba's Race: African-Americans and the Italo-Ethiopian War, 1934–1941.* Bloomington: Indiana University Press, 1993.

Sedgwick, Ellery. "The American Genteel Tradition in the Early Twentieth Century." *American Studies* 25.1 (1984): 49–67.

Semmel, Bernard. *Imperialism and Social Reform: English Social-Imperial Thought, 1895–1914.* London: Allen & Unwin, 1960.

Sexton, Danny. "Lifting the Veil: Revision and Double-Consciousness in Rita Dove's *The Darker Face of the Earth.*" *Callaloo* 31.3 (2008): 777–87.

Shandell, Jonathan. "How Black Do You Want It? Countee Cullen and the Contest for Racial Authenticity on Page and Stage." *Authentic Blackness / "Real" Blackness: Essays on the Meaning of Blackness in Literature and Culture.* Eds. Martin Japtok and Jerry Rafiki Jenkins. New York: Peter Lang, 2011. 155–67.

Sharifi, Majid. *Imagining Iran: The Tragedy of Subaltern Nationalism.* Lanham: Lexington, 2013.

Sharp, William. "The Sonnet: Its Characteristics and History." *Sonnets of This Century.* Ed. Sharp. London: Walter Scott, 1888.

Shaw, Harry B. *Gwendolyn Brooks.* Boston: Twayne, 1980.

Shaw-Thornburg, Angela. "Problems of Genre and Genealogy in African-American Literature of Travel." *Journeys* 12.1 (2011): 46–62.

Shepperson, George. "Ethiopianism and African Nationalism." *Phylon* 14.1 (1953): 9–18.

Shepperson, George. "Pan-Africanism and 'Pan-Africanism': Some Historical Notes." *Phylon* 23.4 (1962): 346–58.

Sherman, Joan. *Invisible Poets: Afro-Americans of the Nineteenth Century.* 2nd ed. Urbana: University of Illinois Press, 1989.

Shockley, Evie. "The Black Arts Movement and Black Aesthetics." *The Cambridge Companion to Modern American Poetry.* Ed. Walter Kalaidjian. Cambridge: Cambridge University Press, 2015. 180–95.

Shockley, Evie. *Renegade Poetics: Black Aesthetics and Formal Innovation in African American Poetry.* Iowa City: University of Iowa Press, 2011.

Shoeman, Charles Henry. "Doubt." *A Dream and Other Poems.* By Shoeman. 1899. 2nd ed. Ann Arbor, MI: George Wahr, 1900. 109.

Shucard, Alan R. *Countee Cullen.* Twayne's United States Authors Series. Boston: Twayne, 1984.

Simeon-Jones, Kersuze. *Literary and Sociopolitical Writings of the Black Diaspora in the Nineteenth and Twentieth Centuries.* Lanham: Lexington, 2010.

Simmons, William J. *Men of Mark: Eminent, Progressive and Rising.* Cleveland: Rewell, 1887.

Smethurst, James Edward. *The African American Roots of Modernism: From Reconstruction to the Harlem Renaissance.* Chapel Hill: University of North Carolina Press, 2011.

Smethurst, James Edward. "The Black Arts Movement." *A Companion to African American Literature*. Ed. Gene Andrew Jarrett. Malden, MA: Wiley-Blackwell, 2010. 302–14.

Smethurst, James Edward. *The Black Arts Movement: Literary Nationalism in the 1960s and 1970s*. Chapel Hill: University of North Carolina Press, 2005.

Smethurst, James Edward. "Lyric Stars: Countee Cullen and Langston Hughes." *The Cambridge Companion to the Harlem Renaissance*. Ed. George Hutchinson. Cambridge: Cambridge University Press, 2007. 112–25.

Smethurst, James Edward. *The New Red Negro: The Literary Left and African American Poetry, 1930–1946*. New York: Oxford University Press, 1999.

Smethurst, Paul. Introduction. *Travel Writing, Form, and Empire: The Poetics and Politics of Mobility*. Ed. Julia Kuehn and Smethurst. New York: Routledge, 2009. 1–18.

Smith, Derik. "Quarreling in the Movement: Robert Hayden's Black Arts Era." *Callaloo* 33.2 (2010): 449–66.

Smith, Gary. "Gwendolyn Brooks's *A Street in Bronzeville*, the Harlem Renaissance and the Mythologies of Black Women." *MELUS* 10.3 (1983): 33–46.

Smith, Robert A. "The Poetry of Countee Cullen." *Phylon* 11.3 (1950): 216–21.

Smith, Virginia W. "African American Travel Literature." *The Cambridge Companion to Travel Writing*. Ed. Alfred Bendixen and Judith Hamera. Cambridge: Cambridge University Press, 2009. 197–213.

Spenser, Edmund. *Amoretti. The Yale Edition of the Shorter Poems of Edmund Spenser*. Ed. William A. Oram et al. New Haven, CT: Yale University Press, 1989. 598–658.

Sperry, Margaret. "Countee P. Cullen, Negro Boy Poet, Tells His Story." *Brooklyn Eagle* 10 Feb. 1924, n. pag.

Spiller, Michael R. G. *The Development of the Sonnet: An Introduction*. London: Routledge, 1992.

Spurr, David. *The Rhetoric of Empire: Colonial Discourse in Journalism, Travel Writing, and Imperial Administration*. Durham: Duke University Press, 1993.

Stanford, Ann F. "Dialectics of Desire: War and the Resistive Voice in Gwendolyn Brooks's 'Negro Hero' and 'Gay Chaps at the Bar.'" *African American Review* 26.2 (1992): 197–211.

Stauffer, John. Foreword. *American Protest Literature*, ed. Zoe Trodd. Cambridge, MA: Belknap Press, 2006. xi–xviii.

Steffen, Therese. *Crossing Color: Transcultural Space and Place in Rita Dove's Poetry, Fiction, and Drama*. Oxford: Oxford University Press, 2001.

Stepto, Robert B. *From Behind the Veil: A Study of Afro-American Narrative*. Urbana: University of Illinois Press, 1979.

Stern, Gerald. *American Sonnets*. New York: Norton, 2002.

Stoff, Michael B. "Claude McKay and the Cult of Primitivism." 1972. *The Harlem Renaissance: A Gale Critical Companion*. Vol. 3. Ed. Janet Witalec. Detroit, MI: Gale, 2003. 255–64.

Stout, Jeffrey. "Theses on Black Nationalism." *Is It Nation Time? Contemporary Essays on Black Power and Black Nationalism*. Ed. Eddie S. Glaude Jr. Chicago: University of Chicago Press, 2002. 234–56.

Street, Joe. *The Culture War in the Civil Rights Movement*. Gainesville: University Press of Florida, 2007.

Sylvanise, Frédéric. *Langston Hughes: poète jazz, poète blues*. Paris: ENS Editions, 2009.

Symonds, John Addington. "Stella Maris." *London Nights*. London: Chriswick, 1895. 40–41.

Szefel, Lisa. "Beauty and William Braithwaite." *Callaloo* 29.2 (2006): 560–86.

Szefel, Lisa. "Encouraging Verse: William S. Braithwaite and the Poetics of Race." *New England Quarterly* 74.1 (2001): 32–61.

Takayoshi, Ichiro. *American Writers and the Approach of World War II, 1935–1941: A Literary History.* Cambridge: Cambridge University Press, 2015.

Taylor, James Lance. *Black Nationalism in the United States: From Malcolm X to Barack Obama.* Boulder, CO: Lynne Rienner Publishers, 2011.

Thomas, Lorenzo. "The Shadow World: New York's Umbra Workshop and Origins of the Black Arts Movement." *Callaloo* 4.1 (1978): 53–72.

Thompson, Carl. *Travel Writing.* New Critical Idiom. New York: Routledge, 2011.

Thompson, Mark Christian. "Aesthetic Hygiene: Marcus Garvey, W.E.B. Du Bois, and the Work of Art." *A Companion to African American Literature.* Ed. Gene Andrew Jarrett. Malden, MA: Wiley-Blackwell, 2010. 243–53.

Thurman, Wallace. "Negro Poets and Their Poetry." 1928. *The Critics and the Harlem Renaissance.* Ed. Cary D. Wintz. New York: Garland, 1996. 34–46.

Tidwell, John Edgar, and Steven C. Tracy, eds. *After Winter: The Art and Life of Sterling A. Brown.* Oxford: Oxford University Press, 2009.

Tillery, Tyrone. *Claude McKay: A Black Poet's Struggle for Identity.* Amherst: University of Massachusetts Press, 1992.

Tillman, N. P. "The Threshold of Maturity." *Phylon* 11.4 (1950): 387–88.

Tomsich, John. *A Genteel Endeavor: American Culture and Politics in the Gilded Age.* Stanford: Stanford University Press, 1971.

Toomer, Jean. *The Collected Poems.* Ed. Robert B. Jones and Margery Toomer Latimer. Chapel Hill: University of North Carolina Press, 1988.

Totten, Gary. *African American Travel Narratives From Abroad: Mobility and Cultural Work in the Age of Jim Crow.* Amherst: University of Massachusetts Press, 2015.

Touré, Askia Muhammad Abu Bakr el. "Introductory Essay: Black Magic!! (A Statement on the Tasks of the New Poetry)." *Juju: Magic Songs for the Black Nation.* Chicago: Third World Press, 1970. 9–12.

Toynbee, Arnold J. *Abyssinia and Italy.* Survey of International Affairs 1935.2. London: Humphrey Milford, 1936.

Tracy, Steven C. *Langston Hughes and the Blues.* Urbana: University of Illinois Press, 1988.

Trethewey, Natasha. *Bellocq's Ophelia.* St. Paul, MN: Graywolf Press, 2002.

Trethewey, Natasha. *Domestic Work.* Saint Paul, MN: Graywolf Press, 2000.

Trethewey, Natasha. *Native Guard.* Boston: Houghton Mifflin, 2007.

Trethewey, Natasha. *Thrall.* Boston: Houghton Mifflin Harcourt, 2012.

Troupe, Quincy. *Embryo.* New York: Barlenmir House, 1972.

Tunnell, Arthur. "On Segregation." *The Crisis* 7.5 (1914): 226.

Turner, Darwin T. *In a Minor Chord: Three Afro-American Writers and Their Search for Identity.* Carbondale: Southern Illinois University Press, 1971.

Tyner, Larry. "On Climbing." *Rhythms of Resurrection.* By Tyner. N.p.: Self-published, 1974. 6.

Umoja, Akinyele. "Searching for Place: Nationalism, Separatism, and Pan-Africanism." *A Companion to African American History.* Ed. Alton Hornsby. Malden: Blackwell, 2007. 529–44.

Van Deburg, William L. *New Day in Babylon: The Black Power Movement and American Culture, 1965–1975.* Chicago: University of Chicago Press, 1992.

Wagers, Kelley. "Race, Nation, and Historical (Re)Form in The Souls of Black Folk." *Arizona Quarterly* 64.1 (2008): 77–108.

Wagner, Jean. *Black Poets of the United States: From Paul Laurence Dunbar to Langston Hughes.* Urbana: University of Illinois Press, 1973.

Wagner, Jennifer Ann. *A Moment's Monument: Revisionary Poetics and the Nineteenth-Century English Sonnet.* Madison: Fairleigh Dickinson University Press, 1996.

Walker, Margaret. *Prophets for a New Day.* Detroit: Broadside Press, 1970.

Walker, Margaret. *This is My Century: New and Collected Poems.* Athens: University of Georgia Press, 1989.

Walonen, Michael K. "Land of Racial Confluence and Spatial Accessibility: Claude McKay's Sense of Mediterranean Place." *Geocritical Explorations: Space, Place, and Mapping in Literary and Cultural Studies.* Ed. Robert T. Tally. New York: Palgrave Macmillan, 2011. 75–89.

Walsh, Rebecca. *The Geopoetics of Modernism.* Gainesville: University Press of Florida, 2015.

Walters, Tracey L. *African American Literature and the Classicist Tradition: Black Women Writers from Wheatley to Morrison.* New York: Palgrave Macmillan, 2007.

Weaver, Michael. *My Father's Geography.* Pittsburgh: University of Pittsburgh Press, 1992.

Weaver, Michael. *Stations in a Dream.* Baltimore: Dolphin-Moon Press, 1993.

Westover, Jeff. "African American Sonnets: Voicing Justice and Personal Dignity." *A Companion to Poetic Genre.* Ed. Erik Martiny. Malden, MA: Wiley-Blackwell, 2012. 234–49.

Wheatley, Phillis. *The Poems.* Revised edition. Ed. Julian D. Mason, Jr. Chapel Hill: University of North Carolina Press, 1989.

Wheeler, Lesley. "The Formalist Modernism of Edna St. Vincent Millay, Helene Johnson, and Louise Bogan." *The Cambridge History of American Poetry.* Ed. Alfred Bendixen and Stephen Burt. New York: Cambridge University Press, 2015. 628–49.

Whitlow, Roger. *Black American Literature: A Critical History.* Chicago: Hall, 1973.

Whitman, Albery Allson. *Not a Man, and Yet a Man.* Springfield, OH: Republic Printing Company, 1877.

Wiley, Michael. *Romantic Geography: Wordsworth and Anglo-European Spaces.* Basingstoke: Palgrave, 1998.

Willard, Carla. "Wheatley's Turns of Praise: Heroic Entrapment and the Paradox of Revolution." *American Literature* 67.2 (1995): 233–56.

Williams, George Washington. *A History of the Negro Race in America.* New York: Putnam, 1882.

Williams, Gladys. "Gwendolyn Brooks's Way With the Sonnet." *CLA Journal* 26.2 (1982): 215–40.

Williams, Kenny J. "An Invisible Partnership and an Unlikely Relationship: William Stanley Braithwaite and Harriet Monroe." *Callaloo* 32 (1987): 516–50.

Williams, Kenny J. "The World of Satin-Legs, Mrs. Sallie, and the Blackstone Rangers: The Restricted Chicago of Gwendolyn Brooks." *A Life Distilled: Gwendolyn Brooks, Her Poetry and Fiction.* Ed. Maria K. Mootry and Gary Smith. Urbana: University of Illinois Press, 1987. 47–70.

Williams, Pontheolla. *Robert Hayden: A Critical Analysis of His Poetry.* Urbana: University of Illinois Press, 1987.

Williams, Wilburn, Jr. "Covenant of Timelessness & Time: Symbolism & History in Robert Hayden's *Angle of Ascent.*" *Massachusetts Review* 18.4 (1977): 731–49.

Williams, William Carlos. *The Embodiment of Knowledge.* Ed. Ron Loewinsohn. New York: New Directions, 1974.

Wilson, Forrest. *Crusader in Crinoline: The Life of Harriet Beecher Stowe*. Philadelphia: Lippincott, 1941.

Wilson, Ivy G. "Introduction: Reconsidering Albery Allson Whitman." *At the Dusk of Dawn: Selected Poetry and Prose of Albery Allson Whitman*. Ed. Ivy G. Wilson. Boston: Northeastern University Press, 2009. 1–15.

Wilson, Ivy G. *Specters of Democracy: Blackness and the Aesthetics of Politics in the Antebellum U.S.* Oxford: Oxford University Press, 2011.

Wilson, Ivy G. "The Writing on the Wall: Revolutionary Aesthetics and Interior Spaces." *American Literature's Aesthetic Dimensions*. Ed. Cindy Weinstein and Christopher Looby. New York: Columbia University Press, 2012. 56–72.

Wilson, Sarah. *Melting-Pot Modernism*. Ithaca: Cornell University Press, 2010.

Winship, Michael. "'The Greatest Book of its Kind': A Publishing History of Uncle Tom's Cabin." *Proceedings of the American Antiquarian Society* 109 (1999): 309–32.

Woodard, Komozi. *A Nation Within a Nation: Amiri Baraka (LeRoi Jones) and Black Power Politics*. Chapel Hill: University of North Carolina Press, 1999.

Woodring, Carl. *Politics in English Romantic Poetry*. Cambridge: Harvard University Press, 1970.

Woodson, Jon. *Anthems, Sonnets, and Chants: Recovering the African American Poetry of the 1930s*. Columbus: Ohio State University Press, 2011.

Wordsworth, William. *Last Poems, 1821–1850*. Ed. Jared Curtis. Ithaca, NY: Cornell University Press, 1999.

Wordsworth, William. *Poems, in Two Volumes, and Other Poems, 1800–1807*. Ed. Jared Curtis. Ithaca, NY: Cornell University Press, 1983.

Wyman, Sarah. "Beyond the Veil: Indeterminacy and Iconoclasm in the Art of Robert Hayden, Janet Kozachek, and Tom Feelings." *Comparatist* 36 (2012): 263–91.

Young, Al. *Heaven: Collected Poems, 1956–1990*. Berkeley: Creative Arts Books, 1992.

Young, James O. *Black Writers of the Thirties*. Baton Rouge: Louisiana State University Press, 1973.

Zafar, Rafia. *We Wear the Mask: African Americans Write American Literature, 1760–1870*. New York: Columbia University Press, 1997.

Index

abolitionism, 14, 17, 29–31, 37, 86

Abyssinia, 68–69, 135n15

aestheticism, 17–18, 20, 27, 98

Africanism, 65–66

Aldrich, Thomas Bailey, 37

Alexander, Elizabeth, 23

allegory, 14, 19–20, 30, 62, 87

anthology, 17, 62, 94, 99–100, 109, 113–14, 139n10

archaism, 20, 53, 69, 73, 84

Aristotle, 120

Asika, Nkemka. *See* John, Frank

assimilation, 36, 38, 51, 101

Aubert, Alvin, "Dayton Dateline," 101

autobiography, 18, 27, 62, 92–94, 121–25

"Back to Africa," 59, 69–70, 92

Baker, Houston A., 11, 38–41, 44, 46–49; *Modernism and the Harlem Renaissance*, 39–40, 47, 90

Bakhtin, Mikhail, 80

Baldwin, James, 85

Baraka, Amiri, 9, 92–93, 101; "The Turncoat," 96

Barrax, Gerald, 98–99, 111; "Poem," 98–99

Baxter, J. Harvey L., 69–73; "Oh, Hang Your Heads, A Voice Accusing Cries," 71; *Sonnets to the Ethiopians*, 72

Beadle, Samuel A., 24–26, 28, 38; "Sonnets to My Love," 24–26

Beethoven, Ludwig van, 37

Berrigan, Ted, 126–28

Bhabha, Homi, 76, 107, 117–18

Bible, 20, 48, 71–72, 136n15

black aesthetic, 84, 92–95, 97, 99, 102, 104, 106, 109, 111

Black Arts, 7, 11–13, 16, 79, 82, 85, 89, 91–108, 109–14, 125, 139n12

Black Atlantic, 70

Black Belt thesis, 60, 69, 92

black nationalism, 9, 12, 55, 69, 72, 91–108, 111, 138n6, 139n8

Black Power, 69, 92

Blount, Marcellus, 7, 9, 34

blues, 77–83, 89–90, 109

Bonaparte, Napoleon, 6

Bontemps, Arna, 39, 113

Bragg, Linda Brown: *A Love Song to Black Men*, 103; "Winter Sonnet," 103–4

Braithwaite, William Stanley, 16–17, 23–24, 37–43, 73; "This is My Life," 18

Broadside Press, 99, 103

Brooks, Gwendolyn, 9, 11, 75–76, 82–86, 89–90, 94–96, 99, 101; *Annie Allen*, 75; *Family Pictures*, 101; "Gay Chaps at the Bar," 82–86; *A Street in Bronzeville*, 84

Brooks, Jonathan Henderson, "Still Am I Marveling," 52

Brown, Sterling, 11, 39, 41, 48–50, 58, 60, 75, 77, 90; "Salutamus," 52–54; *Southern Road*, 49, 54

Brown, William Wells, 31

Browning, Elizabeth Barrett, *Sonnets from the Portuguese*, 22

CPSIA information can be obtained
at www.ICGtesting.com
Printed in the USA
BVHW070709260320
576026BV00004B/8